PRAISE FOR CRAIG MACFARLANE

"Craig's unique passion for life and perspective is inspiring, his optimism is contagious and his work ethic is unmatched...Craig's positive impact on the financial services industry has been widespread and he embodies the true meaning of partnership."

Toby Miller, SVP, National Sales Manager
Leading Financial Services Asset Manager

"Craig MacFarlane is a good friend of mine. I admire his strength, his courage and his enthusiasm. Nobody knows better than Craig what Pride in America is all about. For Craig it means having the desire, the energy and the perseverance to accomplish worthwhile goals which inspire and encourage all Americans. As you listen to Craig you will understand much better what the word PRIDE means."

George H.W. Bush
41st President of the United States

"Craig MacFarlane's life's story is an extraordinary example of integrity, discipline, passion and an unrelenting commitment to excellence. Craig's message is a powerful one that inspires me and, no doubt, everyone who has the privilege to hear him. We are honored to be able to provide Craig a home as he spreads his inspirational message around the world."

Arne Sorenson
President and Chief Executive Officer of
Marriott International

"Craig MacFarlane is a rare and impressive man. His accomplishments themselves are noteworthy but it is the spirit and attitude with which he lives his life that most command your attention and respect."

Bob Costas
NBC Sports

"Craig's life and his journey has been remarkable and impressive. He is a special person who gives so much to others yet asks for little in return. Craig's life's story is truly a remarkable one."

Brad Stevens
Boston Celtics Head Coach

"Craig MacFarlane is the perfect combination of an extraordinary person who experienced adversity, celebrated abundance, and showed gratitude throughout the journey. His speeches are inspiring, his writings are thought provoking, and his audiences are always appreciative."

Dr. Nido R. Qubein
President, High Point University
Chairman, Great Harvest Bread Co

Find Your Flame

Through Purpose, Passion, and Sacrifice

CRAIG MACFARLANE

DEDICATION

I dedicate this book to my parents, the late Earl and Joyce MacFarlane, who have always been my unsung heroes, in life and now in spirit. Without you, I might have thought of my blindness as a handicap rather than just a minor inconvenience.

And, of course, to those who are closest to me and inspire me to be their unsung hero and who tell me I am even when I'm not. The love of my life, my wonderful wife Patti, and our delightful kids, Dalton, Raven, Derek, Ashley, and Morgan, continuously challenge and inspire me to go the extra mile. I lead them from behind and follow them from in front, always giving them their wings and inspiring them to fly.

And, as surprising as it may sound, to all my opponents, who I prefer to think of as simply competitors, who forced me to "walk my talk before I ever knew what my talk was" and, in the process, taught me the lessons I'm about to share with you.

Without a doubt, I must acknowledge my dear friend, Brian Donaldson, without whose inspiration, motivation, and sense of humor, my music I am about to share with you might have been left unsung.

To all the rest of you who put your game face on—I'm about to challenge your "A game."

Let's rock.

Gordie Howe and Craig en route to the 1984 Olympics.

The World's Most Celebrated Totally Blind Athlete Shares a Most Unique Perspective That Led to 35 Years of Business Success in the Sighted World.

A UNIQUE VANTAGE POINT

In a most appropriate celebration of his life, Craig MacFarlane, the World's Most Celebrated Totally Blind Athlete, and a firm believer in the power of a self-lit flame, was invited by US President Ronald Reagan, to carry the Olympic Torch, the universal symbol of the passion that burns in the heart of every Olympic athlete, through the streets of Washington, DC, alongside his mentor, Mr. Hockey, Gordie Howe, as it made its way to the 1984 Olympics in Los Angeles.

Craig transitioned from the world of athletics to the world of business in 1984 without breaking stride and has enjoyed an enviable level of success as he built a remarkable career over the 35 years that have followed.

He told you his story in *Craig MacFarlane Hasn't Heard of You Either!*, but now he's back to share with you the successful lessons he learned from his most unique vantage point that have made him one of the world's most successful inspirational keynote speakers, totally blind or otherwise, and a successful international business ambassador as well.

INTRODUCTION

Imet Craig MacFarlane 25 years ago when I was just starting my career with Edward Jones. Craig's passion and commitment to others' success and potential was immediately evident, and it inspired me.

It touched me. It made me believe that if he could do it, so could I. He delivers an infectious message that still resonates with me today.

I encouraged Craig to write this book because his positive vantage point on life is too unique to be lost. His message and unique perspective is one that must be heard.

Craig's ability to take on the world and conquer it despite his total blindness is a tremendous example for all of us.

Craig will entertain and enlighten you as he challenges you to explore your inner vision and inspire you to ignite your internal flame.

As I am currently in the battle of my life fighting stage 4 cancer, I continue to find my flame through Craig's friendship and the example of how he lives every day.

I remain convinced that with his guidance, through this book and his speeches, everyone who listens can find their flame.

Thank you, my good friend. Keep providing the fuel so that all the flames you ignited never burn out.

Cheers,

Brian Donaldson

Author's note

It is with a heavy heart that I inform all of you reading this book that my dear friend, Brian Donaldson, lost his courageous battle with cancer on August 5, 2019.

Brian, this book never would have come to fruition without your inspiration, coaching, and unwavering belief in me. I will forever cherish our continuous stream of conversation, exchange of ideas, and the never-ending fun and laughter we shared. You will be so dearly missed and never forgotten.

TABLE OF CONTENTS

ACKNOWLEDGMENTS

Everyone should be so blessed to have such remarkable in-laws like mine, Don and Diane Everson, and, of course, my extended family of friends, Mike and Roberta Theisen and Mark Harris, who have all gone the extra mile for me, without hesitation.

This would never have been possible without the amazing assistance of our son Derek and his unwavering commitment to this endeavor. To my wife Patti for her patience, understanding, and always being there for me. It is greatly appreciated. A special thanks to our daughters Ashley and Morgan for their contributions.

Beyond that, I'd be remiss if I didn't acknowledge the world of Edward Jones, which has believed in me wholeheartedly for three decades with no end in sight.

And I can't forget all the extraordinary people who, through their examples, so profoundly shaped my life and empowered the message that I share today with numerous audiences around the world.

Words may be the tools I use to earn my living, but there are not enough words to express my gratitude for all I have been given in my life.

AUTHOR'S NOTE

So, Craig, why are you writing another book? Didn't you already tell us your story in *Craig MacFarlane Hasn't Heard of You Either!*

Yes, I did!

And my purpose is not to retell it here.

This book is the product of six years of answering questions at speeches and appearances and the reflection that resulted as I have been encouraged to expand on, and explain, the messages behind my comments and short essays about success and happiness in the last book.

The purpose of the pages that follow is to elaborate on the principles of achieving a happy and successful life as they have been instilled and ingrained in me as a result of having lived "my story."

You will hear many voices speaking through me, as well as many quotes that have remained inspiring to me throughout my life. You'll also hear a lot of vintage Craig MacFarlane as I pontificate unabashedly over the next couple hundred pages. After 36 years of sharing the stage with many inspirational speakers and entertaining personalities, many of their phrases, quotes, and analogies have become part of my natural vernacular. If you recognize one please accept that I'm adapting it to my perspective and respect that I give complete credit where it is due and full appreciation for having been allowed to absorb the wisdom and share it with you. If you see anything

Life is the art of drawing without an eraser!

—*John W Gardner*

quoted in this book that I failed to credit, please share the message. I'll acknowledge your sentiment.

I hope you take your time with this book. Use the first quarter to, as they say in the world of sports, feel out the opposition. There are just enough flashbacks to help you remember how my perspective evolved, as we build a foundation. Then, let me help you start scoring significant points by enriching, empowering, and enhancing your world with my experience.

I promise, this will not devolve into a pathetic "10-step program" filled with overused sports examples that profess to give you a foolproof formula for success. I'm old enough to know better, and so are you.

On the contrary, I hope you find what follows to be a conversational (after all it is just you and me), easy to read, easy to digest, and hard to resist series of observations and interpretations from a perspective that no one else could possibly offer you.

If nothing else, I hope you find the message of this book to be actionable and applicable in your pursuit of health, wealth, and happiness. Be prepared to internalize who you honestly are today. Otherwise, the pages of this book will be read by blind eyes and a closed mind.

I intend to awaken your theater of thinking. I'm going to bring you face-to-face with your life's real purpose and help you unleash the passion, with sacrifice, necessary to make your purpose your reality.

I intend to:

- Ask you why
- Propel you past procrastination
- Eliminate your need for making excuses
- Awaken your courage
- Raise your standards
- Boost the capacity of your mental toolbox
- Challenge your mental toughness
- Elevate your adaptability

Challenge your own status quo—before someone else does.

—*Ron Kaufman*

- Upgrade your mental processor
- Supercharge your mental transmission
- Turbocharge your Grey Zone
- Give your perception a sense of reality
- Crystalize your inner vision
- Clarify your message
- Embolden your relationships
- Merge you onto the extra mile *and*
- Connect a gasoline IV to the engine that is your inner flame

At the same time, I fully intend to give you the respect and consideration you deserve. So, I'm not going to waste these pages telling you *what* to do. You'll be getting no "magic 10-step" solutions here. What you will get is the most unique set of mental tools, processes, and perspectives that you'll be able to apply to create any result you desire.

Why don't you buckle up, fasten your seatbelt, and remember the driver is totally blind—I promise you'll enjoy the ride.

The person who says it cannot be done should not interrupt the person who is doing it.

—*Chinese Proverb*

Never let people box or paint you into a corner by telling you your not good enough, fast enough, strong enough, tough enough, qualified enough or smart enough. The only person who truly knows what your fully capable of achieving is you. You short change yourself when you throw the towel in the ring prematurely.

Inside every one of us we have a small little torch, how high you light the flame on the torch inside you can only be reflected by the smile you put on your face as you walk through life each and everyday. That is the true power of a self-lit flame.

You can't expect the world to come to you on a silver platter. You must continue to create your own breaks and opportunities.

PURPOSE, PASSION, AND SACRIFICE: SUCCESS BEGINS WITH A SELF-LIT FLAME

Over the past 36 years of corporate life, traveling the world as a keynote inspirational speaker, I've been the beneficiary of more unique opportunities to personally interact with, observe, and learn from more successful people than you can imagine, including three US presidents; Pope Benedict the 16th; innumerable CEOs of Fortune 100 and 500 companies; platinum-selling recording artists; Oscar-, Emmy-, and Tony-award-winning actors; and so many all-star athletes. Can you believe that my move from Canada to the United States was the result of Gordie Howe (Mr. Hockey, look him up), inviting me to live with him and his wife in Connecticut? President George H. W. Bush, and his wife Barbara, actually crashed my 23rd birthday party. I've had the benefit of being mentored by many of these acquaintances and developed many very meaningful friendships, but I can't emphasize enough, at the end of the day, that it has been the ordinary people I encounter on a daily basis who I have observed doing extraordinary things that inspire me to continue to try and inspire you. After all, in my mind, I'm still just an ordinary guy despite all that's happened to me and all I've learned as a result.

Now, that's enough about me. This book isn't about my story, there's another one out there that takes care of that. This book is about what I've

Push harder today than yesterday if you want a different tomorrow.

learned, from my very unique perspective, over the course of building a very satisfying and happy life, and it all starts with the lesson I've continued to confirm from my association with these very special people. Their operating systems were driven by purpose, passion, and sacrifice.

This book is called *Find Your Flame Through Purpose, Passion, and Sacrifice* because those are the fundamental elements of accomplishing anything worthwhile. They are the overarching bedrock ingredients that you continually return to over the course of a successful, satisfying, and happy life.

Sure, there is a huge subset of skills and attitudes that you're going to need to tap into along your journey, and I'll be discussing many of those in the following pages, but without purpose, passion, and sacrifice, most people never get out of the garage let alone get in pursuit of the extra mile.

Without a substantial, absolutely essential purpose, you're limiting yourself. Now, I'm not talking about goal setting here. You are going to set and achieve many goals on your success journey and over time the nature of the goals is going to change and evolve. How you achieve those goals will also change over time as you mature and develop. The goals you achieve that support you on your journey will often be set as necessities to continue the journey, and many will become key components of your ultimate achievement, but it is the ultimate achievement that is your purpose. Your purpose is what gets you up and keeps you going. It is the big picture that all your efforts and accomplishments will build to. It is the most important thing in the world to you, even though, occasionally, you will need to remind yourself. In other words, it's your reason WHY.

Once your WHY is clear, you'll need fuel to propel you along your journey. The fuel is your passion. It is the energy and excitement that you feel inside when you remind yourself WHY. It is the force that propels you through the challenging times and accelerates you during the good times. When you get your WHY right, you'll find that your passion is always burning and ready to respond to any request you make of it. You'll also find

> **In every single day, in every walk of life, ordinary people do extraordinary things. Ordinary people accomplish Extraordinary things.**
>
> —*Jim Valvano*

that your passion is voracious. It wants to grow and get stronger, and if you feed it, it can take you farther faster than you can imagine right now. Your responsibility is to feed your passion with all the personal development, skill development, and knowledge acquisition you can in your continuous program of self-improvement in pursuit of your purpose. Your passion is manifested in the actions you take in pursuit of a successful life, but remember, *action* is just a word until you give it meaning and purpose and take it to heart.

Fueling your passion comes at the cost of sacrifice, which doesn't have to be a bad thing. If you are truly, genuinely, sincerely passionate about your purpose, then the sacrifice will be a labor of love. It will be about investing the time, effort, and energy needed to gain the knowledge and develop the skills that you know will bring you closer and closer to achieving that purpose.

Sacrifice is about doing the work. It is about putting in the time, it's about being the first to arrive and the last to leave, it's about extending the day, it's about going outside the boundaries of the clock, so that you can do more inside the boundaries. It's about continuously taking action, without taking shortcuts, that has the effect of throwing logs on the fire of your internal flame, which feeds your passion. Sacrifice is not about giving up everything that matters to you except your success, but it does demand that you find ways to push your limits. You'll need to develop skills in that list of subsets in order to cope, because you have to do the work, but remember, the goal is still a happy, satisfying life, and you can have both. Just do the work to learn the balance.

I firmly believe that we all have a flame within us that is waiting to be ignited. The spark that ignites that flame is your purpose, and that part of the equation is totally up to you. It must be a self-lit flame because only you know what truly excites you. I can't overemphasize that it must "truly excite you." After all, you're not chasing my dream. A false flame will burn out, no matter how much fuel you try to feed it. You have to be honest with yourself

If you can't figure out your purpose, figure out your passion. For your passion will lead you right into your purpose.

—*Bishop T. D. Jakes*

and engage in some serious soul searching to be certain that you know what your purpose is and why you want it. I'm not suggesting that this a clinical, cut and dried, set a purpose and go for it equation. It's not a definitive process, but it is one that you need to take charge of because if left to chance, you'll be chasing false dreams forever.

Many ideas can excite us in a moment, but only a true calling can sustain us. I know this not because one of my many mentors told me, but because I was brought face-to-face with having a major purpose and knowing why I was making the sacrifice at a very early age. When I was only six years old, by law, I was required to attend the Ontario School for the Blind, which was 500 miles away from home. From the moment I was deposited there, all I wanted was to go home. When I found what I thought would be my vehicle, I worked relentlessly because I was afraid that if I failed, I might never get to live at home again. I understand this now, in retrospect, but it doesn't change the reality. I had a purpose that ignited my passion so strongly that I would do anything to achieve it, and, ultimately, I did. You can, too, if your purpose is true.

You are going to evolve as a person over the course of your journey, and your purpose will evolve too. You are going to achieve some ambitions and recalibrate your purpose as you continue to move upward and onward.

My purpose today is very different, but just as inspiring. Yes, I still speak at major events and interact with senior executives, but I have also spoken at more than 3,000 high schools and almost as many community meetings and service clubs. I thrive on my time in the sighted world, interacting with people just like you and me, honest people doing an honest day's work, and the most rewarding experience, which is meeting ordinary people who are doing extraordinary things. I do the work I do today hoping that I can contribute to your next extraordinary accomplishment by providing a dose of inspiration for you to overcome whatever is holding you back and just try,

Passion eats depression for breakfast, feeds on sadness for lunch, devours procrastination at the dinner table, and gobbles up excuses all day long.

without fear or trepidation. It is in the trying that everything great becomes reality.

My purpose is to help your flame burn a little brighter and hopefully inspire you to continue feeding your passion.

Here's a few pieces of kindling to throw on your internal flame:

- Have a clear vision of how your purpose will look when you arrive and absolutely understand WHY you want to get there.
- Make whatever sacrifice is necessary to keep your passion burning brilliantly.
- When your purpose, passion, and sacrifice are flying in unison, there will be no challenge you can't overcome and no ambition you can't make reality.

Have the passion, take the action and magic will happen.

—Bar Rafaeli

IN CASE YOU MISSED IT

Some of you will have already read my previous book, *Craig MacFarlane Hasn't Heard of You Either.* For those of you who have, welcome back and thank you. You may want to skip these next 45 pages, as what follows is a summary my life story, as told in that book.

For the rest of you, I encourage you to keep reading. Much of the wisdom that follows in this book comes from a most unique vantage point, as I learned my lessons through practical, hands-on, real-life experience long before I was introduced to the academic lessons and associated principles. Consequently, having an understanding of my story is helpful, if not critical, to seeing the applications

CLOSE YOUR EYES

You already know that I'm blind. What you need to understand, if much of what is to follow is truly going to resonate for you, is that I'm totally blind. Let me explain.

There is one thing that it is critical we both understand on the same terms. If we can establish that starting point, it will punctuate everything else this book has to offer, in the most dramatic way.

In a moment I am going to ask you to try an experiment, but first, please let me establish some ground rules.

I am going to ask you to close your eyes. NOT YET! You need to read this first, but in a moment I will ask.

Life's lowest moments can be the strength of your greatest gifts.

Once you have closed them, there are a few more things I would like you to do. First, eliminate any sense of light or shadow that may be filtering through your eyelids. No grey, no light or dark, no motion whatsoever. Try to eliminate the blackness too. I honestly see absolutely nothing. I have no knowledge of color. I don't know what blackness is, or redness, blueness either. I have absolutely no vision. Can you create the equivalent of that in your mind, just for a moment? GREAT, but not yet.

Once you do, imagine that you have no memory of any images at all. You know what absolutely nothing looks like. All the mental images your imagination is about to create on the inside of your eyelids to compensate for your lack of vision do not count. They do not exist. You have never seen a toothbrush, bar of soap, or a shower (or a toilet for that matter.) You don't know what a cereal bowl looks like, or a spoon. You have no reference for your imagination to create any images to help you with the tasks you must do or learn. Even if you have read, or have a verbal description to draw on, the chances of your imagination, working without reference, creating the right picture are slim. Can you have faith in the picture?

Let's start out, first thing in the morning. You have just awoken and need to start your day. How are you going to get ready? How will you tell the shampoo bottle from the conditioner, or, if your partner is like mine, the other 14 bottles and cans and tubes and bars in your shower? How will you set the water temperature? How will you shave, be it your legs or your chin? How will you be sure you are putting toothpaste, not hemorrhoid cream, on your brush? How will you be sure it's your brush? How will you comb your hair or make sure your part is straight?

Once your shower is finished, how will you dress yourself? How do you make sure your clothes coordinate? Remember, you've never seen a dress or a suit, but you have to decide what works. You have no idea what red or yellow or black are. How will you tie your tie? Is it the right tie? Can you

> The definition of darkness is the absence of light. You cannot see darkness. Darkness cannot exist without light. Darkness cannot be explained. Darkness only comes when everything else has gone. Darkness is nothing...then darkness is everything.

find your shoes? Are they the right ones for this outfit? Will you be confident when you're done? Will you be ready to face the world?

Imagine preparing your breakfast. How do you know you're pouring Raisin Bran in your bowl and not Fruity Pebbles or elbow macaroni? Are you sure that cereal bowl is clean? What about the milk? All gallon milk jugs feel the same. Is that white or chocolate milk you are about to pour?

And where is your phone? Where did the kids leave it?

Now you are out in the world. You would like to try your hand at golfing. Problem is you have never seen a golf club, let alone somebody swing one. What would you do if you were handed one now? How would you learn the swing? How would you learn to model something you've never seen a person doing?

Not interested in golf? How about skiing? You've never seen skis or a skier. What is your starting reference? What does a crouch look like, feel like? Can you translate this experience to waterskiing, or wrestling, or throwing a javelin, or changing a diaper?

This is the one thing I hope you can understand about me. I am not visually impaired. I am totally blind, with no visual memory that I can access.

Now, please close your eyes and try to imagine learning and doing in a complete vacuum, void of any light, shadow, color, or motion. Try to imagine getting out of your house in the morning, or out of your hotel room. Try to imagine learning to golf, ski, throw a javelin, run in a straight line, or waterski jump and do it at a highly competitive level. Just try.

I hope you can read this book from that frame of reference and really listen to the thoughts that come.

That's all I ask. Now, if you are ready, let's go!

So, now you know that I'm totally blind. What you probably don't know yet is that I wasn't born this way. I lost my eyesight in an accident when I was two years old. Initially it was only one eye, but we lived in a small town in Northern Ontario where ophthalmologists were rare commodities, and by the time the doctor at the nearest hospital had returned from a medical

The darkness that surrounds us cannot hurt us. It is the darkness in your own heart you should fear.

—*Bernardus Silvestris*

conference he was attending, a sympathetic condition had caused the sight in my surviving eye to be lost as well.

I grew up in Desbarats, Ontario, which is a small town, and I do mean a really small town. Even today, the population of the township where my hometown of Desbarats is located is only 750 people. It was a charming place to grow up, where everyone knew everyone, and everyone helped everyone. When I lost my eyesight, everybody in town knew about it.

After my accident, which so many people still want to call a tragedy, but which I have come to think of as a minor inconvenience, my home town supported my parents through the struggles of my recovery, through the long trips to Sick Children's Hospital in Toronto, over 500 miles away, and the cost of being away for weeks at a time and the lost income and all that stuff. When I finally came home to stay, the moral support for me and my brother and my parents was tremendous. So was the result.

It all came down to my mother. Over the years she has often been quoted as saying, "We didn't know how to raise a blind kid, so we just raised a kid." My mother and my father just expected me to be part of everything, and I was. I learned how to bake pies with my mom. I learned how to hunt and trap and make maple syrup—hey we are Canadians—with my dad. I learned to climb trees with my friends. I learned to skate. I went tobogganing. I had my own bicycle and rode it wherever I wanted. I ultimately had my own horse, which I took care of and learned to ride. I learned how to walk to my grandma's house, which was about half a mile away, on my own. I even had my own car, which I drove into several ditches, although that was years later.

The point is this: I grew up as an everyday, run-of-the-mill, normal—if there is really such a thing— kid, in every respect, and I fit in. I belonged. I wasn't pampered or protected or over-sheltered. With very few exceptions, I was just part of the family, one of the gang. I had a happy life in the sighted world, and I loved it.

Then, I turned six. Now, turning six, in the province of Ontario, in 1968, meant I had to start school. Being totally blind and turning six in

We didn't know how to raise a blind kid, so we just raised a kid.

—Joyce MacFarlane

Ontario meant that I had to start school at the Ontario School for the Blind, which was the only school for the blind in the entire province. Actually, it was the only school for the blind in the entire country at that time.

The Ontario School for the Blind is located in Brantford, Ontario. Brantford is a nice enough place, but it is also 717 kilometers (459 miles) away from my hometown of Desbarats. I was being forced to leave my home and my family and my friends and my pets and everything to live in a strange place with strange people where I was going to have to follow a whole bunch of blind kid rules. It was the law, my parents had no choice, but to me it was punishment.

Can you imagine being forced to send your son or daughter, especially your handicapped son or daughter, almost 500 miles away from your home just because they had to start first grade? Can you imagine turning over care and supervision of your child to a group of total strangers who would be with them day and night while you were reduced to one ten-minute, long-distance phone call once a week? Remember, this was 1968. There was no Internet, no Facebook, no Messenger or WhatsApp or Viber, and long-distance phone calls were expensive. Certainly, there were no webcams, so you wouldn't see your child grow and develop, and they can change fast at that age. You might be picking up a child who barely resembles the one you dropped off months earlier, and you'd have missed it all. I have five children and I can't imagine going through that. It must have been so hard on my parents.

I still remember when my mom said goodbye to me the day Dad drove me there. I still didn't know what was about to happen, and I couldn't understand why she was so sad. Finally, Dad hurried me into the car, and after a couple quick side trips to say goodbye to my grandparents, my dad and I were off.

Dad just kept driving and driving and driving. He was so quiet, and I was afraid to say anything. It was a long, long, long, eight-hour drive. Finally, we got there, and he took me upstairs and dropped off my luggage in this strange room. It was then that I realized that he didn't have any luggage, that they had only packed for me. Still, Dad stayed for a couple hours, and we wandered around. It was a big place, but I didn't care about that.

How can I miss something if I have no memory of having it?

Then it came time for Dad to go. Remember, he still had to make that eight-hour drive back home, so he took me back to my room. By now I knew it was just going to be my room, not our room, not his and mine anyway. My roommates were there when we got back to the room. There were introductions and Dad explained to me that I would be staying with these new friends because this would be my school. He told me that he needed to go home because he and Mom still had to work. He told me that I would be coming home at Christmas and Easter and maybe Thanksgiving, and he and Mom would come and visit, but that I needed to stay there.

It all happened so quick and, all of a sudden, he was gone, and I was, at least to my six-year-old way of thinking, alone and in prison. For the first time in my life, I didn't have the safety, security, and familiarity of my family, friends, and home. It left me feeling not only scared but sick to my stomach. I had never even been around another blind person before. This was a totally different world.

I CAN'T, I'M BLIND TOO!

I found exactly how different the next morning. I got up early and went off to try and find the cafeteria for breakfast. Dad had taken me there the day before, and I was trying to retrace my steps. Then, while I'm just walking down the hall, another kid runs right into me, knocking us both sideways. I get myself back together and call over my shoulder at the other kid, "Hey, watch where you're going." He replied, "I can't, I'm blind too." Talk about a reality check. Truth is, that wasn't a unique experience. In my early days at the School for the Blind, class change always looked, and felt, like bumper cars until we all learned to always walk down the right-hand side of the hall.

It was in my second year that I saw my opportunity to prove I deserved to live with my family in the "sighted world." During that time, I got okay grades, but I did become a master mischief maker because I was bored. I didn't see the need to follow all the rules. I didn't need to be coddled and protected.

Thanks to the way I grew up, I was an independent spirit who could get around freely, without always walking on the right or holding the bannisters

I was forced to walk my talk before I ever knew what my talk was!

or waiting to be led through the commons. I had skills. I had learned to navigate for myself in the forest when my dad took me hunting and trapping. As my hearing started to become more acute, I had even developed a skill I now call "echo location." Simply, I learned to make a loud clicking sound with my tongue off the roof of my mouth and could tell where things were around me by listening to the echo bounce back to me. I was so good at it that I could move around the forest without bumping into trees, so dealing with the occasional lamppost was no problem. Sensing the freedom that came with not needing the rules to function or cope, I was a genuinely effective, or so I thought, practical joker. What I didn't realize was that I was developing a reputation.

By the end of first grade, the teachers in the athletic department decided I needed some constructive direction, and they made me an offer, one that I really couldn't refuse, that changed my life. That was the start of a lifetime of learning and practicing the laws of mental toughness. The mental toughness was emotionally motivated at first, but I had guidance from my coaches and later my teachers. As I became more and more committed to my vision, my powers of mental toughness and emotional resilience became firmly embedded in my character. The lessons were emotional, if not almost spiritual, in my younger days, which is why I refer to learning the principles of mental toughness as confirmation. By the time I learned the principles, I had been living them for years.

I became a member of the Ontario School for the Blind wrestling program. My teachers saw this as a way that I could "act out by the rules." Being a high-energy, restless type, I welcomed the opportunity to roughhouse and play without worrying about being disciplined, but this wasn't a lot of fun in the beginning. I was the youngest member of the team, and the smallest, at the tender age of seven. It was hard because I didn't know what I was doing, yet, and that meant struggling to compete with kids much bigger than me, who were better. It also meant having those bigger kids knocking me down and falling on me, kicking me in the head, and bending me in ways the body doesn't bend, which left me feeling exhausted and battered at the end of practice. Just imagine how you'd feel after spending an hour on a wrestling

They had meant to break my spirit, or at least rein it in...

mat with a bunch of blind kids who don't know what they're doing. You don't know when you're going to get hit, or where.

That was perfect in the minds of my teachers. Exhausted was their goal for me. They had meant to break my spirit, or at least rein it in, while giving me a little constructive direction. The battered part they didn't worry about. They just expected that would come to an end as I got better, and bigger. That didn't reassure me very much. I wasn't enjoying it much at all, but I was a competitive kid who didn't like to lose so I stayed at it, thinking I'd eventually get my chance to pay back those bigger kids who always beat me in the early days.

That mind-set changed, and the evolution of my reputation for mental toughness and emotional resiliency was put in hyperdrive, when our coach announced that we were going to compete in a tournament. At first that intimidated me, because I still wasn't winning very much, but then I learned that at the other school I'd be competing against kids my size, or at least my own weight. That made me feel better, but what really turned on the switch was when I found out I'd be competing against kids who can see!

Ironically, that was the news that my coach thought would scare me the most, but to me that meant that this would be like going home. I wrestled and roughhoused, and sometimes just plain fought, with my friends and even my brother, and all of them could see. I had always been able to give as good as I got and won my share of battles, so if these kids I was going to wrestle against were all my size, thanks of course to weight classes, then I figured I had as good a chance to win as anybody. I was getting excited.

When my excitement about wrestling a sighted guy came through, my coach explained that the Ontario School for the Blind was the only school for the blind in the entire country. That meant that every match I wrestled in competition would be against sighted opponents.

What excited me the most was the idea that when I got my call from Mom and Dad on Sunday, I wanted to be able to tell them that I wrestled a kid who could see, and I won. That excited me because my next question

You can hear a smile over the phone. That's good. The problem is you can also hear a frown.

was going to be, "If I can learn wrestling good enough to beat a sighted kid, why can't I come home and be on the wrestling team with my friends?"

Do you see what was starting to happen, even if I didn't know it yet? It wasn't the winning that mattered as much as what it represented. In my mind, even at eight years old, I was already thinking that if I could prove I was able to learn wrestling good enough to win against sighted kids, maybe that would prove I deserved to live in the sighted world, in my world, back in Desbarats, like all my friends.

Well, I did win in that first tournament and then I had the accolades to deal with, and the medal. They awarded me a medal. They said it was gold and I just took their word for it, that didn't matter. That first medal was the most important medal I ever won. It was the one I cared about the most, the one I really cherished. I kept it under my pillow, slept with it, and held it in my hands, sometimes next to my heart. That medal became my symbol of hope that if I kept winning more gold medals, just like that medal, that someday they'd let me live at home again. I didn't even know who they were, but I was quickly convincing myself that if I kept winning in the sighted world, they'd have to let me back in, they'd just have to.

To me, hope is like kindling. The more you have, the brighter the flame that burns inside you, but remember, you can't live on hope. Action throws the logs on the fire that sustains the flame that drives you. My action was the competition with myself. I really believed that if I was the best I could be, if I pushed to have any advantage, even being able to do one sit-up more than everyone else, that I could achieve my goal.

Making sense? Can you understand how, all of a sudden, I didn't just want to roughhouse with the big kids in practice, I wanted to learn what they knew. I wanted to learn how they did those moves that let them beat me. I became determined to get up every time they knocked me down because if I got up enough times, this might just be my ticket out, to get back home.

That was my first experience with knowing WHY and the beginning of having to "walk my talk before I ever knew what my talk was!" But I was

If you feel you reside on the outskirts of hope, maybe it's time to change your zip code.

motivated. I sensed opportunity and was starting to believe that I didn't have to give in and accept this fate.

"GIVE 'EM HELL RIGHT FROM THE START"

That was the start of the mental toughness that would define the rest of my athletic career. I went back to school with a determination to become the best wrestler I could be, so I could keep winning until they allowed me to go home. I also became determined to be the strongest, fastest, best-conditioned wrestler I could be because I had been very surprised by how hard some of those other kids were willing to fight to try and beat me. After all, nobody wanted to lose to a blind kid. Plus, Grandpa's strategy to "give 'em hell right from the start" was exhausting, but I was on a mission. I just knew, at some deep-down level I didn't understand yet, that this was my ticket home.

After that, truth be told, I became obsessed. I was the first to arrive at practice every afternoon and I never wanted to leave. I did every exercise the coaches told us to do, tried to sneak in a couple extra reps of everything we did, bugged the coaches about extra exercise I could do, and I wrestled. I wrestled every kid I could in every weight class. I didn't resent the bigger kids anymore. I wanted to battle them. My thinking was, if I could beat them, I would beat the kids in my weight class for sure. I even wrestled in the locker bay during class change and in the cafeteria line. *Oops!*

And I did start winning, but winning never became my purpose. It was my vehicle, my passion, but not my purpose. Initially I was motivated not by winning but by a fear of losing. I was totally afraid that if I started losing, even just a little bit, that it might derail my dream of going home, so I became determined to win. Many people, most in fact, didn't understand this, and my coaches and my parents would sometimes be asked if they thought my allegedly obsessive fixation on winning was unhealthy. They knew better and would reassure all those concerned that I was fine. They knew, I wasn't driven by gold medals, trophies, or the eventual headlines.

In a way, it was perfect eight-year-old logic, and it forever changed my life and how I thought about it.

My coaches taught us a discipline of no excuses! Let's face it, we all had a built-in excuse, if we wanted to fall back on it, and to ensure that none of us were tempted, they didn't accept any excuses at all. They also taught a culture of no exceptions. Part of the mental toughness that developed in many of us was the discipline of doing our homework. We couldn't go to practice if it wasn't done, and we couldn't go to tournaments if we didn't have good grades. That taught us responsibility, which is another cornerstone of mental toughness.

As time went by and I began to gain some recognition as a successful wrestler, I began looking for ways to accelerate my ambitions. I had worked hard to become a skilled wrestler, but I had always credited my success to my grandpa's formula. With that thinking, I had developed the habit of doing 100 sit-ups or more, over 100 push-ups, and a bunch of chin-ups every day, in addition to the work we did at practice. I didn't do them all at once, but throughout the day I'd get them done, firmly believing that every rep I did was one the competition wasn't doing. As I got older, I also started sneaking out at night, after homework was done, and running extra laps at the school track. The School for the Blind had a track with a special handrail that we used as a guide. This not only kept kids from running off the track, or into each other, but it meant, for me, that I could run a hard as I wanted with no fear of getting injured.

I was learning two very important lessons or developing two very important character traits during these six years of my life. We didn't have the fancy terms for them back then, but my coaches, and through their support, my teachers and my parents, certainly knew how to instill the principles, which I still carry with me now, although they manifest themselves a little differently these days. Those principles are emotional resiliency and mental toughness, and they both came to play bigger and bigger roles in my life as I got older.

I made another discovery as a result of doing all that work, and it helped me accelerate my ambitions, although not in the way I anticipated. I discovered, in the process of running all the additional laps, night after night after

If you ever hope to do what you want to do, keep doing what you have to do!

night, that I not only had great stamina as a runner, but I could also run exceptionally fast.

This added another dimension to the pursuit of my ambition. I began running for the school track team. I began winning in another arena. I began developing a backup plan in case my plan to earn my way home as a championship wrestler fell through. And, I began winning.

My fears proved to be unfounded as I kept winning in both sports. I started winning national championships and accumulating more gold medals and getting more recognition, which lead to publicity, which lead to opportunities to argue my case to return home.

GOING HOME

Ultimately, as a result of sheer hard work, supported by the emotional resiliency and mental toughness my coaches instilled in me and fueled by my passion to live in the sighted world, my dream became reality as I did return home, joining my friends as I became a freshman at Central Algoma Secondary School in Desbarats, Ontario.

By this time in my life, my purpose was starting to change. I'd made it home, but that was just the start. I became concerned with how I'd stay there, especially after I finished school. I started to think about careers and how I would earn a living. This became an even more intense mental exercise as it became time to start picking electives and planning curricula at school. I was looking for ways to change and adapt, anticipating the eventual end to my athletic career and being determined to find a way to support myself and carry on when those days were over.

What I knew was this: "What was good enough to get me here wouldn't be good enough to keep me here." I had learned to always be looking forward.

Of course, I continued my athletic pursuits while I was in school. I continued to win tournaments and gold medals and blind national championships and even participated as a member of Team Canada in a number of international events, and that opened some interesting doors.

What was good enough to get me here might not be good enough to keep me here.

When you win the blind national championship after competing all year where the majority of your competition was able to see, you attract a certain amount of notoriety. That was never really my pursuit, but it was a useful tool in attracting attention to my story and creating higher-profile platforms to present my case, but as a very young man from the School for the Blind those opportunities showed up as rare human interest stories in the local newspapers or a mention on the sports page of a newspaper in the town where we traveled to for our latest tournament, and maybe a mention on television after a national event, but it was never enough to distract me from my prime directive.

Once I was home, and older, I began to receive requests to give speeches, to tell my story, at local service clubs, chambers of commerce, other schools, and such. I'm an outgoing type and I enjoyed being able to tell my story and answer questions. After the Canadian Television Network (CTV) had done a feature on me for its version of *Wide World of Sports*, which was the third national documentary done on my life before I had even turned 19, I started wondering if being a public speaker might be a great career option. Of course, school and training still dominated my time, but I filed the idea in the back of my mind and continued to accept every request to speak that I was offered.

I also started coming to grips with the issue of time. I was succeeding in my new life, but there was a certain lack of freedom that I found frustrating and that my hard-earned superstar status among the sighted couldn't compensate for. I was happy, yes, but apprehensive too. I was entering my junior year and, as always, was concerned about being ready for the transition to an independent adult life. Maybe I was looking to maximize my advantages, but of all things—and it even astounded me at first—I longed to go back to the School for the Blind.

The idea really began to sink in with me that spring. The School for the Blind was where I had been truly the most free. I had carved out a life for myself there where I could roam at will. I knew every nook and cranny of that place. I'd learned and achieved things that I hadn't at Central Algoma.

Life isn't about finding yourself. Life is about creating yourself.

—*George Bernard Shaw*

I was a better student, for one thing. The School for the Blind has special things like raised maps for learning geography and Braille books, which was something I never had my entire freshman year. Academically speaking, that kind of help really makes a difference.

Even the athletic facilities gave me an advantage. The School for the Blind had an indoor track that I could run on alone. I could ramp up my training in ways I simply couldn't at Central Algoma. I thought I was going to find independence in a sighted school, but many of the methods that were set up in Brantford actually gave me more freedom to learn. I missed all those hours on the outdoor rink playing hockey with the tin can and our tin can hockey league, something I didn't have in Desbarats either.

I returned to the School for the Blind for my junior and senior years, continuing my athletic pursuits full speed while ramping up my academic standards to ensure acceptance to university and getting active in student politics as I prepared for the next phase of my life. It was a two-year, nonstop whirlwind of activity that took a large degree of mental toughness to do all the work and to do it all when it should be done, as it should be done, while staying in the best possible shape to continue outlasting ever increasingly more skilled competition on the wrestling mat and adapting to the constantly changing and unexpected demands of being president of the student council for two years. It was a blur, but it paid amazing results.

In 1980, when I graduated from the School for the Blind, I travelled with the Canadian team to Arnhem, Holland, to compete in the Worldwide Olympics for the Disabled. I competed in wrestling, sprinting, and goalball, a sport that was developed for the blind.

TURNING A PAGE

As I turned the next page in the adventure that has been my life, the transition to my career as an inspirational keynote speaker was getting underway.

There were, however, still a few memorable and event-filled athletic quests yet to be pursued.

If opportunity doesn't knock, build a door.

—*Milton Berle*

The next adventure was a combination of athletics and entrepreneurism as I decided to hold an event of my own, and in 1982, I hosted the Craig MacFarlane Charity Celebrity Tennis Tournament in Sault Ste. Marie, Ontario. This was easily the biggest thing I had ever undertaken, and most gave me little chance of pulling it off.

I knew I could do it because this had the right reasons WHY. First, I could give something back to the Soo and Desbarats, the places that supported and believed in me and my family when we needed it most, and still did, and does.

Second, it was, in my mind, a great way to connect with influential sports personalities who could help me explore my marketability. All I needed to do was attract them.

Once I had my major sponsor, and a budget (what a budget) from Molson Breweries and Adidas to work with, I set my sights on attracting a major name as my honorary chairman. I set my sights on Gordie Howe. To me there was no bigger name in Canadian sports. As a Canadian kid, there was no bigger name in sports, period! Wayne Gretzky may have been on his way to legendary status, but Gordie already resided there. He wasn't just a legend in hockey, he was a *god*.

It wasn't the first time I had asked something of Gordie, either. When I was in third grade, I had written Mr. Hockey a letter:

Dear Mr. Howe,

I think you are one of the greatest hockey players in the NHL. Can I have an autographed picture of you? I am a pretty good hockey player myself.

Sincerely,
Craig MacFarlane

I wrote my letter in Braille of course, and my teacher, generously, had underlined the script and written in the words.

I was ambitious, even in the third grade, and absolutely intended to become the first blind hockey player in the NHL. I didn't realize that dream,

You have to have a plan, but be prepared for the detours.

but I did touch the heart of one of my hockey idols. Gordie remembered receiving my letter. In fact, he had kept it. I was determined to be just as memorable at age 19.

Gordie's wife, Colleen, most often related the story. She would later talk about how persistent I was at trying to get Gordie to be my honorary chairman. It was Colleen who finally said to Gordie, "You know this kid is not going to give up, we might as well do it. Who knows, it might be fun."

After the tournament, the night it ended actually, I sat up with Colleen and Gordie past 3:00 a.m. talking. Colleen, showing a motherly concern already, was interested in what I wanted to do with my life. I told her and Gordie that I wanted to take my athletic experience and create some form of business path that I could follow and build. I also shared that I didn't know how I was going to do this yet, and I was now researching and networking, looking for the right contact or opportunity.

Colleen's enthusiasm and the fact that Gordie (despite being the roughest, toughest, and possibly meanest player in any professional sport) had a warm, kind, considerate heart, led them to say yes to my tournament. That was a major turning point in the success of the tournament, and as it turned out, in my life. After that, everyone else was on board. Restaurants, businesses, celebrities all made donations or agreed to participate in one way or another.

Later that month, Gordie and Colleen invited me to their second home at Bear Lake outside Traverse City, Michigan.

HOWE I CAME TO AMERICA

That day, the Howes made me an incredible offer. The Howes actually invited me to come and live with them in their home in Glastonbury, Connecticut, just outside Hartford. Gordie obtained a position for me with the National Hockey League's Hartford Whalers, working alongside him in the community relations department. I was able to learn more about sports marketing, a field of great interest to me, while I got my feet under me in the United States and got serious about a future.

Success is the progressive realization of worthwhile goals, while staying well adjusted.

Gordie got serious about my future too. He challenged me one day: "If you don't want to be just another blind athlete, if you really want to be the best ever, why don't you win 100 gold medals? Why stop now?" He was basically saying that if I wanted to build a career using my athletic success as my springboard, then punctuate it, leave no doubt about it. One hundred gold medals would be a tremendous milestone. It was a worthy goal and when I considered the accomplishments of the man who suggested it, I was inspired. I was going to do it.

I prided myself on staying in top physical condition, so I was ready for this challenge and decided that the quickest route to winning seven more gold medals would be in track and field. In that same month that Gordie challenged me, I entered the US Blind Nationals in Long Beach, California. Having set the goal, it was important to take action, right away. Otherwise, goals have a way of becoming delusions, and I have never been delusional.

I was not to be denied and I won four gold medals in California. That left three more to 100, and the next event I could get to was the New Jersey Invitational, two months later in November. I went in feeling confident that this would be the day my milestone accomplishment would be reached, but my confidence took a hit early in the competition.

The New Jersey Invitational was a huge lesson for me in mental toughness, not just because I felt like I was trying to find fuel in an empty tank early in the meet, but because my focus was thrown for a loop early, and I had to battle the mental distraction as well as the physical challenge.

Here's what happened: The first event was the 60 meters, which was an indoor event in New Jersey that year. The competitor immediately before me had veered off the course and ran head-on into a steel post, knocking himself senseless, unconscious actually. I swear I could still hear the post ringing in my ears as I was loading myself into the starting blocks. That mental image and sound does not create a confident feeling, particularly when you are expected to hurdle yourself down the same course, at breakneck speed with reckless abandon, in pursuit of nothing but sheer velocity, running

Giving up on your goal because of one setback is like slashing your other three tires because you got a flat.

toward a disembodied voice at the end of my lane. It affected me. I lost. By three-hundredths of a second.

That left me with my own mental challenge to deal with. I had a strategy in my mind going into New Jersey. I really wanted to win the 60 meters. That would take a little internal pressure off. It would still mean winning two of the next three events but now, to reach my 100th gold, I had to win three in a row. I couldn't let that take my focus off the next event. Let's face it, I couldn't win the javelin toss until I ran the 400 meters. I still had to do this one event at a time, but my spirits were down, for a second anyway.

The best-laid plans don't always go precisely the way you would like them to. More often than not what happens isn't what you hoped for, but it isn't what happens to you, it's how you react to it that ultimately counts. I had to find a way to boost my confidence, but that, too, was a challenge. Next event for me was the 400 meters, and my energy tank didn't seem to be full that day. Sometimes you just have to gut things out and this was feeling like one of those days.

I managed to win the 400 meters, but it wasn't a pretty picture. I didn't cruise to the finish line that day. It was a neck and neck struggle right down to the finish line, or so I'm told. What I remember is running the entire race with the sound of footsteps just off my left shoulder. As hard as I pushed, they just refused to fall behind, and I was being driven by my determination not to let them pull ahead. It was about then that the Grey Zone kicked in. It wasn't that I somehow magically summoned it, it was always more involuntary, like an extra gear that let me draw on all my years of conditioning and practice and hard work to push me just a little bit further. I don't even remember the end of that race. I remember dropping the guide rope, and that was it. It was as if I had thrown down the gauntlet. It was now or never. My friends and coaches told me later that the determination was written all over my face as I broke the tape. Truth is I didn't know where the tape was, and I didn't actually stop running until I was 20 meters past

Only those who will risk going too far can possibly find out how far one can go.

—T.S. Eliot

it. Didn't matter, I won the race in a photo finish. That still left two more events, but the drama was over.

I won the javelin purely due to benefits of years of strength training and practice. I had spent hundreds of hours every summer just throwing the javelin. To me it was all about refining my technique, like a baseball player taking hundreds of extra swings in a batting cage. On that day I just grunted and twisted harder than anyone else and let the muscle memory do its thing. Nobody else in that event had my motivation that night and it showed.

That meant only one more race stood between me and my 100th gold medal, and it was my favorite race, the 200 meters. That might have had something to do with it, but I doubt it. By that point, I had shaken my early mental distraction and, fueled by pure adrenaline, I'm sure my tank was full of energy again. I was not going to be denied. In my greatest tribute to my grandpa ever, I gave them hell right from the start. I burst out of the blocks and left the field in the dust.

I had done it. I had my 100th gold medal!

That was a monumental high point, not just in my athletic career but in my life. It marked the end of one era and the transition into the next. It was the time when I faced the reality that my life was changing and that I needed to find my own way of coping with the feeling, and taking advantage of new opportunities without resting on my laurels.

When I returned home, I could hear the smile in Gordie's voice, and that bear hug he gave me reminded me just how powerful this man was. His power went beyond his physical strength, and the inspiration he instilled in me still resonates with me to this day.

Fortunately, I already had a job with the Hartford Whalers and that was bringing me numerous chances to accelerate the advancement of my inspirational speaking career as well. I loved the job, and the fact that I was not only working beside Gordie Howe, but living in his house, prevented me from breaking stride. I couldn't let myself disappoint Gordie. In a sense, I was still being motivated by my fear of failure.

When you subscribe to a philosophy of being consistently good, occasionally you will have gusts of greatness.

THE RESTLESS SPIRIT PERSISTS

There was something else going on as well. I was getting restless. I had always led a physical life and I needed something to do. Not competition necessarily, at least not against others, but I needed a way to vent my energy. I still had that desire to push myself and challenge my abilities, so I started looking for a hobby that would satisfy this yearning.

For most blind athletes, their careers, and often their athleticism, come to an end when they leave school. The vast majority of blind athletes compete in individual sports because the traditional pursuits like joining a pickup basketball team or baseball team or any other team sport simply weren't practical. I did get to go on the ice with Gordie after Whaler practices, but that was too tame. I wanted something more intense.

Games like tennis or badminton or even golf weren't an option either, although I do joke with my friends who play tennis that "I have a great serve but a lousy return." The logistics alone were a deterrent, but the desire to find a challenging physical distraction, one where I could at least compete with myself, was insatiable.

Then the idea of skiing popped into my head. I had memories of the sound of skis chattering on the snow and the excitement of the commentators' voices when my dad would watch skiing on *Wide World of Sports*. I liked the idea of a sport that required a high level of physical coordination deployed at a high rate of speed where I could continually challenge myself. The idea slowly grew into an obsession, and I started researching the possibilities.

I didn't know much when I started looking around for opportunities, but soon found out that there was a large, well-respected, blind skiing program in Kirkwood, California, near Lake Tahoe, and another in Winter Park, Colorado. I also learned about the Blind National Snow-Skiing Championship that would be held the following April in Alta, Utah, and that really set my

---

If you become restless, speed up. If you become winded, slow down. You climb the mountain in an equilibrium between restlessness and exhaustion.

—Robert Pirsig

imagination on overload. This all sounded fabulous, but I was a young kid, in a new job, in Connecticut. There was no way I could afford the money, let alone the time, for either of these options. I settled for an option closer to home and contacted the best blind skiing program on the East Coast, hosted at Smugglers' Notch, in Vermont.

Smugglers' was a great place for my skiing adventure to begin, mostly because I was introduced to a wonderful man, George Spangler. I was told that George was a particularly good instructor, but he turned out to be much more. Without him I suspect that my skiing story could be very short, and possibly tragic.

I was restless, but I wasn't reckless. The danger element of learning to ski was appealing as part of the bigger package that came with the desire to feel the adrenaline rush of performing my best at the fastest speeds possible began to consume my imagination once again, but I didn't have a death wish. I knew there was going to be a lot to learn, and George focused me on just how much.

Still, the idea of the Blind National Snow-Skiing Championship in April was playing on my imagination too. I thought I was done with competitive sports, but who knew. So, the first time I talked to George, on the phone, I told him that I didn't just want to learn how to ski, I wanted to learn how to ski fast. I told him I wanted to learn how to race. I wanted to discover if I had enough talent to make it worthwhile to do the work necessary to learn to race.

What happened over the next four months was the greatest series of lessons in mental toughness and emotional resilience. Sure, it was a blur of adrenaline-fueled, testosterone-powered adventure after adventure but it was also a continual series of triumphs and failures and discoveries, reevaluations and challenges, self-doubts and affirmations, bumps and bruises, and pain and pleasure that makes even the most intimidating roller coaster ride look like a kiddie coaster in comparison.

The difference, this time, was my maturity. This was something new, and while I craved the new physical challenge, it came with coaching on a

I was restless, but I wasn't reckless.

level that opened my eyes and made me think, not just do. It was truly mind opening.

It took me over 60 pages to tell this story in *Craig MacFarlane Hasn't Heard of You Either*. It's not my purpose to retell the entire story here. However, it is a defining period of my life, even if it did only last four months. Let me share the headlines with you and the lessons I learned. You can decide if you want to read all the details after that.

Once I made up my mind, with skis and boots and gloves and googles and my snowsuit stowed in the luggage compartment of the bus, I headed off to Smugglers' Notch in January 1983.

I arrived in the evening, so there was no skiing, but George was there. He greeted me with a smile in his voice and immediately started building my confidence. I still remember how he grabbed me by the shoulders, stood me up, and said, "You're built just like a bulldog, this is going to be a breeze."

I'd been competing long enough to know exactly what he meant, and I was encouraged by the fact he understood too. Riding the residual benefits of all my years wrestling, I was still in excellent shape, and I am, after all, built rather low to the ground. I knew how to take a hit, or a tumble, and get up and do it again. I was looking forward to it actually. It encouraged me that George recognized that, because that defined so much of my skiing evolution.

I had my first skull session with my first coach before I ever got near my skis. Over dinner in the lodge at Smugglers' Notch, where I found that I quite appreciated the culture of the skiing world, George walked me through what I could expect over my four-day visit. He sprinkled this with frequent reassurances—maybe I looked worried—but he was calm and engaging, and when I went off to my room, I was convinced this was for me. Little did we know that his plan and our reality would have very little in common.

The next morning, I came face-to-face with how unprepared I was for this adventure. I may have been excited about learning something new, but when it dawned on me just how much there was to learn, I began asking

You cannot lead a battle if you think you look silly on a horse.

—Napoleon Bonaparte

myself, "Do I really want to do all this?" Maybe Colleen had been right, I should just take a scholarship to Yale and study law. Still, the thrill of conquering the mountain was calling to me. I decided to be an adult and learn my lessons, so I could experience the rush I was anticipating.

That didn't mean getting on a hill right away and being taught how to snowplow though. No, for me, as an absolute neophyte, that meant learning how to put on my equipment. My only qualification as a skier was that I understood snow. I grew up in Northern Canada. I played hockey, so I knew what it was like to have slippery things on my feet, and I'd even helped shovel the Desbarats River to make hockey rinks. I loved the environment but was intimidated when I learned that I really knew nothing about skiing.

My first morning as a skier was spent being introduced to my equipment. I mean, I was okay with the jacket and pants and the gloves, but I didn't know how to put on ski boots properly, let alone my skis. That was humbling because I felt like a I was a 20-year-old on display learning what everyone else on the hill learned when they were 6. Still, despite my impatience, George was methodical and thorough. By day four, I was already appreciating that lesson, because I never needed help or instruction again.

Once I had the skis under my feet, a whole world started unfolding, and it was awesome, scary, and intimidating, but awesome. The first hour on skis, I didn't even move. Well, at least not by myself. George moved me. He was explaining various moves I'd need along with the instructions he would be giving me, and he would physically move me, so I could get a sense of what he expected. After an hour or so of this instruction, he finally said, "Okay, that's enough for now, let's go have some fun."

That got my juices flowing, but I didn't make it very far. We were off to the bunny hill, which meant we had to take the rope tow to get to the top. I made it, maybe, 10 feet. Then my skis twisted and I was down for the first time. Then the lessons started. Not the skiing lessons but the advanced training in mental toughness and emotional resiliency.

> **Talent is God-given. Be humble. Fame is man-given. Be grateful.
> Conceit is self-given. Be careful.**
>
> —*John Wooden*

George remined me that this was something new. If I wanted to pursue my goal of going fast, a casual attitude wasn't going to get me there, even on the bunny hill. This meant a change in mind-set for me, because I was used to being the best, and now I wasn't even qualified to play.

I gave my head a shake and got my game face on. We made it to the top of the hill and had a reasonably good time. I made it down that little slope two out of three tries without one wipeout, and when we reached the bottom the third time, George asked me if I wanted one shot at the big hill before the sun went down.

My first thought was to say, "Does a frog jump?" but I realized I'd only known this man for two days, so I just said, "Let's rock!"

That led to the second, or was it the third, humbling experience of the day: the chairlift. Even in Vermont, you don't get to the top of a mountain on a rope tow, so I had yet another new lesson to learn, on day one.

Fortunately, George had a technique to help me get on the lift, which worked, but George had been so focused on me that he missed my chair and wound up on the chair behind me. I still remember the euphoria that came from the sense of floating in midair, but the way that thing rocked back and forth was seriously unnerving. With George yelling at me from behind almost as soon as we were in the air, there wasn't much time for the experience either. My focus almost immediately went to how I was going to get off this crazy thing.

Without him beside me, I would have to rely on him telling me when to launch myself off the chair. Ideally, I was just supposed to push forward at the right time, and I would glide ahead on my skis. Didn't quite work out that way. George started a countdown, but in my apprehensive state I jumped the gun and pushed off a step early. The result was a spectacular fall, fortunately into a big snowdrift, with my skis flying off in multiple directions. I'm sure it looked worse than it felt, but that doesn't mean it didn't knock the wind out of me.

> **That sounds like a horrible day to me. If you're not having wipeouts, it tells me you're not trying very hard.**
>
> —*Another ski instructor*

For a split second I was wondering if people really enjoyed this sport, and one more time that day, I found myself thinking, *Why am I doing this?* I remembered the answer, got up, dusted myself off, and got back on my skis.

We made it down the mountain without meeting any catastrophe, and I was okay with that. I was having fun, but I knew by the end of that first day that I wouldn't be setting speed records anytime soon.

I arrived at the bottom feeling a little bruised but not battered. When we were done for the day and milling around at the bottom of the mountain, socializing, as skiers often do, another instructor came by and asked how my day had gone. I told him it had been pretty good because I hadn't fallen much. His response, once again, set me back and made me think. He said, "That sounds like a horrible day to me. If you're not having wipeouts, it tells me you're not trying very hard." That perturbed me.

I brought it up with George at dinner. I asked how I was going to honestly evaluate if I had the talent to become a racer if I wasn't stretching my limitations? He cautioned me that part of his job was to keep me alive, and I told him I respected that, but I didn't come here to dip my toe in the water, I wanted to jump into the deep end and leave the life jacket on the deck.

He, reluctantly, agreed that we would push the envelope on day three, but I had to listen and not go radical. I agreed and when I went off to bed, the adrenaline was back, stronger than ever.

The next day was a real learning experience—and I'm not talking about my equipment.. I was up early and ready to ski when George showed up at the bottom of the chairlift. This time there were no incidents, and I was at the top of the mountain, bright and early, ready to start skiing for real.

Considering my skill set at the time, what it meant was that I was going to go tree line to tree line in an almost horizontal pattern, making sharp turns and focusing on staying upright. George was following maybe twenty feet behind me, yelling instructions. His goal was still to make sure I didn't get up too much speed before I was ready. I was focused on maintaining my crouch, turning when instructed and not falling down.

Often the greatest opportunities exist just beyond the reach of those who stop trying.

This was working fairly well, and I was starting to feel more stable on my skis, which might have been the problem because while I had become used to George yelling instructions, "HARD right" or "EASY left," I was shocked when he yelled, "SIT, SIT, SIT!"

I dropped immediately and came to an abrupt stop with snow flying in my face. George was behind me in an instant, and I barked out, "What the hell was that?"

He just told me to extend my arms to my sides, and I immediately felt the trunks of two enormous trees. Apparently, I'd become too casual with my turns, or overconfident, but speed had overtaken my skills. If I hadn't dropped, I might well have been dead.

Anyway, we made run after run after run. I had my share of spills, but I had my share of clean runs too.

Later in the day, we did push my limits, and I spent much of the afternoon on my backside, or my face, or once on my shoulders with my skis—at least one of them anyway—in the air. I didn't mind because even when I wiped out, I could sense that I was gaining some ability. I was getting better each run, although something wasn't entirely right.

I ended the day by colliding head-on with a snow hydrant. Fortunately, I had my head up so I took the blow directly in the chest, but it still knocked the breath out of me, and resulted in a trip to the hospital.

I had managed to slightly crack a rib. Enough to be tender, but not enough to keep me off the slopes. After the doctors taped me up, George and I returned to the lodge for dinner, and I told him I wanted to change our routine. I told him I wanted to follow him down the mountain instead of trying to execute his instructions from behind while hurtling into the unknown.

He resisted, but then, in a profound demonstration of emotional resiliency, showed a remarkable ability to adapt to change, after I explained my reasoning. You see, my entire sprinting career had been spent running in the direction of my coach's voice and my entire life navigating by sound. Additionally, I could follow the sound of George's skis along with his voice. With him in front of me, I knew if there was anything to run into, he'd run

Why the hell do we make simple things so difficult?

into it first, so I wouldn't have that worry, or the apprehension. I convinced George that my way would work better, and we went to bed in agreement to try it in the morning.

The benefits of the change were evident on the very first run. We started having successful run after successful run. We began to gain speed and both of us were gaining confidence, him in me and me in myself.

Once it was working, we just kept skiing. My body was aching from pushing an entire set of muscles I had never used as a wrestler, but once I could ski down that mountain without fear that my mortality was at risk, I wanted to see just how good I could get.

By the time day four was over and I was packing to return to Connecticut, my mind was made up, I wanted to race at Alta in April.

Both Gordie and Colleen were happy that I made it home alive, but they weren't so impressed with my plans. Colleen kept telling me I had nothing left to prove, but I believe Gordie understood the nature of the competitive beast and wished me luck.

Of course, one four-day trip to Smugglers' Notch wasn't enough training to make me a competitor for the Blind National Snow-Skiing Championships, but it convinced me that with continued training and practice, I could make a credible showing at a minimum and maybe even win it.

I had three months left and I was determined to become the fastest blind skier in the world, or at least the United States. I reached out to the country's elite blind skiing program in Kirkwood, California. After several calls and telling my story repeatedly, I was connected to an amazing coach named Cliff May.

Cliff was a former ski racer who respected that my mission was not to learn to be a recreational blind skier who had enough ability not to fall down. No, he understood that I wanted to push the limits of how to go faster, and faster.

Cliff's passion led us to try many new techniques. We often skied down the hill in tandem, connected to each other using a pair of 10-foot bamboo poles. With Cliff in front and me behind, I was able to feel his rhythm and

The speed of ski racing is addictive. It pumps so much adrenaline into you that the race becomes a blur you almost can't remember but never want to forget.

how he shifted his weight. Some days we wouldn't even use the polls. We simply skied with me holding his hips, my skis between his.

We developed so many techniques like this—focused on the tactile experience of syncing me with Cliff—and it proved to be a great method of accelerating my development. After all, you can explain skiing to a blind person all you want, but Cliff's techniques took the message out of my imagination and made it tangible and real in a way that I could translate into more and more speed.

That, of course, was the objective. This wasn't about tight turns and bleeding off speed in the name of safety. This was about going for broke, about seeing how fast we could get down that mountain, and it worked. In no time at all I was able to gain Cliff's groove, his tempo, and as a result, more speed.

Not every run was brilliant. You can't go for speed without an element of risk. With risk comes collisions, and we had more than our share. I ran into Cliff from behind, I flipped over his back, got my skis tangled with his—so many wipeouts. Cliff had the patience of Job. He never complained about any of the trouble I caused him or any of the help that I needed. He simply stayed focused on the goal and kept reminding me of what we were about to accomplish.

We lived and breathed skiing, 24/7. We spent every possible minute we could on the mountain. When we weren't skiing, we were talking about skis or poles or boots or bindings or wax or snow conditions, and when that conversation slowed down Cliff would read me articles about skiing. It was like being in military boot camp. We were totally locked and loaded, possessed with my wacky idea of winning the blind national championship, and as a result I'm sure I learned more about skiing in a few weeks than most learn over many years. We were totally invested. If I didn't win, we were certainly going to make sure that it wasn't from lack of effort. We left everything on the mountain, every day.

To make a long story short, that was our routine for the next three months. It was an intense, relentless, repetitive test of my mental toughness.

Once your Grey Zone learns the lesson, repetition reinforces that skill.

Even in my wrestling career, while there may have been daily practice, there were still other classes and activities. There were ways to keep your mind fresh, alert, and undistracted. Even in practice, there were different activities, so it wasn't just the same thing, over and over and over again.

This was three months of 8 to 10 hours a day doing the same thing, over and over and over, whether I felt like it or not. And I had commitments I had to live up to. I had a sponsor and I didn't want to let him down. I had the Howes and everyone back east who were pulling for me to win, or at least make a good showing, in Alta, and there was Cliff. He was working so hard that I simply couldn't let him down, so I had to develop that toughness to just do the work.

And beyond all that, I still had my self-respect, and disappointing myself was simply not an option.

There was one distraction that happened about halfway through my training and it helped refuel my tank, but it was still about skiing.

Kirkwood hosted a blind skiing event called the Kirkwood Invitational, and we started training as if we were preparing for that event. The Kirkwood Invitational would be a good measuring stick. Was I ready to play in the majors or was I still a minor leaguer? Cliff and I were both anxious for an answer, and by the end of that event we would have it.

I was pumped, eager to go. It was a one-day competition with the giant slalom in the morning and the downhill in the afternoon. When it was over, I had come in third in the giant slalom and won the downhill, quite handily in fact. I don't remember the exact times, but I do recall that I won by more than six seconds in a field of 23 skiers.

Now we knew. From then on, it was damn the torpedoes, full speed ahead until April. Then it was time.

THE BIG RACE

We arrived in Alta, Utah, a few days early. I wanted to learn the mountain and get mentally prepared to unleash everything I'd learned when I went down that hill in pursuit of the championship.

> **Competition with others tells you if you're ready for the big leagues, but it's competition with yourself that gets you there.**

My fuel tank was full again and I was bubbling with enthusiasm, but we didn't give in to all the distractions that were available to us in this amazing place. We could do that next week. We went right back to the same routine, seven to eight hours a day on the mountain. We traversed all over the slope, I heard all the sounds and got my bearings, but most of all we skied. Maybe too much.

That's when I came face-to-face with the biggest challenge to my mental toughness and emotional resilience. It was getting to be late in the day on Friday. Well for everybody else it was getting late. By our standards there was still time for one more run. By this point we would have felt like we were cheating in our preparation if we didn't leave it all on the mountain every day, and that meant we had to do this. Looking back, I realize now that I didn't need it. After 100 days of run after run after run, I was ready, but the mountain was calling. By the time that run was over, I wished I hadn't been listening.

We decided not to go for broke but to have a technically perfect, confidence-cementing final trip down the mountain, which was still going to involve speed. That's what all the effort to perfect our techniques had been focused on, so it was going to come, we just weren't going to push it. Unfortunately, when you tempt fate once too often, well...

We were coming to the end of the run and moving well. As we entered the last turn I could hear Cliff yelling, "Tuck, tuck, tuck," and then all of a sudden—nothing. Some guy had started up a snow groomer (probably somebody who couldn't believe a couple of yahoos were still skiing in that weather), and the noise instantly drowned out Cliff's voice, and all other audible references.

We were seconds from the finish line, which in competition was marked by two clusters of bamboo poles sunk into the ground on either end of the finish line. I didn't have a reference to follow between the poles, and my left ski slammed right into the middle of one of the clusters. I twisted severely, slammed my forehead into the bamboo, lost my skis, and went down in a tumble.

My head hurt but I knew right away that something much more serious had happened. The pain exploding out of my left knee was excruciating,

Don't be afraid of what you can't see, unless you can't hear it.

nauseating. It was bad, there was no question about that. My greatest challenge had just arrived.

Cliff was livid. He was screaming at the driver of the snow groomer. "How could you be so stupid? Can't you see these vests? There have been blind skiers out here all week, they need to be able to hear, they need silence, you..." I finally got Cliff's attention.

I was angry, too, but I wanted Cliff to cut the guy a break. Yes, what he did was wrong, but Cliff and I were really to blame, we shouldn't have been out there. I was so mad at myself, at the weather, at the world probably, but now I wanted answers. How bad was this? What was I contending with? I never considered not skiing the next day, but I am a realist. I needed to know so I could strategize in my mind how I would fight through this.

It seemed a side trip to Salt Lake City was in order.

The news wasn't good. It was a badly torn medial collateral ligament. I might be able to avoid surgery if I stayed off it for six to eight weeks. Not just take it easy but completely off it. This was hard to hear, not because it made me consider quitting—that thought never entered my mind—but in that environment it was hard to summon up the resolve to struggle on.

Fortunately, I had learned one big lesson in my life.

Everything I had achieved up to that point, and since, was the direct result of a decision, and I was always in control of the decision. At that moment I decided I was going to ski tomorrow, and I was going to win. I had all summer to recover, but only one chance to race and that was tomorrow.

That was a long and difficult night. The pain was off the charts. There was no doubt left about how serious this injury was. My knee was hot to the touch and I continually felt sick to my stomach, but eventually even agony becomes just a state of mind. The challenge that evening was mental, with gusts to spiritual.

If 90 percent of blind skiing was mental, I decided the time had come for me to get my mental game face on. It really is a decision. You can take control of your state, regardless of your situation, and be just as happy, positive, and confident as you want to be. It is that simple, but that doesn't mean it's easy.

Showing up may be half the battle, but if you don't show up, nobody will care about the second half.

I was never unclear about my purpose. I was there to win, I was there to succeed, not only on the slopes but in the "sighted" world. Now I had something to prove to myself as well.

So, I spent the night envisioning myself winning. I knew the course, I had physical memory to call upon, so during that long night, when I wasn't lucky enough to be enjoying a few minutes sleep, I visualized myself winning this race, over and over and over on the cinematic screens inside my eyelids. I saw my knee performing perfectly, I felt my left leg pushing off when it needed to—again perfectly—I saw myself crossing the finish line and even Cliff hugging me and jumping up and down in celebration.

When morning finally arrived, I was ready. I won't lie and say I wasn't in pain. Heck, every morning started with pain. We had skied so much and so hard that my body ached every morning. I ached in places I didn't know I had before this began, but this morning was different. It was still agony, but I had reduced it to a dull roar in the background that you could tolerate, if not ignore.

The slope was icy and that buoyed my spirits. Icy meant speed, and I always liked that, but it also meant the best sound. It would be easy to follow Cliff. The stage was set: icy slopes, 10 degrees Fahrenheit, and very little breeze. I couldn't ask for more. Now the show was all mine.

There were new sounds, too, at the top of the mountain that day. There was a public address announcer, the chatter of other skiers, the murmur of the crowd. I thought, *What a wonderful venue for this. This is what it's all about.*

I could also hear some of the competitors' comments, such as, "Hey, there's MacFarlane. I thought he wasn't supposed to be here," or "He's done, we don't have to worry about him." As I heard these words, I was also enjoying the melody of some birds singing in the trees nearby. The inspiration of nature, in that moment, overwhelmed the negative commentary from the peanut gallery. If I wasn't ready enough, the words of my competitors put me over the top. It was as if they metabolized four months of experience into one irresistible force. Now I had something to prove to more than just myself.

Eventually even agony becomes just a state of mind. The challenge that evening was mental, with gusts to spiritual.

Then we made our first run, and we got all the way to the bottom. Everybody seemed to be ecstatic that I had made it because so many others had wiped out or gone off course. Problem was, I wasn't ecstatic. My knee bobbled on me for a split second about two-thirds the way down the mountain, and Cliff and I lost the pocket for a second, literally. That was enough to push me down to fifth place after round one, and I was livid. I hadn't come this far to only get that far!

I had one more run and I had to pull it together. I now needed a perfect run if I was going to take home the gold, and I was going to take home the gold. I had made up my mind. I was going to leave everything I had on this mountain in my final run.

I barely remember getting into the starting gate again. I was totally in the Grey Zone now. Once again, we found the pocket instantly, and from that moment to the bottom of the hill, I was locked onto Cliff's voice, following his skis like freight cars on rails. Cliff's voice was inside my head, guiding me like a heat-seeking missile, taking this most intense moment to an even higher level. We sliced down that hill, cutting some gates so close they whacked my shoulder. Jumping headwalls in perfect form. It was like riding the wildest roller coaster, dropping almost in free fall but landing without missing a beat. The exhilaration was off the charts. The sensation of the wind stung my face, keeping me locked in despite our almost unbelievable speed. I didn't feel the pain in my knee at all. I was in total unison with the mountain. If I didn't win, I would owe no apologies to anyone, including myself. We left everything up there this time.

I knew I had it by the time I was two-thirds of the way down. I could tell from the chatter of my skis that I had never gone faster in my life, yet by that point it almost seemed like a practice run. This fast, furious, some said death-defying race down this huge mountain was now playing in my mind like a dream. We cruised to the finish line, at breakneck speed.

Then we finished in spectacular fashion, almost apropos, and anticlimactic, but appropriate considering the events of this adventure.

When someone underestimates me, the advantage becomes mine. It wakes up my Grey Zone and puts fuel in my tank.

I knew we were reaching the finish line when I heard Cliff yelling, "Tuck, tuck, tuck!" Cliff crossed the finish line and began to slow down, but in all his excitement he forgot to tell me. I crossed the finish line at the speed of light, ran into Cliff once again but this time did a double-binding release and started sliding backward down the mountain. Before I could stop, I had taken the legs out from under a camerawoman and actually became her "human toboggan" for a few seconds before we came to rest.

Fortunately, this time, nobody was hurt, and we were laughing out loud and joking as we untangled limbs and equipment and regained our feet. I even remember saying, "This gives a new meaning to the term *close-up*."

Cliff was more animated than ever, "Whoa man," he was shouting, "we pushed the envelope this time, and you stayed right with me. That was incredible." I turned to him and said, "Well, you know my motto. If you're not living on the edge, you're taking up too much space!"

Then I heard my time. I was still shaking the snow out of my hair and thought it must be in my ears as well. Could that be right? They were saying I had skied 11 seconds faster than the leader of the race. We were still marveling in disbelief when this guy came running over to me and said, "Hey, I run the speed gun. I was on the steepest part of the course, and when you came through, the gun said you were in excess of fifty miles per hour."

Over 50 miles per hour, with absolutely no idea what was in front of me except for the chatter of some skis and one voice yelling at me, until he forgot to. Was I ambitious, competitive, or just plain crazy?

Didn't matter in that moment. All that mattered was that I had won. I was the US Blind National Snow-Skiing Champion. I wouldn't have traded that experience for anything, not then, not now!

The rest of that day is a different story. I got through the afternoon, but my adrenaline pump had turned off by then and I felt like collapsing. I was buoyed by Cliff's enthusiasm and there was also the banquet that night. We all expected that to be a good time. Little did we know.

If you spend too much time looking in the rearview mirror, you're going to miss your turn.

The banquet brought with it another round of pomp and ceremony over the day's events and the announcement of the US Blind Snow-Skiing Team that would be competing in Switzerland.

I wasn't named to the team. I was the 1983 US Blind National Snow-Skiing Champion and had apparently set a speed record in the process, but I wasn't named to the team. Let's face it, I am from Canada and I was not a member of the blind skiing fraternity, but I was still a champion.

I went back to Connecticut as an utterly defeated national champion and resumed my career. Fortunately, I had a great new chapter to add to my inspirational speaking ambitions, which made putting the disappointment behind me easier. Think about it, how many people do you know of who went from neophyte to national champion without even experiencing one birthday? I had a story that galvanized audiences, and turned pages.

A DIFFERENT SET OF SKIS

I was back in Connecticut, licking my wounds, when I received a rather unexpected phone call. It was the conversation of that phone call that cemented in my mind the real lesson that I took away from Alta, and which still guides me today. Don't worry about the things you can't control. As I've said a million times, and will again later in this book, play the hand you were dealt. Focus on what you can control and stop worrying about what you can't. It can only add more years to your life.

The call was from Cypress Gardens in Florida. They were looking for a spokesperson for the Blind National Water Skiing Championships in late November. That set off bells. I was honored, of course, but immediately I thought, *Spokesperson? Heck, let me compete too!*

We came to an agreement instantly and I was in the competition. That meant I had one entire month to train for the national stage. Not a big deal, I already had the formula.

I didn't come this far to only get this far.

Find the best available coach, commit my days to nonstop training, immerse myself in the fine points and mentally prepare each evening, work relentlessly without rest, and take a break when the competition was over.

Simple, and in this case, I thought a little easier than snow skiing. At least I had been on water skis before, skiing on the perpetually icy water that most of you call the Great Lakes, since I was 11 years old. I mean, we could see Lake Huron from the kitchen window. I was certain that my snow-skiing experience would help too. I also thought the collision factor would be lower.

I did all that and won another national championship at Cypress Gardens in November 1983, but that is just where this story begins.

Basking in the afterglow of the medal ceremony, still sitting on the dock at Cypress Gardens, some yahoo in the crowd yelled out, "Hey MacFarlane, have you ever tried water-ski jumping?"

That got my attention. I'll tell you the story about that first jump later in the book, but for now, what you need to know is that I made the jump and didn't crash and burn. Because of the configuration of the Cypress Gardens water-ski basin, I had to make two jumps, and lived to tell the story.

I firmly believe that luck is what happens when preparation meets opportunity, and that day, they had a monumental collision. After watching me win a national championship and then demonstrate enough courage (or insanity) to attempt and land two successful jumps, Cypress Gardens offered me a place on their world-class water-ski show-jumping team.

My entire life had been spent in pursuit of a real job, a professional job, in the world of sports, but who could have selected a curriculum for this position when they were talking to their high school guidance counselor?

All I really knew how to do was to never give up. I had pursued every opportunity, learned every lesson, licked my wounds when I was down and got back up, and kept running for as long as I could when times were good to get as close to my goal as circumstances allowed.

Sometimes your ultimate dream is just on the other side of a death-defying feat.

I wanted a career that allowed me to leverage my athletic accomplishments, but I never imagined becoming the only gainfully employed professional totally blind athlete in the history of the world, or at least so I've been told.

Imagine, waking up every morning, and as the warm-up to your job, your morning run was through the most fragrant orange groves. Then water-ski for the rest of the day, learning how to barefoot, riding ramps and jumping into no man's land, and get paid for it. Could life get any better?

Imagine if I had quit the first time a kid 40 pounds heavier than me fell on my back at wrestling practice?

I had made it this far by always pushing the envelope, and that mind-set didn't change now that I was a professional. During my first year in the show, my next bright idea came to me.

I decided I was going to try a backflip off the water-ski ramp. Little did I know that when you are in the air rotating, it becomes incredibly difficult to judge when to pull out of your spin without the use of sight. I had an excellent teacher in Scotty Clack, who was a world champion in freestyle jumping and who would be my partner as I attempted this stunt, but unfortunately, that wasn't enough.

I did this live in the show. No rehearsals, no practice. I think I knew that this was a seriously high-risk stunt. If it was going to be a one-time thing, why not let the paying customers get the benefit?

I got the countdown to the ramp and went into my rotation. I may have had too much speed, too much enthusiasm, or maybe it was just a judgment thing, but I did a 390-degree rotation instead of 360 degrees. I got off my axis and got my axis kicked.

I smashed into the water in a horrific, cartwheeling, out-of-control crash. I bent my body in ways it was never intended to bend, and that came at a price. Instantly I knew this was bad. I heard a voice from the crowd, a kid saying, "Look mommy, he's hurt!" and I thought, *You don't know the half of it, kid!* This wasn't a small hurt. I felt like my body was totally paralyzed.

If you're not living on the edge, you're taking up too much space.

As I had done so many times before, I shortly found myself on the way to a hospital, this time in Winter Haven, where my worst fears were confirmed. My ribs were cracked, my collarbone was broken, and my hamstring was torn completely away from the bone. Incapacitated was an understatement.

My career at Cypress Gardens came to an end with that injury, but I wasn't quite finished on skis. You see, this time when I won the national championship, I was named to compete at the world championships, but, thanks to my horrific spill, I wasn't at my best. Heck, I wasn't even in the area code.

After my recovery was as complete as it was going to get, I decided to go back into training for one more national championship, just to fill the void so I could move on with no regrets.

Fortunately, between my Cypress Gardens notoriety and my national champion status I had been retained by Eagle Wetsuits as a spokesperson. That funded my training and kept me busy as a keynote inspirational speaker.

Eagle Wetsuits was based in Houston, Texas, where I found myself living for a while. I loved Texas, but it was such a departure from Desbarats, Ontario. For example, my training in Texas was conducted at a place called Camp Strake. All you need to know about this place is that before training each day we had to do a gator run!

More than once my coach would say to me after a successful day on the lake, "Man, you're so lucky you're blind, you don't want to know how many pieces of luggage you almost hit today."

Anyway, I kept skiing by day and giving speeches at night, and I won another national championship. By now you know that means another shot on the national team, and this time, on the fjords of Norway in August 1985, I won the Blind World Water Skiing Championship.

I finally had my world championship, but I also knew that I had to keep my ear to the ground because my speaking career was gaining traction, and this was when the transition happened for good. My days as a competitive athlete needed to fade into the rearview mirror. That was okay, because you

The only thing you have to fear is fear itself, and alligators.

drive looking out the windshield and you never usually crash into something behind you.

It was time to move on, to focus on a business career. Maybe start a family. Reap the rewards and take advantage of the opportunities that my athletic career had exposed me to. My speaking career had begun to gather serious momentum during the past year and now it deserved my full attention. When I left Norway, I was on my way to speak to more than 21,000 at the Lions Club International convention in Dallas, Texas.

Forgive me for such a long opening chapter, but I wanted you to know that I learned my talk by walking it first. What follows is how these experiences have defined the life that followed and how I hope my experience will have a positive impact on yours!

Here are some pieces of kindling to help you walk your talk with your head held high. Throw them on your internal flame:

- "First, they ignore you. Then they laugh at you. Then they fight you. Then you win." —*Mahatma Gandhi*
- If people are trying to bring you down, it only means you are above them.
- There will be naysayers, haters, doubters, nonbelievers, and then there will be you—proving them wrong.
- You can't expect the world to come to you on a silver platter. You must continue to pursue and create your own breaks and opportunities.
- Hope is not about taking your next breath, it's about conquering your mountain. Hope is everything.
- The scariest moment is always just before you start. —*Stephen King*
- Ambition is the path to success. Persistence is the vehicle you arrive. —*Bill Bradley*

The past is where you learned the lesson. The future is where you apply the lesson.

EMOTIONAL RESILIENCE...
MENTAL TOUGHNESS

The most inspiring speeches I've ever heard haven't been about dreams or goals or ambitions. They have been confrontations, almost always delivered to me one-on-one, or staged one-on-one in a movie, or written with a one-on-one tone.

The most inspiring speeches I've ever heard weren't given by people at the top of their game or the height of their success. They were given by people who were facing a challenge or dealing with a failure or suffering a loss, by people who had dealt with more challenges or recovered from more failures or suffered more losses.

The most inspiring talks were given by my mother or my father or one of my coaches or my doctors or my wife. The most inspiring lessons were the ones that helped me remember WHY I had to keep trying, WHY I had to pick myself up, and WHY I wasn't going to quit. The most inspiring people were the ones who reminded me that I'm good enough, smart enough, courageous enough if I just refuse to give in. The most inspiring teachers were the ones who taught me that problems and challenges and failures and losses were normal, that they were reality and I needed to embrace them and soldier on because the successes would come, too, if I refused to surrender. The most inspiring lessons were the ones that taught me not blame others for my troubles or care about what others thought but to overcome my

Every sunrise brings with it new opportunities worthy of the extra mile, if you do the work.

problems with my inner vision. The most inspiring speeches were the ones that reminded me, in the words of Rocky Balboa, that "the world ain't all sunshine and rainbows, it's a mean and nasty place."

The more inspiring speeches were the ones that taught me that it's not how many times life knocks you down that matters, it's how many times you get back up. The more inspiring quotes were the ones that taught me it's not the size of the dog in the fight, it's the size of the fight in the dog. The more inspiring lessons were the ones who reminded me that it's not the strongest that survive, or the most intelligent, but the ones most resilient and responsive to change. The more inspiring speeches were the ones that taught me: "It's not what happens to you, it's what you do about it." The more inspiring messages were the ones that taught me: "It's hard to beat someone who never gives up." The more inspiring mentors were the ones who taught me that the strongest are those who win battles we know nothing about. The more inspiring coaches taught me that you can't get much done in life if you only work on days when you feel good.

The greater motivation for me was that as I learned these lessons throughout my life they served as confirmation that I'd been doing it right, and that was even more inspiring.

There is a bigger message though that I came to understand over time, as the common denominator became crystal clear. That message is that there is one characteristic that stands above all others as a necessity if you have any ambitions that you intend to accomplish in your life.

You could accomplish a great deal if this was the only characteristic you possessed, but I'm sure you are too deep and substantial to be such a one-dimensional person.

Nonetheless, you could be the most well-educated, brilliantly skilled, well-intentioned person, but without this single, critical characteristic, I don't hold out much hope that all those skills and smarts are going to take you very far. Depending on your profession, you might not go anywhere.

When something is important enough, you do it even if the odds are not in your favor.

—*Elon Musk*

I am certain that without it, I would not have gone anywhere, let alone this far.

For those of you who have read my story, in my previous book, or the abridged version in the previous chapter, you might already be getting a sense of what I'm talking about because my story is, at its essence, the personification of this characteristic.

It is important to make a significant differentiation here, early. There will be a lot of discussion in this book about talent, and skill, but what I am talking about here is very specifically a characteristic. It is a core quality that exists at the heart of every successful individual. It begins for most as a conscious decision, but when made repeatedly, without exception, grows into an attitude, and when that happens, at whatever age, it becomes the antimatter needed to pursue your life's ambition at warp speed. In the vernacular, this characteristic is called mental toughness.

From the age of two years old, before I understood anything, mental toughness has been my catalyst. I won't retell the stories, but there are so many times where I know I would not have survived, let alone succeeded, if this wasn't "part of me."

Here are just a few of the highlights:

- Completely losing my vision when I was two years old.
- Being forced to leave my family and live 500 miles away from home, with total strangers, at age six.
- Continuously training to live up to Grandpa's theory as the only way I was sure to reach my goal.
- Maintaining my path as a high school freshman in a "sighted" school.
- Running, and promoting, my first charity celebrity tennis tournament.
- Becoming a public speaker.
- Moving to a new country and starting a new career, with Gordie Howe as the yardstick of character I felt obligated to measure myself by.

It is not the strongest of the species that survive, nor the most intelligent, but the ones most resilient and responsive to change.

—Darwin

- Training for the US Blind National Snow-Skiing Championship and overcoming injuries considered too serious to continue.
- Training for the US Blind National Water Skiing Championship.
- Performing under contract as the world's first totally blind professional athlete and overcoming even more serious injuries that were supposed to end my athletic career.
- Training for the World Blind Water-Skiing Championship.
- Elevating my platform to the nationally televised audience and international stage.
- Having my 23rd birthday party crashed by the vice president of the United States.
- Spending time in the Oval Office with the president of the United States.
- Being invited to meet Pope Benedict the XVI at the Vatican.
- Becoming an ambassador for a major financial corporation.
- Launching my own charity.
- Writing multiple books.

And, of course,

- Walking my talk, both publicly and for my family.
- Consistently challenging myself to raise the bar on behalf of my wife and kids.
- Flying more that 4 million air miles, around the world, as an inspirational keynote speaker.

There are roughly a million or so adjectives and metaphors that are thrown about, rightly or wrongly, to describe this characteristic. Adopt whichever one that resonates with you:

- Relentless
- Tough as nails

The greatest pleasure in life is doing what people say you cannot do.

—*Walter Bagehot*

- Iron fist in a velvet glove
- Always finds a way
- Can't keep a man down
- Never gives up
- Doesn't know the meaning of the word *quit*
- Rolls with the punches
- Has the heart of a champion
- Overcame the odds

At the end of the day, what all of these adjectives and metaphors are trying to describe is the characteristic of mental toughness, and its younger brother, emotional resiliency.

Mental toughness is absolutely where it all starts, and if you don't have it, where it all ends.

Mental toughness: The unwavering commitment to yourself that you will persist with all the effort, focus, integrity, concentration, commitment, and emotional investment needed until you succeed in your pursuit or, figuratively of course, die trying.

I'm not talking about physical persistence here. I admit that in my athletic days I had a reputation for fitness and endurance and stamina, but that's not what I'm talking about here. You see, physical strength only measures what you can do. It's your mental strength that measures whether you'll actually do it.

That's what I'm talking about, and not just in athletics. Mental strength is not the exclusive property of the athletic world. It's your mental strength that measures whether you'll do it or not, in every aspect of your life, period.

The question isn't, Can you do it? I firmly believe you can do anything you set your mind to do. The question is, once you've decided what you want, Will you do everything in your power to accomplish what you set out to do and refuse to quit until you succeed, regardless of what obstacles, setbacks, losses, injuries, illnesses, detours, failures, and criticism you encounter along the way?

> **You've got to say, I think that if I keep working at this and want it badly enough, I can have it. It's called perseverance.**
>
> —*Lee Iacocca*

Is any of this resonating with you yet? In the world of motivation, inspiration, and achievement, you're going to be told that you can achieve anything you want, but if you only read the headlines, it will never happen.

Yes, it's true, you can achieve anything you want, but it is not your talent, or your knowledge or your dreams, goals, and ambitions that are going to get you there.

It is your mental toughness that keeps you going when you want to quit. You have to become the personification of mental toughness. You have to live it, breathe it, and embody it if you want to rise above the masses, if you want to get to the extra mile.

It is your emotional resilience that enables you to pick yourself up when life kicks you in the teeth, and it's your willingness to make the sacrifice and do the hard work that nobody else is willing to do that makes anything possible.

That's what mental toughness is all about. You have mental toughness when you can find fuel in an empty tank. Mental toughness is being able to suck it up and finish the job. Mental toughness is doing what you have to do, when you have to do it, the way it should be done, whether you like it or not. Mental toughness means not throwing the towel in the ring prematurely or quitting in the face of adversity.

That's why mental toughness is a characteristic. It is the resolve that empowers you to develop your talents, skills, and knowledge to whatever superior levels you need in order to employ them relentlessly, with the utmost integrity, for as long as it takes, to achieve your goal, regardless of what that goal might be.

You all know somebody like this. No matter how subtle, or overt, their behavior is, they just seem to never stop working, never stop improving, never stop giving. They always seem to be doing the right thing, the right way, at the right time, for the right reasons. They always give the impression that they know what they want, they know how they're going to get it, and they will not accept failure.

That's the emotional mind-set that needs to become instinctive. Isn't it interesting that these mentally tough, never give up, no surrender people

Mental toughness is being able to find fuel in an empty tank.

are actually the ones who experience the most failure? That's because failure is part of trying and reaching out and challenging yourself, but more about that later.

The fortunate thing is that mental toughness has a younger brother, emotional resiliency, who is always there to help with the obstacles, setbacks, losses, injuries, illnesses, detours, failures, and criticism. Sometimes he'll step up and give your mental toughness a chance to refuel, if you treat him right.

Emotional resiliency is embodied in Vince Lombardi's famous quote, "Success is not final, Failure is not fatal, it is the courage to continue that counts." To me that says that it's okay to enjoy your success today, but you have to have your head screwed on right because tomorrow is another day and you need to do it again. Same thing with failure. It's going to hurt, but if it didn't kill you, you still have tomorrow, and if you soldier forward and give your best again, you may find your next success. The key is to adapt and carry on. It's the lessons learned and applied that provide your progress, assuming you get up and use them.

Mental toughness is what will allow you to persist and, in the famous words of Winston Churchill, "Never give up!" Emotional resiliency helps you bounce back and refocus when you hit a setback, reroute when you encounter a detour, create plan B if plan A fails, while helping you maintain confidence that you will succeed long before you run out of letters. Mental toughness is the ability to continue moving when you are feeling scared, fearful, or lazy. Emotional resiliency means learning that the occasional loss isn't the end of the world. The world will go on and so will you. It is the knowledge that you can recover and adapt while still charging forward that gives you significant advantages in making your purpose reality.

Here are some more pieces of kindling to help you fuel your empty tank:

- It is really wonderful how much resilience there is in human nature. Let any obstructing cause, no matter what, be removed in any way,

Sometimes emotional resilience will be all you can count on to carry the day.

even by death, and we fly back to first principles of hope and enjoyment. —*Bram Stoker,* Dracula

- Success is not final, failure is not fatal, it's the courage to continue that counts. —*Vince Lombardi*
- You didn't come this far to only get this far!
- Ambition without mental toughness is like trying to drive a race car with an empty gas tank.
- Mental toughness will ultimately define who you become.
- You're never too old, or too young, to summon your mental toughness. It's there if you have the courage to call on it.
- If you are not passionate about your WHY, how can you ever be resilient?
- It's not how good you are, it's how good you want to be.

MENTAL TOUGHNESS

Mental toughness is the ability to face adversity, failure, and negative events without a loss of effort, attitude, and enthusiasm. Everyone works hard when they feel good. Everyone is enthusiastic when things go well. A person who is mentally tough does not let circumstances dictate who they are at that moment. You control mental toughness!

Some days there won't be a song in your heart. Sing anyway.

—*Emory Austin*

KNOWING WHY

"**R**emind me again, why am I doing this?"

We've all heard someone say this, usually in a state of frustration or exasperation, always when they are doing something that challenges them or that they find unpleasant or that they are not very good at, yet.

To me, hearing these words always brings a sad feeling because almost invariably, even though the person who uttered them thought they were being witty and probably they were deflecting attention from their failure, that person is about to give up on a goal.

That's sad because they couldn't have asked a better question to bring them to success.

Why do you want the goal you are striving for? That is the critical question. If your answer is clear, specific, detailed, and, most of all, inspiring, to you, on your terms, then you'll know the value of every task required to accomplish it, no matter how minor or how difficult. You'll have the strength, the resolve, the energy to take on every aspect of your plan, and your goal will become real. In essence, if your WHY is right, your HOW will take care of itself.

Of course, defining WHY is only the beginning. Once you have defined WHY, once you are excited by WHY you want to achieve your goal, then you have to get focused, you have to get obsessed, you have to get eager, and you have to stay that way. If you don't, all the goal setting and achievement advice and strategy is useless.

Have a clear vision of how your purpose will look when you arrive and absolutely understand WHY you want to get there.

I don't want to make this sound like I have a secret on/off switch for setting and achieving goals. You are still going to have to do the work, all the work. What I am telling you is that if you want to stay the course, keep your energy, and remain excited regardless of the task required to reach of your objectives, the first and most important discipline of goal achievement is the focus on *your* reason WHY.

Please note I said the discipline of goal achievement. That is not a casual comment. So many people that I meet think the power of WHY is all about inspiration, but the reality is that the inspiration comes from the discipline. Goal achievement is a process. The motivation to execute the process is your understanding of your reason WHY!

By the way, *execute the process* is synonymous with taking action. Now, understand that any action is better than no action, but if you're in tune with your WHY, you'll realize your best action.

Staying focused on WHY is something that you must do with intent and repetition. You need to write your goal down, in detail. You need to spend time with your goal every day and visualize it. You need to remind yourself daily of the steps you will take to make that goal a reality. You also need to celebrate your progress to stoke your internal flame.

You need to find your version of that gold medal that you sleep with under your pillow, just like I did. If you lose your focus, find some creative ways to reignite your passion. Keeping your inspirational reasons WHY at the forefront of your thoughts is essential, so much so that there is never a need to be reminded, never any doubt, never any second thoughts about the importance of every action you have deemed necessary to reach your goal.

Maybe a practical example or two would help make my point.

Every year I'm invited to speak at numerous sales conferences and conventions. I work on an almost daily basis with financial sales professionals and have for more than 25 years. I deal with the question of how to increase sales virtually every day of my career. The question I always ask, of every salesperson who ever asked me how to increase their sales, from senior account executives to entry level financial advisors, is always the same. WHY?

Don't focus on WHAT you want. Understand WHY you want it!

In almost every case, they answer a different question. They tell me they would make more money or qualify for higher bonuses or be able to apply for a promotion. All nice benefits that could result from making more sales, but it wasn't until we got to the real reasons, their reasons, that their sales started to go up.

After they were finished with their initial reasons, I ask them to describe how achieving their goal would change their life. I ask them what their life would look like in a year's time if they were achieving their goal. I ask them how their house will look, what kind of car they will be driving, what school their children will be going to, how would their relationship with their spouse be affected, what type of office will they be working from, where their stress levels will be, how will these things make them feel?

The answers to those questions define the reasons why you want to achieve your goal. They are not the goal itself. That is easy to identify, but the answers to these questions are the inspiration that will take you where you want to go. This is what should drive you from the moment your feet hit the floor in the morning, until you return for a well-earned night's sleep.

If your goal is a new car, you need to know how owning that car will make you feel. What benefits will that car bring to your life? How will your world be better with it than without it? When you are focused on those reasons why, doing whatever is necessary to get there will be simple for you, not necessarily easy, but simple for you to follow through.

If your goal is to lose weight (haven't we all had that one), the focus is not on how many pounds you want to lose or have lost. The focus has to be on how you will feel when you have achieved your perfect weight. What kind of clothes will you be able to wear? What will other people say? What will happen to your confidence? Where will you go that you may have avoided? How will your health improve and what will that do for your energy? Won't those thoughts inspire you to do the extra sit-ups, run the extra lap, or skip dessert more than the thought of losing a pound? Can you visualize yourself at your perfect weight? Try it, you'll soon be more motivated than ever.

Think about it. HOW would achieving your WHY make you feel?

If you want to stop drinking or smoking, move to a new home or back to your old home, earn a degree or a license or a promotion, take a trip, have a child, win the US Blind National Snow-Skiing Championship, or any other worthwhile pursuit that matters to you, I promise that if you understand WHY and discipline yourself to stay focused on all the good things and feelings that will happen in your life when your goal is achieved, you will get there easier, faster, and with less stress.

Knowing why is everything, but it has nothing to do with how or what. Knowing why is the emotional turbocharger that will keep your pursuit focused and energized and relentless regardless of how you determine you need to perform or the what that you will acquire or possess when you arrive. The only thing that is ultimately going to matter, and therefore motivate you, is how you are going to feel when you finally achieve your goal. If it is all that matters, it should be all you focus on. Most goals represent achievements and acquisitions that you really want to have, but don't have to have. Your reason WHY represents an achievement or acquisition you really want to have with a feeling you can't live without. Focus on the feeling.

There is another benefit that will happen for you too. Nothing can give a more positive boost to your self-esteem, to how you feel about yourself, than setting and achieving a personal goal. And don't forget, success breeds success. Finding the discipline to achieve your goal becomes easier the more you do it. Achieving future goals becomes easier as a result and feeling good becomes a way of life. Put that image on the screens inside your eyelids and never stop visualizing yourself, in your perfect world.

Remind me again, Why are you doing this?

And, don't forget, as you become more successful, understand that your goalposts are going to move. You will forever need to recalibrate your WHY, because what's important to you today will not have the same sense of urgency three years from now. Don't let yourself get stuck in the world you've already outgrown.

It's the feelings that come with achievement that propel your pursuit. The reward is in the journey, not the arrival. Your feelings are your reasons WHY.

Here are some pieces of kindling to identify the feeling that should fuel WHY:

- Don't focus on what you want, focus on how it will make you feel. Focus on the benefits you'll achieve rather than just the goal itself. That's WHY you want it.
- Write out your reasons why in detail and spend time with them every day. Your WHY should be your cause, your belief, and your purpose.
- Celebrate your success, large and small. That will ensure that your internal flame never dims.
- You have to know WHY! Take the time to clearly define why you have put your life on this course. When the WHY of your life is in focus, the HOW often takes care of itself.
- When you know WHY, your reservoir of mental toughness is always full.
- You will forever need to move your goalposts and recalibrate your WHY. What's important to you today will not have the same sense of urgency three years from now.
- Your goal might be material, but your WHY is always emotional.
- Don't let yourself get stuck in the world you've already outgrown.
- Define it. That's the vision. Describe it. That's the feeling. Demonstrate it. That's the action.
- An impassioned, emotional vision of WHY is the best motivation to take care of your health, which is your greatest asset to achieving anything.

I can teach anybody how to get what they want out of life. The problem is that I can't find anybody who can tell me what they want.

—*Mark Twain*

NEVER LET YOUR FEARS CONTROL YOU

All of us are afraid of something. You might be afraid of the dark, you might be afraid of spiders, you might be afraid of snakes, you might be afraid of wide-open spaces, you might be afraid of closed spaces. You're probably afraid of public speaking too. If you say you're not, you're probably kidding yourself about a bunch of other fears as well.

For all of us who have ever been entombed by fear, for any reason; for all of us who have missed out on opportunity because we were paralyzed by fear; for all of us who have watched life pass us by because we felt too much fear to participate in every way we wished we had; for all of us who have regrets because we surrendered to our fears, I have good news.

You have the capacity to resurrect yourself and resurrect your dreams. You have an asset, a weapon, a resource that far too many of us have never unleashed because we listened to that inner demon called fear. That weapon is called courage, and it is infinitely more powerful than fear, if you will just make the effort to harness it!

Your courage is, without a doubt, stronger than your fear, but without use, it can go dormant. You need to be aware of your fears, real or imagined (more about that later). You can acknowledge your fears, or at least the feelings, and then you need to confront them, little by little, until your courage is fully awake and engaged. That is where it starts.

You have the courage to accomplish anything you really, truly, absolutely want to do, but you have to build it, develop it, experience it. It is a process, like exercising a muscle. The more you decide to be, and act,

Being fearless is easy to say but still scary as hell. Fortunately, your courage will devour your fear, if you just let it have the first bite.

courageous, the stronger your courage will become. There is no limit to the development of this muscle, and fear will wither and retreat in its presence.

So, I ask you, What would your life feel like, as you look toward the future, if you earnestly decided that you are not going to allow your fears to stop you?" What would your future feel like if you knew what you really wanted, with an undeniable desire? What would your life become if you have your dream for your life clearly in focus and your desire powers your courage to propel you past all your fears?

The truth is, if you will risk that first slightly tepid, timidly bold step to call on your courage, if you will just face one fear that is holding you down and test your courage enough to get started, you will find that you have the courage to achieve all you want. You just have to get started!

Will it be easy? No! It will not be easy. Can you do it? Yes, without a doubt. So how do you get started?

I'll give you credit right now that you have read the previous chapter, "Knowing Why," and that you have some reasons for where you want to take your life and what you want to achieve and acquire. If you've done that, and you've made some quality decisions about why you're here and what you want from your life, then you're ready to get started.

Now, understand this, it is okay to have fears. We all do. What is not okay is to let your fears own you! It is not okay to let your fears run your life!

What are the fears that are holding you back? Have you acknowledged them? Have you defined them? You'll need to do that, not because your fears are real, but because you can't defeat them all at once. You need to take inventory of your fears because you're going to prioritize your fights, at least for now.

I'm not professing to be an expert on overcoming fear, but I am an expert on my own life, so let me share some of my experiences dealing with my fears, and when you grow up without eyesight, there were plenty.

It's not my mission here to give advice on how to overcome fear. That's too personal. What ultimately works for you will be unique to you. My mission is to break your pattern, give you a new perspective, help you laugh,

Fear can only thrive in a mind that won't confront it.

or maybe embarrass you, all in your own mind, of course. After all, that is really the point. All of your fear resides in your mind.

Now, let's get rid of this pop-psychology merry-go-round of polite theories and trending platitudes and talk some reality. My reality is that I grew up afraid of not confronting my fear because I was afraid of disappointing my parents and losing my privilege to be a real kid. I grew up afraid of what I couldn't see, and, because I've never had any visual imagery to draw on, I was also afraid of what I couldn't imagine.

As I grew older, I became afraid of failure. I had fears in the moment, I had fears about the consequences of failing in that moment, I had fears that my failure now would result in failure later. I had fears that if I didn't continue to win, that if I didn't continue to deliver in the moment, every moment, that not only would I never reach my goal, but I would be denied even the opportunity to continue the pursuit.

I grew up with fear feeding fear. I grew up afraid that I would be boxed into a corner and, through no fault of my own, be stereotyped and left behind by a society I knew I belonged to. I grew up afraid that I might die with my music still in me, with my voice having never been heard and my potential forever left untapped.

How's that for a starting point? How much comfort do you think that person would have taken from glib reassurances like, "It's all in your imagination," "Your courage is stronger than your fear," or "What's the worst that could happen?" I already told you I had no references to draw on, never did, so if I was left to deal with a fear that was all in my imagination, the worst that could happen was what always happened. I was plunging into complete darkness with no light period, forget at the end of the tunnel. Even the proverbial train coming at me would have been something, but I was always plunging into the complete unknown.

That's what life was like for me. I was an ambitious, high-octane kid who didn't want to be left behind but was constantly dealing with a sense of fear because giving in to it meant being left behind for the rest of my life.

Follow your heart but take your brain with you because comfort zones are wonderful places, but nothing grows there.

I grew up in the days before self-help books, videos, workshops, and seminars and social workers became part of our daily reality. That was probably the best thing about how I grew up. There was nobody coming around to check on us, to caution us, to reinforce my fears and help me and my parents cope with my tragedy.

No, the best thing for me was that we didn't know any of that stuff. We didn't know what we didn't know, and we didn't know it before the industry learned it. What my parents knew was that they didn't know anything about raising a blind kid, so they just raised a kid. What I knew was that no matter how much fear I might be dealing with, I could always trust my parents, maybe not my brother (he couldn't trust me either) but always my parents. We had that trust and we ran with it. It became our foundation.

The end result was that I was just expected to do everything they did. I wasn't pressured but I was expected. That's where my first juxtaposition with fear started to develop, even though I only understand that now, at my advanced age, but the results were all that mattered back then, and the results came from our actions.

It was really my parents' actions first. They encouraged me to try but not from the mental expectation that I would be afraid. They encouraged me just like my brother, no special treatment. It was, "This is what we're doing today, let's go," and off we went. I never wanted to be left behind, so off I went. You see where my fear of not confronting my fears got started. Do you also see how that fear was a complete product of my imagination? Do you think my parents would have left me behind, ignored me, forgotten me? Do you think that fear was real, or imagined?

Do you know that when you were born you only had two fears? It's true, all of us, as babies, only suffered from two fears. The fear of falling and the fear of loud noises. Every other fear you've experienced in your life you had to learn or create. It's the classic example of perception becoming reality. For most of us, it's

> **Let the word and legend go before you. Let the world go before you. Let your shadow grow. Let it grow hair on its face. Let it become dark. Given time, words may even enchant an enchanter.**
>
> —Stephen King

the construct that we have built in our mind, often over long periods of time, that create the mental monsters we call fear. They are all products of our imagination.

Now, I'm not saying some fears aren't real. If you're facing a situation where one of the results is that you could die, then you should be afraid. Even then, you can't let your fear control you because that might very well lead to your death. In the face of any fear, you have to take control and act appropriately. I'm just saying that sometimes that reaction will have to be extreme with a greater adrenaline rush than you're used to, and sometimes the best reaction is to simply not go there. The problem, as I see it, is that far too often, we choose to go there.

So how do you qualify if a fear is real? Ask yourself this: Will facing this fear kill you or cause you grievous bodily harm? If not, what are you afraid of? Will facing this fear land you in jail or get you fired? Then maybe it is not a fear, just a mental guardrail; respect it but know the difference.

If you are not going to die from facing your fear, what's holding you back? For most, it's that construct we've built in our mind that lets fear raise its ugly head in a place where it doesn't even exist.

I don't remember exactly when I found my perspective on dealing with fear. Obviously, I grew up with the habit of being a hard charger in the face of fear, and it served me well, but it didn't make it easier. Even those people you perceive as being courageous are often terrified on the inside. They have just made the choice to saddle up and ride into battle even while their stomach is doing backflips and beads of sweat are popping out on their forehead.

I was like that—scared to death but unwilling to suffer the consequences of not trying. Then, one time, in the course of an everyday casual conversation with a sighted friend at high school, it was mentioned to me that most sighted people are afraid of the dark.

In that moment, in that instant, my entire perception of fear changed. When I learned that more of you than not have a fear of this place where I spend 100 percent of my life, I realized just how silly some of our fears can be, or least some of mine.

It was mentioned to me that most sighted people are afraid of the dark. Really?

That was a significant moment for me. I'm talking momentous, note-worthy, maybe even life changing. Now, to understand why this was such a powerful message to my still developing mind, you need to understand this: I don't know what the dark is, not really. I don't know what light is. I have no concept of shadows or shapes. If I can't feel the sun on my face I wouldn't know if it was day or night without my watch. I don't just live in the dark. I live in a complete absence of everything.

When I realized that so many people have a fear of something that they can cure most of the time with a simple flick of a switch, a light went on for me. Not like that, my world is still dark, but I woke up to a life-changing realization. I can't comprehend being afraid of the dark, it's normal for me. I have flown all over the world, in the "dark." I skied down a mountain at 50 miles an hour, in the "dark." I let someone pull me behind a speed boat and water-ski jumped off a ramp at Cypress Gardens, in the "dark." I carried a woman in a wheelchair down more than 20 flights in a smoke-filled stairwell during a hotel fire, in the "dark." I empty our dishwasher and put everything in its place, in the "dark." I'm not saying I was completely fearless every time, but I wasn't afraid of the dark.

And consider this too. Truth is, so I'm told, most people never experi-ence that complete and downright total absence of light that I am calling darkness, unless it's self-inflicted. Most of the time, tell me if I'm wrong, there is usually a streetlight or some stars in the sky or nearby lights reflect-ing off the clouds. Enough light that in a moment or two you can get your perspective, you can gain some focus or see at least shadows. So, as long as you're not afraid of shadows, you're still better off than me.

Your fears, my fears, all our fears are almost exclusively the product of our imagination. They are harmless phantoms we let go unchecked because we can't summon up a moment of decisiveness to deal with them, and over time they can become intimidating. The good news is, these phantoms of fear that lurk in our imaginations are just bullies, and like all bullies, they cower and back down, if not totally capitulate the second you take some kind of action to deal with them.

Courage lives in the heart of those who are willing to try.

My biggest fears have always arisen from what I didn't know. I wasn't unique in that I felt fear, often considerable fear, about trying something for the first time, especially because I'd never seen it done before.

Visualization, by the way, is a great technique for overcoming fear. If you visualize yourself performing a task or job or action perfectly in your imagination, and replay that vision over and over, with an imagined sense of strong emotion of success or happiness or elation or even just satisfaction, you can anchor that image in your subconscious and create the courage (remember we talked about that at the start of the chapter) you need to try.

It doesn't even matter if your visualization is true to life, it just has to be true to you. Let's face it, I use visualization all the time, and I have no idea what true to life looks like. I have no idea what anything looks like. Try enough times and you will develop the courage that propels you to make that imagined image real and bring you the success you desired, often at a higher level than you dreamed of.

All the experts said to visualize, and supposedly I couldn't, so I was doomed to failure, right? You know better. I said earlier that we have to find our own unique ways of overcoming fear. Let me share with you some of my strategies, and maybe it will wake up some ideas for you.

I want to tell you a story. I mentioned earlier in the book that I was a water-ski jumper at Cypress Gardens. That was an adrenaline rush and a half, but the first jump came with as much apprehension, or fear, as any "first time" in my life. The experience of that first jump taught me a tremendous lesson about dealing with that kind of apprehension and re-channeling it as courage. Let me share the day.

Now, water-ski jumping was a challenge that would test my abilities as a water-skier. I had no idea if I could or not, but at that point in my life I had also developed the fear of humiliation and I thought, *If I don't try, I won't like how I'll feel.*

That was enough. A buzz started running through the crowd. I heard one-person yell, "Yeah, let's see him do it!" Then somebody responded, "No way, he can't, he'll kill himself."

Adrenaline can catapult you beyond any fear in the blink of an eye.

Kill myself? I doubted that, but there had to be an adrenaline rush attached if the crowd was thinking that way. Now, I had to try this! But first, I needed knowledge, and I had to get some facts straight in my mind.

I got my wish. Ricky McCormick, a world water-skiing jump champion, lived nearby. Ricky had been so successful as a water-ski jumper that he had even appeared on *Johnny Carson*. (For those under the age of 26, look Johnny up, he was the king of late-night TV. Many think he still is!)

They brought Ricky over to Cypress Gardens. I couldn't believe how fast he got there, and let me tell you, meeting Ricky was a rush. I felt like I'd met my match. I was an energetic, outgoing guy, but here was Mr. Energy personified. This man had a heart of gold and knew water-ski jumping like the back of his hand, or bottom of his feet. He lived it, he breathed it, and he was excited to share it.

Ricky was totally into the idea in a moment. Almost before I knew what was happening, he had Donny Croft pull up the boat, and we were on our way to inspect the ramps. It was as if Ricky had been in touch with my snow-skiing instructors. He seemed to instinctively understand how to take the imaginary vision of a blind person and turn it into a tactile reality. He started teaching right away, and my adrenaline levels started to rise.

I can't say enough about Donny Croft, either. Ricky was an amazing teacher, but we also had the best boat driver in the world. Donny was incredible then and he was at Cypress Gardens forever. Legendary wouldn't be an understatement to describe his status. Trust is another essential element to confronting your fears, or summoning your courage, and Donny made that part easy.

So, to the ramp we went. No skis, no equipment. We just climbed out of the boat and walked around on the ramp. I was able to get a sense of how wide it was, how long it was, how high it was, and even what it was made of. I tested the approach of the ramp to see how much was submerged in the water where I would enter. I even jumped off the end to get a sense of what kind of drop to expect. Of course, Ricky explained that I would go higher

Don't rely on what your eyes can see. Your inner vision gives you the real picture.

in the air due to the speed of the approach, but it was still vital information for me to have. Now, I could start to develop a clearer mental picture of what would be expected of me.

Within minutes of meeting Ricky, I actually had hard knowledge that I could use to envision and translate what he was about to teach me. That proved invaluable because this was all happening at such a whirlwind pace, literally just moments after the medal ceremony. I doubt I could have connected all the information Ricky started to feed me with what I was physically about to attempt if I didn't have the physical reference from my tour of the ramp.

Understanding what was expected of me before I tried to do it was always critical. It helped me harness the nervousness and pent-up energy. I would refocus that through visualization, and my courage would start to grow. And remember, too, I had no idea what a ramp looked like. I seriously needed this reference. Of course, that makes us seem like geniuses now. In the moment, it was all instinct, but once I realized why it worked, I never forgot the lesson.

Instructions seem to be coming fast and furious:

- Make sure you're not leaning too far back or you'll fall on the ramp.
- Make sure you're not leaning too far forward or you'll face-plant.
- Keep your skis together or you'll become a whirlybird.
- Remember the boat will pull you to the right, so compensate.

Ricky was telling me all of this as he and Donny took me back to the dock and helped me into a set of jump skis. They were wider than normal water skis and I was surprised how heavy they were, but they felt solid. At that moment, in the midst of all that frantic activity, a touch of solidity was reassuring, somehow.

The butterflies were swirling in my stomach now. I had to take a deep breath, several deep breaths, and take that swirling mass of butterflies and harness the energy until they were all flying in unison. I retreated inside my imagination and let my subconscious paint a picture inside my eyelids of me

The world doesn't make sense, so why should I paint pictures that do?

—*Pablo Picasso*

landing a successful jump. It probably wouldn't look like a Picasso, or from what I'm told maybe it would, to you, but it made my spirits rise.

The buzz from the stands was growing. It was as if nobody had left. It seemed that a bigger crowd was assembling to watch the "blind kid" try and kill himself. More people were there now than had been present for the Blind Nationals. Even *PM Magazine* and *The CBS Morning News* and other shows were still there. They had set up again and had their cameras rolling. I am certain they really must have thought there was serious risk to life and limb, mine in particular. Why else would they stay to film a lark like this?

Donny fired up the boat again and we were off. Ricky skied beside me on a separate rope, the same length as mine obviously, and was going to guide me into the ramp. He would give me a five-four-three-two-one countdown, and I'd be off. He kept shouting last-minute instructions to me, repeating everything we already covered, but I really didn't hear him now. I was waiting for the countdown with just two instructions in mind:

1. Jump
2. Don't die!

I never really expected that this was going to result in any horrible tragedy. After all, it was just a ski jump. I'd jumped hundreds of headwalls in snow skiing and landed practically all of them. I couldn't see my landing point then either. I just expected the skills to translate. (I have always found positive expectation beats negative expectation every time.) Ricky didn't express any serious concerns, either. If he had, maybe I would have hesitated, but this was a definite go in both our minds, right from the beginning.

If there were any concerns, it was too late now. Ricky started the count-down. "FIVE...FOUR...THREE...TWO..." I barely heard him say, "ONE." I heard, and felt, the chatter of my skis across the ramp and in an instant I was airborne.

It wasn't a long flight. I splashed down almost right away and not in a terribly graceful manner. My skis hit the water and my butt splooshed right

The key was to take that swirling mass of butterflies and harness the energy until they were flying in unison.

down on top of them. Fortunately for me, I had the strength (residual benefit from the years of training as a wrestler) to fight my way back to my feet and ski away. What a rush, I had just landed my first jump.

A cheer went up from the grandstand. Good to know they were excited for my success. I was hooked on that sound as soon as I heard it. It just added to that adrenaline rushing through my system, but not as much as Ricky's reaction. He was beside me again in a second, giving me a high five and embracing me, at least as much as he could considering he still had a rope to hang on to.

"That was just awesome!" he yelled.

Now that might just sound like the reckless pursuit of a headstrong, hard-charging, high-octane young man who should have known better, but consider this: I had some experience on skis, both snow and water. I had the confidence of being in decent physical condition. I had just won the US Blind National Water Skiing Championship. I was not a neophyte on water-skis. I just knew nothing about jumping on water-skis. I needed knowledge.

The knowledge I gained from visiting the ramp with Ricky and jumping off the top and inspecting the approach and riding around with Donnie and having a chance to stand up on the jump skis gave me the input my sub-conscious needed to believe I could do this. My conscious mind wanted the adrenaline rush and the cheers and the satisfaction, but my subconscious had the resources. My subconscious knew my qualifications, knew the benefits of my previous experience that it would use to ensure I succeeded. I am confident that my subconscious mind, playing older brother, guided me to my awkward but successful landing and just let my younger, more immature, conscious mind revel in the short-term rewards.

So, what were the lessons I never forgot? First, it was that I still needed to confront my fear of not confronting my fears. Second, it was the realiza-tion that I am probably more prepared to deal with my fears than I realize. You have a life of experience recorded in your subconscious, and if you

You already know more than you can possibly remember, but your Grey Zone never forgets. Face the fear and your Grey Zone will win the day.

act confidently in your conscious mind without resisting your subconscious mind, you are capable of far more than you can believe with your own eyes. I have come to call that the "Grey Zone" and I've learned to depend on it.

There was an additional lesson that was taught to me that day, although I didn't learn it until later in my life, but, as Jack Canfield so eloquently wrote, "Everything you want is on the other side of fear." I had, from my earliest days, always wanted to be independent and self-reliant. Summoning up the courage to make that, allegedly, reckless jump led to a contract and a job, a real job, as a professional athlete on the world-class, water-ski jumping team at Cypress Gardens. What's waiting for you on the other side of your fears?

One more story, in case you might think all my stories are about athletics and that I'm coming from a rarefied world of elitism. I admit I reveled there for a while, but the proudest moment of my life, and the scariest, happened when the benefits of all I had done came together in a way that nobody could ever have imagined and kept me going in the face of a life-threatening situation I never would have thought I was prepared for.

Now, before I go on, understand this. I'm only telling this next story to show you how all the events and experiences of your life have already prepared you to face and overcome any fear, challenge, or obstacle you might encounter. You are strong enough, resilient enough, and equipped enough to take on any challenge life can throw at you. Your Grey Zone has been preparing for it for years.

When you travel as much as I do, there is one sound you get used to but never want to hear—that ear-piercing blare produced by a hotel fire alarm.

Fortunately, in most cases, before you've shaken off your slumbering haze and taken your mental inventory (it seems most fire alarms go off in the small hours of the morning), there is an announcement that it was a false alarm.

But, as I said, that is only most cases. That was not the case early one morning in late 1985. I was awoken by that loud staccato squawk that I had

Use your fear, it can take you to the place where you store your courage.

—*Amelia Earhart*

become so familiar with. Never taking a fire alarm for granted, my mind did its quick inventory. I was on the twenty-third floor of a Los Angeles hotel. I had a great view, or at least so I was told, but all I could think in that moment was that it was a long way to the ground.

I threw on a pair of pants, grabbed a shirt, and forced my feet into a pair of loafers. Fortunately, I keep hotel rooms perfectly organized, nothing out of place, ever. I have to, not in anticipation of a fire, but because it is the only way for me to cope. If I have a five a.m. wake-up call, I don't have time to read the carpet, like Braille, looking for my socks or shoes.

There was nothing else to worry about. The only important thing to do in that instant is to get out. Of course, I was expecting that calm voice on the intercom telling everyone that this was a false alarm, but it never came. What I heard were panicked voices in the hallway, plenty of them. This was a large hotel, and there were a lot of people looking for the exit.

The exit! OMG, I hadn't bothered to locate the exits. You'd think someone in my situation would orientate himself, but after almost a million air miles I had become rather blasé about such details. That was one attitude adjustment I would have to deal with later.

For now, I just exited out into the hall. I quickly realized that if I just followed the crowd, I would be led to the exit. That part of my plan worked. I found the staircase and was on my way down when I realized something was wrong. Not with me, but I could hear something.

A voice, a soft-spoken voice, but one that was in trouble. Everyone else just kept pushing past, making their way to the ground as quickly as possible. Nobody else seemed to hear this, but I was always hearing things nobody else did. By age 23 my hearing had become very acutely developed. Tonight, that became more a godsend than a compensation. There weren't that many people left in the stairwell. We were close to the top floor, and it seemed all the guests were already below me, at least in my stairwell.

I had only gone a couple of floors when I heard this. I couldn't ignore it, but I couldn't find anyone else to check it out. I decided I better do it

Fear is a reaction. Courage is a decision.

—*Winston Churchill*

myself. I exited the stairwell at the next landing and quickly found this voice. It was a woman's voice, coming from close to the ground. I followed the sound and quickly found a woman in a wheelchair. "Please help me," she said. "The elevators aren't working. I don't know what to do."

Of course you can't take the elevators during a fire, but how was I going to help this woman? I don't think I even took time to strategize. There was no time. I pushed her wheelchair through the door into the stairwell landing, turned her around, and picked her up, chair and all. It was the only way I could think to get her to the ground level. There was certainly nobody left to help us at this point. This was all up to me.

"Don't worry ma'am, if I make it out of here, you will, too, and I fully intend to get out of here."

It wasn't long before I realized it was going to take every ounce of strength, energy, and resolve I could muster to get the two of us to safety. By my calculation, we had around 20 floors to go. It wasn't long before my arms started to ache, and I felt my equilibrium slipping away, or at least my orientation. We were going backward, eight steps, around the corner, eight steps, around the corner. Again and again and again.

I wasn't going to put this woman down. I didn't think we had the time, and I didn't want to startle her any more than she already was. We maybe had 10 flights left now, or 12. How much longer could I carry her? I was in great shape, yes, but I wasn't a weightlifter. I stayed toned through push-ups and chin-ups and cardio. I had to keep going, but how?

I was praying for that calm voice on the intercom. These are always false alarms, right? Maybe we still had to get down these stairs, but how urgent was it? Just as I was thinking this, the smell of smoke hit my nostrils. No announcement today. I picked up my pace, maybe a little panic setting in, recognition of the urgency to get out, certainly. And the fear of the smoke. I may have been blessed with the refined instincts to maneuver in the dark, which translated well to a visually impaired, smoke-filled stairwell, but that

Never look backwards or you'll fall down the stairs.

—Rudyard Kipling

doesn't mean the smoke still didn't burn my eyes too. I knew you could suffocate through smoke inhalation. Yes, I got a little scared, for both of us.

I was starting to rush, moving as fast as I could while staying under control. There were beads of sweat bursting out on my forehead and dripping into my eyes, which obviously didn't cloud my vision, but my sweat was soaking through my shirt at the same time. I knew I could have been outside in a heartbeat if I was on my own, but I was starting to worry about how much stamina I had left to get us both to safety. All I could think to do was to hurry.

My quickened pace brought with it an adrenaline rush, a small burst of energy to get around those last five or six corners. My god, don't these stairs ever end, I thought. Then I felt it. A break from the heat, a blast of cooler air on my back. We hit the final landing. I set her chair down, swung it around, and stumbled out the side door onto the street. We were safe. Thank God!

Fortunately, it was a small fire on one of the lower floors that never amounted to much. Turns out it was more smoke than fire, but isn't that that so often the case? I didn't get all the details, didn't really want them. I was just happy the two of us got out safe and there was still a chance for a couple hours of sleep before checking out in the morning.

I have thought, since that night, if there isn't always a bigger plan in God's scheme than we ever realize, or ever could. I may have been the most qualified, appropriately experienced person, in that moment, to save this woman's life. Maybe it was just fate, who knows?

I'm not saying this to brag. I'm not a superhero, but I am, or at least was, particularly qualified to perform an athletic deed in a stairwell with the lights out. I was still riding the residual fitness benefits of my competitive athletic days, including those days at Carleton University when I trained by running the stairs of the YMCA Tower in Ottawa. Was it pure luck or some divine intervention that this woman was found by maybe the only man, certainly in that hotel that night, who had run up and down 20 floors of stairs, over and over and over again, for no particular reason than just to be "in shape."

Sometimes you don't have a choice. The moment will demand greatness from you. Will you be ready?

And, how ironic is it, that I don't believe that woman ever knew I was blind! That really didn't matter.

It was as if I had been training my entire life for this night. All the inconveniences were nothing more than training for the most important race I would ever run.

Think about it. The simple, virtually random accident that took my sight at age two, may well have saved another person's life two decades later. The way my parents raised me to be as normal as possible, hunting, setting traps, riding my bike, throwing bales of hay, created a man who was anything but fragile when the chips were down. Those nights Eric and I used to sneak out of the third floor of the boy's residence at the School for the Blind, then creep along the ledge, and climb down the corner bricks to the ground, must've been preparation for the treacherous flights of stairs I somehow made it down through the smoke. And the strength I was driven to create in my upper body and legs for wrestling—few people in that hotel could've maneuvered that woman in her wheelchair the way I did.

And think about this. A sighted person may well have become completely disoriented when the smoke filled the stairway and visibility went to zero. Not me. I was perfectly equipped to maneuver in the dark, especially walking backward carrying a wheelchair.

I don't say this to boast. I say it to drive home one point. If I can do it, so can you. If I can live the rewarding life I've lived, so can you. And if everything in my life led me to this point, then ask yourself, Where is your life leading you? What special duty are your inconveniences leading to? What special duty are you in training for right now?

The simple truth is that your courage is stronger than any fear you will ever face, and that the resources you have accumulated through your life's experience are available to you if you will just take the first few timid steps to confront your fear. You are capable of far greater, more heroic accomplishments than you have ever imagined, but you won't know what you can accomplish until you try. Never sell yourself short.

When challenged, your faith and inner strength will always be your best ally.

Here are some more pieces of kindling to help you harness your fear:

- When a door opens, and your Grey Zone is sensing opportunity, you have to confront whatever fear might be stopping you from stepping through that door. Everything you ever wanted could be one step away.
- How many fears do you have that could be cured by a little education?
- I believe that the world doesn't owe us anything. It has provided unlimited opportunity, and the rest is up to us. Do you have the courage?
- What is provoking that sense of fear in your imagination now? Have you ever conquered such a fear before? If you could do it then, you can do it now! Listen to your Grey Zone!
- "Fear is being scared to death and saddling up anyway." —*John Wayne*
- "Fear is a reaction. Courage is a decision." —*Winston Churchill*
- Having fear is normal, surrendering to fear is fatal!
- I grew up afraid that I might die with my music still in me, with my voice having never been heard, and my potential forever left untapped.

Fear can become a tornado unless you take the wind out of its sails.

THE GREY ZONE

When I was a young man and still a competitive athlete, I knew the Grey Zone as an involuntary reaction that could only be triggered by fear, desire, or exhaustion in the heat of competition. The best way I can describe it is with an example.

From *Craig MacFarlane Hasn't Heard of You Either.*

"We didn't say much as the chair ride began. Cliff asked, "How are you doing, buddy?" I quietly mumbled something like, "I'm almost ready," and I was. All of my mental rehearsal, my visualization, my focus was coming to its apex. There is a point in mental preparation that I call the Grey Zone. It's that place where you consciously surrender to your instincts, where you let your subconscious take over and trust your ability without hesitation. It's:

- what allows Michael Jordan to play better than the rest of the NBA even when suffering from a devastating case of the flu
- what gives Kirk Gibson, despite a pair of knees both probably worse than mine, the capacity to hit his bottom of the ninth game-winning home run in the first game of the 1988 World Series
- what makes it possible for Bobby Baun to overcome the pain of an ankle, broken by a Gordie Howe (yes the same one who brought me to the United States) slap shot in the third period, to score the overtime winner in game six of the 1964 Stanley Cup playoffs

The person who thinks it cannot be done hasn't met their Grey Zone, *yet!*

- what would allow me to plunge down that mountain in total darkness without hesitation or pause and take my speed from a cautious 35 mph to a potential 50 or 55 mph

I had been there before. I was often in the Grey Zone by the championship match of wrestling tournaments, relying more on instinct and preparation to battle through injuries and exhaustion to win most of my gold medals. It was my ultimate advantage.

It came to me about halfway up the lift. The worry of the moment just left me. At that moment I was ready to totally give in to my inner vision and preparation, ready to go for broke.

Now don't get me wrong. I'm not saying that there is some supernatural, Zen-like voodoo mind magic that takes over, and if you just show up you win. Not at all. Focus and awareness and concentration were still the key, but the willingness to believe your body to be able to perform whatever was demanded of it, and trust in your subconscious to process all the data that comes in too fast for you to think about was critical. Then it is just damn the torpedoes, full speed ahead.

My Grey Zone led me to winning the US Blind National Snow-Skiing championship that day and taught me numerous lessons.

That was how it used to be. I was this competitive, ambitious, some said driven, testosterone-filled, adrenaline-fueled athlete who had found success by pushing the envelope until his extra gear kicked in. I knew I had to win because if I lost, I might fail in pursuit of my bigger goals and that was not an option, so I just pushed, and, more often than not, seemed to come out on top. That extra gear, which I began to call the Grey Zone, served me well in competition, but I really didn't understand where it came from. In those days, I just knew it was there.

It wasn't until my athletic career was coming to an end that I started to seriously question this phenomenon of the Grey Zone. I was curious if the

People who are crazy enough to think they can change the world understand the power of the Grey Zone.

experience would translate to a business career, and if so, how? I understood that it comes to an athlete when physical and mental preparation, it takes both, are refined and focused through repetition and hard work until excellence becomes involuntary. When I had done the work, the Grey Zone paid benefits. But, to be perfectly honest, it all seemed a little supernatural.

My dilemma was that up until that time in my life, I attributed my extra gear to having superior stamina and conditioning. That's why I did all the sit-ups, push-ups, chin-ups, and squats and ran lap after lap after lap.

I needed the confidence to know that if anyone was going to beat me, it wasn't going to be because they were in better shape than me. I had assumed that they all had the same coaching and learned the same moves and techniques. Hadn't all of my competitors had good coaches too? So, at that age, my simplistic understanding of the Grey Zone was that if I could simply push harder and longer than my competitors, it would be when they got tired that I would get the opportunity to win the competition. I would be in the last race of the day when I would have one extra ounce left in my tank and get to the finish line a stride sooner.

It wasn't until I met my coaches and started training for the 1983 US Blind National Snow-Skiing Championships that my understanding of the Grey Zone benefitted from some enlightenment. Until that time all the competitive experience in my life had taken place on solid ground. I was limited by physical size, speed, and gravity. What I mean is that on a wrestling mat or a running track, you are only able to move with the speed of human resistance. Even if you look at a sport like soccer or football, there is a physical limit. In my experience, even if the speed of the competition was maxed out, you could sort of consciously keep up.

When I got on skis for the first time, I almost instantly understood what my friends like Gordie and Wayne Gretzky and Bobby Orr and Phil Esposito and so many other great hockey players I have met (hey, I am Canadian after all) meant when they said that their game took place at a different speed. Usain Bolt, the fastest man in human history, has been clocked at 28 mph,

Your Grey Zone is the extra gear in your mental transmission that unleashes the awesome power of your subconscious mind.

which is impressive, but also elite, under controlled conditions, in a straight line. Bobby Hull, in 1962, was clocked at 29.2 mph under game conditions, which means he was passing and shooting and checking all at the same time at a faster speed than the fastest man in the world on dry ground and today. It is generally accepted that hockey is even faster now and the players are bigger, and if you think you are going to survive if you are only dependent on your conscious grey matter, you're nuts. The Grey Zone isn't just a benefit, it's a necessity.

The Grey Zone may not have an on/off switch that you can control but it can be cultivated, and, if you want more from this world, you need to respect it.

My first, brutal, amateurish attempt at skiing down a hill, a bunny hill, took place at a speed that was faster than anything I had ever experienced. Cliff, my coach, told me later that it is hard to snowplow pedestrian speeds if you're on a serious mountain, so I was in a zone where I would be processing input and executing at a speed that exceeded anything I could relate to.

I don't want to dwell on the athletic experience. It is unique and some would say exceptional, but I want to make this point. To win the 1983 US Blind National Snow-Skiing Championship, I had to implant enough experience through constantly improving repetition that I could trust my Grey Zone to process while reacting to input being received at 50 mph even though, before getting on skis, I have never traveled at even half that speed without vehicular assistance.

That's when the light went on and I understood all the experience that got me to the top of that mountain. It was also the beacon, or maybe it was the brass ring, but it was the driving force behind my 10 to 12 to sometimes 15 runs a day down that mountain. I realized that I needed the muscle memory, fine-tuned to as elite a level as I could achieve, within the time constraints I had saddled myself with, if I was going to be able to leave it all on the mountain.

My focus was on not killing myself. Cliff was focused on the chatter of my skis and if the runs were getting smoother. I skied behind him so he was

If you do not manage your Grey Zone yourself, someone else will.

never able to actually watch me. As my skis got quieter, he increased the level of difficulty, introducing me to jumps and sharper turns. We developed our unique form of communication as we developed our own unique style, which was me following him and listening to the sound of his skis and his verbal commands.

This was great but the secret to winning was the constant and never-ending improvement that resulted from run after run after run. We did all the dry land training, too, and brainstorming sessions, which the physical runs translated into the Grey Zone, but in the end, it was just the total accumulation of work that led to success.

I've also studied the Grey Zone, which I suspect that most of you would call it the subconscious mind. I'll give you that, but I think that the world is too casual about the power and impact of the subconscious in our everyday lives.

Personally, I believe that we effectively live in our subconscious minds. If we had to consciously think through everything we do, day in and day out, we'd go nuts and accomplish almost nothing. We'd be in a constant state of frustration, if not total rage, completely unsocial and entirely defeated.

Think with me for a moment about any experience, skill, or behavior that you were learning for the first time. Did you enjoy it? Did you get frustrated? Did you get snippy? Probably.

I remember when I bought my first car. Obviously, I couldn't drive it, but I had some savings and thought that if I had a car, my friends and I could go out whenever we wanted. What I didn't realize was that driving a manual transmission was so much more difficult to learn than driving an automatic. I bought a big car so that it could seat all my friends, but it was older and had a manual transmission. All of my friends were licensed in automatics.

I had to ask my dad to teach my buddies how to drive manual. We'd go out together—me in the back seat—and we'd hop and jerk and stall, over and over as we tried to drive down the street. I remember joking about it

Keep doing what you can, trust that your Grey Zone will do the rest. Keep doing more of what you can, and your Grey Zone will do the rest even better.

being jackrabbit lessons and my friends would snap at me, sounding angry, but really they were just frustrated.

Now, here's the lesson. The first day out it honestly felt like I was losing a friend. My friend would be in such a bad mood within an hour and go home without even saying goodbye. Three months later though, we'd be out, and he'd be tuning the radio and opening a stick of gum while making a left turn and waving to girls on the corner while changing gears like it was nothing. Why? Because once his Grey Zone had learned the lessons, he didn't have to think about it anymore. Be aware of it, yes, but his Grey Zone could do it better without his interference.

Here's a more real-life example. My best friend was blessed with twins. Having an instant family—he had a boy and a girl—was wonderful, but, as he tells the story, for the first two years of the twins' lives, if you walked into his house and all the blinds were drawn and the curtains were closed, you couldn't tell if it was noon or midnight. It was a constant and frenetic environment, which meant "all hands on deck."

Now, as much as it may sound stereotypical or judgmental, the truth is that most dads have an aversion to changing diapers. At least they try to make excuses to not do it, justified or not, that's just reality. Some get away with it, some don't, but when twins enter the equation, dad is enlisted, like it or not.

My buddy has regaled me with his stories about diaper duty. He admits he often wonders if his wife went through the same challenges, but, at 12 dozen diapers a week, it was always one of them or the other, so he doesn't know what it was like for her. With all due apologies, I'm sure every new mother can appreciate what I'm saying, especially if you've been blessed with twins.

What my friend admits is that the first few weeks, maybe even a month, was a dreaded experience that you would only endure for your child. He also brags that by time he had changed a thousand diapers (remember, that was only two months) he could do it blindfolded while singing a lullaby and leave his child perfectly happy with all the residue in exactly the right place

We are what we repeatedly do. Excellence then, is not an act, but a habit.

—*Will Durant*

at two o'clock in the morning and go right back to sleep because he never really woke up.

If he could become that proficient at something he didn't want to do and never studied and sometimes, maybe often, did in a comatose state, imagine what he, meaning you, could do if you pursued something you wanted to do and consciously planted the benefits of such experience in your Grey Zone until your autopilot became so proficient that all your frontal lobe had to worry about was progress.

On a personal level, beyond my athletic experiences, my Grey Zone has been my single greatest, most significant advantage. It has taken my efforts to develop compensatory skills and, over time, but not that much time, elevated those efforts into almost superpowers, or at least that is how some people have described them, maybe just because they haven't worked to develop the same powers.

The two "superpowers" I've come to rely on are my hearing and my memory. Let's face it. I can't just make a note and refer to it later. I can't write things down for future reference. I can't just go with the flow and wait for the visual clues or landmarks to come into view to guide my navigation as I travel. No. I have to *remember* everything and constantly listen to changes in my environment to have any awareness of my surroundings and location.

The simplest example is telephone numbers. When you ask someone for a number, you probably write it down or save it to your phone. I can't. I have to remember it. Most times I will not have an opportunity to have someone look it up for me later, so I have to be able to recall that number when I need, as often as I need, purely from memory.

I have the same challenge with space and distance. I have to rely on my hearing and facial perceptions to tell me where I am, my proximity to my surroundings and the movement and happenings I'm operating in.

My Grey Zone has elevated these two skills to a level that makes my life seem effortless although that is far from the case. It also causes many people

Everyone has a photographic memory; some just don't have the film.

—*Steven Wright*

to express levels of amazement at my capabilities that I sometimes find almost embarrassing, but at the same time totally naive, on their part.

I only have these "superpowers" because I cultivated them, relied on them, and listened as my Grey Zone refined them. You could have the same powers, if you wanted to, but you developed other skills because you could. I didn't worry about the gifts I didn't have. I worked to make the most of the gifts I did have. We all have to play the hand we were dealt.

Think about it this way. Many, if not most, people think of blindness, especially total blindness, as a disabling handicap. My Grey Zone has empowered me to such an extent that I just consider my blindness to be a minor inconvenience. That's the power of the Grey Zone.

Your Grey Zone is your navigator, it's your shepherd, it's your guardian angel! You already know more than you will ever be able to remember. In truth, you've probably forgotten more than your competition is ever going to learn, although if you ever need it, your Grey Zone still knows it.

Your Grey Zone is your reservoir of wisdom. Everything you've ever learned or experienced is there. Your challenge is to cultivate it and build the avenues, the reflexes, that bring that knowledge and coordination to the surface when and as you need it. It will always be there, if you have the faith to draw on it.

Let me explain. I had the privilege as a young man to be a member of the world's preeminent water-ski jump team as a member of the show at Cypress Gardens, Florida. I retired from the team after suffering an injury in 1984. Almost 30 years later, I was invited by a friend to vacation at his newly purchased cottage in northern Ontario. I loved the idea, but once I arrived my son Dalton informed me that my friend had a speedboat.

Dalton was excited to see his dad on skis, and even though I was suffering a total lack of enthusiasm to get back on the water, it wasn't long before I was doing single ski slalom and I even barefooted on the boom. My point is that the Grey Zone never forgets.

Not only is my short-term memory horrible, but so is my short-term memory.

Not only does your Grey Zone never forget, it never stops learning. In fact, it never stops studying! It is a voracious sponge that consumes and retains every iota of information that your frontal lobe is ever exposed to, and it processes it. It organizes it, it refines it, and it improves your use and understanding of it. It consumes everything from every source. It doesn't care if you're gathering knowledge from conversation, audio, video, encyclopedias, the Internet, or physical experience. It has built a file of knowledge and experience for everything you have ever done and cross-references everything to help you improve, even if you didn't realize there was opportunity for improvement.

I won a gold medal snow skiing before I thought of waterskiing, but I understand now that my Grey Zone already had me up on water skis in my subconscious mind the instant I first thought about it. It took one file of knowledge and experience and transferred it to my new thought process without even being asked, but I know now that could only have happened because I had a Grey Zone full of raw material.

You have the same Grey Zone, at least in structure and function. Yours might have files on cooking, woodworking, computer programing, taxes, investments, politics, landscaping, teaching, or science instead of skiing and wrestling and public speaking, but only because that is more relevant to you. You might have files on all of those subjects, and more, or maybe your files are more limited, but now that you know you have this amazing capacity functioning inside your head, the question is, Are you maximizing it?

You have a Grey Zone for everything you do. It is limitless in power and capacity, and it is running 24/7. It can and will take you to whatever level of proficiency you desire if you feed it enough input for it to learn and guide you. Once you start the feeding process, it will start to learn for itself. It will listen to your sixth sense and take in ancillary information, which it will merge with your focused study and action to accelerate your competence, once you open the file.

I remember every lyric of a song I heard 35 years ago. Why can't I remember all five things I went to the grocery store for?

Said another way, your subconscious has a filing system where every iota of data that has ever passed through your experience is recorded in its appropriate place. For most of us, the challenge is with our recall programming. I believe your Grey Zone is the ultimate recall program because it will pull all the necessary files; assemble them in the most effective, actionable format; and deliver them to your frontal lobe with a turbocharged kick that will send them to the right muscle group, be that your arms, legs, or mouth, at exactly the right time, if you just learn to listen.

You can achieve any level of competence you desire by educating your Grey Zone. You control how much information and experience you feed each file and, if you pay attention, your Grey Zone will feed that information and experience back to you in ways that are calculated to accelerate your growth and success. This sets up a cycle, and the faster you use the feedback from your Grey Zone and create another deposit in that file, the faster it will respond. Getting the picture?

You need to give your Grey Zone enough raw material for it to take you to the level of success and competence you desire within each file, and you need to listen to and respect the feedback. All I'm trying to say here is that if you want to be adequate in any particular area, make sure your Grey Zone has enough knowledge and experience to get you to that level and keep the file fresh enough to maintain your requirements.

This is probably going to be the case for most of the mental files you maintain, but there will be a few passions, your career for one, where you need to deluge your Grey Zone with knowledge and experience because the benefits will be amazing. You may never develop the ability to turn it on and off, at will, but if you develop the habit of nurturing your Grey Zone, it will always be at your side, ready to come to the surface and elevate your performance, when it senses the opportunity.

The more you feed your Grey Zone, and the greater the focus, the faster the turnaround. I'm not saying this is a secret formula or mystical shortcut. You still have to do the work, but if you're listening to and learning from

Not only does your Grey Zone never forget, it never stops learning. In fact, it never stops studying!

your Grey Zone, it can process a huge amount of work in a very short period of time.

So, if you're not growing fast enough, if you're not achieving new levels of success as quickly as you want, keep studying, keep practicing, and if that isn't enough, up the intensity. Your Grey Zone will absorb everything you can give it. It will assemble and analyze everything and continually give you the resources to improve and succeed.

After all, that self-lit flame that fuels the successes and passions of your life is sustained by your profound belief in yourself, which resides and thrives in your Grey Zone.

Here are some more pieces of kindling to help you connect with your Grey Zone:

- Remember, your Grey Zone is your reservoir of wisdom. Keep gathering the fresh kindling that feeds the fire in the furnace of your Grey Zone. At the same time, vehemently protect your Grey Zone. It absorbs everything, so do all you can to keep the input positive. Garbage in, garbage out still applies.
- Don't be afraid to let your Grey Zone dictate to your conscious mind. It knows you better than you do.
- How many things do you do instinctively without thinking? The instinct is your Grey Zone.
- You rely on your Grey Zone. Embrace it, listen to it, feed it, Nurture it, Respect it! Give it what it needs and enjoy the journey.
- That small silent voice inside you will often be the difference between success and failure. Don't ignore it.
- You may think you live 100 percent in your conscious mind, but you are at the mercy of your IMAX-oriented, Technicolor, 3-D, Panavision, Sensurround, multidimensional, guided-missile-targeted, organic-supercomputing Grey Zone. Listen to it!

You already know more than you will ever be able to remember, but your Grey Zone knows.

INNER VISION

"You can't depend on your eyes when your imagination is out of focus."
— Mark Twain

Inner Vision is not as mystical as you might think. It is simply how honestly you understand yourself. As simple as that concept might sound, it is critical to your success and happiness as you try to navigate this journey we call life.

During my life, as I have tried to envision my future and visualize my success, the only vision I have ever had to rely on was my Inner Vision. That may very well have been my only competitive advantage, in athletics, in my career, and throughout my life.

I say this because I've observed that most of the well-rounded, successful people I have known had a profound, crystal clear understanding of themselves and an unwavering belief in their abilities, and potential, due mainly to that fact that they didn't function in a world of perception. They take action based on a clear-cut understanding of their reality. How honest is your understanding of your reality?

Your Inner Vision is the compass of your Grey Zone. It's the conscious input to your subconscious filter that sorts fiction from reality in terms of where, what, and how you project your life through your imagination. Your Grey Zone is brilliant, but it will accept whatever input it receives through your Inner Vision. Do you have the integrity to supply the accurate intelligence?

The only vision I have ever had to rely on was my Inner Vision.

Your Inner Vision gives you the reality check needed to tell you what is truly possible today, next week, next month, and next year based on who you really are right now, or who you "think" you are right now. That's your choice—your Inner Vision is going to use whatever input you provide.

But, that's the key. The most successful people I have known are always making the most of the hand they have been dealt. They don't just complain about their cards and give up or strategize based on the wish that they will be dealt the winning card and then wither in false hope. No, they go forward with a plan, based on their knowledge of what they are best at right *now*, while recognizing the limitations of the moment and then taking actions to improve their weaknesses while always maximizing their strengths.

In a very practical sense, that is what has led to the success I have experienced in my life. I learned early that I had some qualities that were valuable to my desire for a "normal" life. I developed those qualities with a focus on my goal. Even at age eight or nine, I wasn't languishing in self- pity waiting for a miracle or dreaming about what life would be like if I could see. I thought I had found a means of achieving my goal doing something that was available to me.

The fact is that I was strong, durable, and energized. I craved physical activity and someone in my life had the sense to recognize how that fit with wrestling. Once I was connected, I focused on developing those gifts of strength, durability, and energy so I could best take advantage of my opportunity. For me, that focus on developing the gifts I knew I possessed in that moment paid huge dividends and led to more opportunity, as you are reading about in my stories.

Let me make myself perfectly clear, if I haven't already. Your vision for your future without a clear, honest, uncensored Inner Vision of yourself is just a pipe dream. It comes down to accepting your own reality. Unfortunately, most people live their lives in the pipe dream. That's sad because it means you're living your life like a bottle rocket—full of energy, bursting out in every direction but just putting on a big show before burning out far too soon with very little to show for the effort.

Inner Vision sees the potential that is illuminated by the self-lit flame that exists in all of us.

We all have God-given talents (remember, God doesn't give out skills, you get those by working at your talents) and attitudes that, when properly aligned and slyly exploited, give us the opportunity to do truly amazing things. Your Inner Vision knows what those are, and if you will listen to the unvarnished message and adapt accordingly—honestly—your Grey Zone will guide you to heights your imagination can't perceive because it's running on faulty data.

This is what I was referring to when I said, "If your WHY is right, the HOW will take care of itself." I know I'm not the first person to say that, and I won't be the last because it's the truth, and you need to have your order of operations set in the right priority.

If you have an honest understanding of yourself, your assets and liabilities, your strengths and weaknesses, your advantages and disadvantages, and you are focused on an overwhelmingly compelling WHY, then the WHAT and the HOW will come into focus.

You'll understand HOW to make the most of WHAT you can do today while becoming aware of WHAT you need, if you want to accomplish more tomorrow.

Then you focus on being the best at what you are while complimenting your skills and knowledge with the outside resources that provide what you're not, and you keep playing your hand. Learn to develop your God-given gifts, don't worry about the ones you don't have and focus on the ones you do have.

I could go on, but my driver is waiting. Play the hand you were dealt.

Here's some more pieces of kindling to brighten your Inner Vision:

- Have the courage to know who you are today, so you can be who you want to be tomorrow.
- Your Inner Vision knows the coordinates of the harbor where your WHY resides. Follow it and you'll never be off course. After all, it is your internal GPS system.

Inner Vision will show you your ultimate potential if you are just brave enough to look.

- Sight without Inner Vision is like driving blindfolded!
- We all know that hindsight is 20/20. Think of Inner Vision as your hindsight of the future. Instead of a perfect picture of where you've been, it's the perfect picture of how far you can go.
- "The only thing worse than being blind is having sight without vision." —*Helen Keller*

How honest is your understanding of your reality?

DON'T COMPETE WITH OTHERS: MAKE THEM COMPETE WITH YOU

If you can't resist the need to compete, compete with yourself. You might well experience the instant gratification of a trophy or a medal or a standing ovation or a big commission, but if you don't learn the lesson, you might never experience it again.

A little competition is never a bad thing. It forces you to get focused, bring your best game, and strive to succeed in that moment. The problem is that for most of us, when the moment is over, the value of the moment is lost on us, even if we won. Heck, even if we lost, there is value in the moment, but only if you understand who you were competing against.

Now, don't get me wrong, we all like to win. Once the competition begins, a true competitor must be willing to do whatever it takes to leave the competition battered, bruised, broken, and utterly defeated. You have to be willing to go that hard because your competition isn't just going to roll over and play dead. If they are worthy, they want to leave you battered, bruised, broken, and utterly defeated as well. In the end, you're both going to take your lumps, and someone will be declared the winner, but there is no loser if you understand the value of the battle.

The value of head-to-head competition is not whether you won the battle. It is whether you became more likely to win the war. The battle is a measurement tool, nothing more. So, let me warn you right now not to get lost in the accolades of winning the battle. They can be distracting and

The real value of competition is the knowledge you gain about your own competence.

exciting and, at least temporarily, profitable, but there will always be someone coming who thinks they can knock you off your throne, and if beating
the next opponent becomes all that matters to you, eventually somebody
will.

The real value of competition is in the knowledge you gain about your
own competence. It tells you how close you are to playing in the big leagues,
competing with the best of the best, and advancing confidently toward your
goals as a result. But, understand this. If you have a clear vision of where you
want to go in your life, what you want to achieve, the price you are willing
to pay and WHY, then you should have been competing with yourself, and
only measuring yourself against the elite in your field.

If you want to be the best there ever was at what you do, more power
to you, I hope you make it. In fact, I fully support every effort you make to
get there, but I want you to be aware of one crucial fact. If your motivation
to be the best of the best at whatever you do is simply to be better than who
or whatever is the best right now, you may very well find that when you get
there, you wasted your time because the results don't match your expectations.

You need to know why you want to be the best. You need to measure
yourself today against yourself yesterday, without concern for where the
competition might be. You need to be sure you are improving, that you are
growing and becoming sustainably more competent. More importantly, you
must be sure that your improvement is taking you in a direction that will
ultimately place you where you want to be, on your terms.

Model your competition, learn from them, learn what made them successful at what you want to be successful at, but don't do it just to compete
with them. Do it to arrive at your vision of success, which is almost certain
to be different from theirs.

Let's face it, you don't want to put your ladder up against the competition's wall just to find out, when you finally get to the top, it's the wrong
wall. Climb your own wall by competing with yourself to get better every
day. Learn from your competitors, become better than your competitors,

**As you get better, you stop modeling others. They start
modeling you.**

but don't compete with your competitors, compete with yourself. If you win that battle, you'll come out on top, on your terms, and there is no better place to be.

What I'm saying is: *Don't compete with others, make them compete with you.*

Now, having said all that, I acknowledge that competition was a major factor in my formative years. The first third of my life was defined by competition. I competed as a wrestler, I competed as a sprinter, I competed as a downhill snow skier, I competed as a water-skier and even performed professionally as a water-ski jumper. When I wasn't in a formal competition, I was competing with my friends playing hockey and football, and I played golf in charity tournaments too. When we were bored, we competed chugging bottles of Coke. I was so competitive that I even got into races on stationary bicycles.

At the risk of sounding a little conceited, I have to admit I became quite good as a competitive athlete. I won multiple national championships in multiple sports in Canada and the United States. I won medals in international competition and I even won a world championship. There are many people who would say that competition defined me, that it made me who I am today, and in a way they are right, but they always get the reason wrong.

A cursory glimpse at my story shows the picture of an obsessed young man who appeared driven to win, at any cost. It comes across, without reading the fine print, as if all I wanted were medals and trophies and photo ops. I can understand how it might appear that way because, in the arena that presented my best opportunity to achieve my goal, my victories were always public, with awards, ceremonies, and notoriety, but that picture didn't tell the whole story.

Yes, it's true that I did hundreds of sit-ups and push-ups and squats and chin-ups and ran dozens of laps every day. I was relentless but it was solely a competition with myself. I felt driven to do a little more today than I did yesterday, and I felt that way every day, especially on those days I didn't feel like it. It was about pushing myself to be the absolute best I could be, at that time doing the thing that I felt had the best chance of achieving my next, or

I was so competitive that I even got into races on stationary bicycles.

at that time, my first major life goal. I had a reason WHY I was pushing so hard, but it wasn't simply to beat someone else. I just wanted to go home.

As I got older, I became more aware of what I had been doing and got smarter at it. I began to realize the value of doing hundreds of sit-ups a day, and I did them wherever I was, whenever I could, unless of course, I was doing push-ups or chin-ups. By the time I was a teenager, my obsession had grown to 500 sit-ups a day. I simply would not let anybody outwork me. I even used to start sneaking out after hours to run laps on the school track, which had special railings for us visually impaired kids. The railings let me run harder and harder because I didn't have to worry about directions or obstacles.

I think it was all those extra laps that led to my track career, but that wasn't why I was running. I was running because I wanted the bragging rights that let me ask, every time I won, "Could I go home now?"

That's the power of WHY!

I never could have trained that hard with that much focus and intensity just for trophies. When I reached the point where I didn't need any more trophies to prove myself, when my reputation, which I didn't even antici- pate, grew to where I had street cred, I took more pleasure in giving the trophies away and would look for fans at tournaments who were even more handicapped than me and give them the trophy. Maybe it would inspire them, or maybe it would just put a smile on their face because due to cir- cumstances beyond their control, they could never win one on their own. It didn't matter, I wasn't there for the trophies.

I wasn't there for the accolades. I certainly used the newspaper articles and occasional television interviews to build my case, but I never would have pushed that hard just to get my name in the paper. I did it because it gave me more evidence to justify my desire to go home. I did it because I knew, at some level deep down inside, that if I was the absolute best I could be, then "they" would have to pay attention.

A dream doesn't become reality through magic; it takes sweat, determination and hard work.

—*Colin Powell*

I did eventually get to go home and attend high school with my friends. Once I proved myself, I became a member of the wrestling team and got to go wrestle at some international tournaments in the states that border Ontario. It felt like I had arrived, but you can't stop progress, and my life certainly moved forward.

I began to get requests to speak at local service clubs and dinners, and that was a new experience. It was different from being interviewed for a newspaper or a television station. It was a spotlight where I was being encouraged to talk about my journey and, slowly, I began to realize I had a message. When I told my mother how I felt about these speaking experiences, she suggested that maybe I had identified my future career.

When Mom said that, I got nervous. I loved the idea, but what if I wasn't interesting enough? What if I wasn't entertaining enough? I realized I had to write my message as a speech. I had to develop a trademark and make it compelling. I began to write my thoughts and structure the message I shared in those speaking opportunities. That is what lead to my message of PRIDE: Perseverance, Respect, Individuality, Desire, and Enthusiasm. These were the characteristics that typified how I behaved in my life. They made my world work. Once I had my message, my persona so to speak, I rehearsed, and I listened to other speakers and had my parents get me tapes of other speakers from the public library. I may have had some talent, but just like in wrestling, track, skiing, waterskiing, and even golf, I worked on my speaking until my talent became a skill. In other words, I competed with myself as a speaker.

A word of caution here. I don't want to leave anybody with the impression that competing with yourself is just about study, preparation, and practice. There is a great amount of truth to the famous saying that "He who sweats most in training, bleeds least in battle," but if you never do battle, you will never come anywhere near your potential in anything. If you want to reach your full potential, or at least some reasonable rung on your potential ladder, you are going to have to bleed.

Why get out of bed in the morning if you have nothing to compete for?

The first time you step out into the real world of competition, you are going to find it difficult. It will feel like amateur hour. You'll be confused. You might panic. You'll be thinking too much. You will invariably struggle, but you will also grow.

Like I have said elsewhere in this book, failure is part of success. Failure is part of growing. Failure is part of learning. The secret, if you can call it that, is to step back from each experience, lick your wounds (I did say you're going to bleed, even if only metaphorically, although I did bleed real blood a few times on my journey, and I'm not alone in that experience), learn a lesson or two, and find the mental toughness to try it again. The focus should not be on winning, or succeeding, just on being better than last time (i.e., bleeding a little bit less). How soon you stop bleeding altogether will be determined by how much work you do and how hard you do the work.

As a totally blind person, you realize at an early age that your career options are somewhat limited. When I conceived in my mind that I could actually be a success in the "real," sighted world as an inspirational speaker, I had a new WHY that drove me just as much as my first WHY.

Then I realized that no matter how good you are as a speaker, if nobody knows who you are, they'll never want to hear you speak. So, I turned back to athletics. I was determined to maintain as high a profile and earn as much respect as I could from demonstrating my commitment to excellence, which meant continuing to be the best I could be, and maybe better, in the arena of competitive athletics.

I continued to push myself to be good enough to win national championships in wrestling and sprinting, but now I also endeavored to develop relationships with the important people I met at those events.

To me, it was a means of keeping my visibility high enough to get requests to speak. And I worked on my speaking skills too. So, there I was, constantly pushing myself to be the best athlete I could be just to earn opportunities to prove that I was the best speaker I could be. You could say I was working to build a reputation as "the best inspirational speaker you've never hired, yet."

You'll never be a .300 hitter if all you face is batting-practice fastballs.

Ultimately, I won that World Blind Water Skiing Championship, which was the crowning glory of my athletic life and the last significant competition. I admit, I played in many charitable golf tournaments after that, and actually shot a 91 once, but it wasn't about the game anymore.

Before I went to Norway, I had spoken, for what turned out to be the first of three times, at the 1984 Republican National Convention, and before I even returned from my world championship I had been contacted and called to Dallas, Texas, where I would speak at the Lion's Club International Convention. Shortly after that, I was asked to speak at the Rotary International Convention in Calgary, Alberta, Canada. My public speaking career was off and running and, if I do say so myself, with a spectacularly exciting start. Looking back, it's hard to imagine three more inspiring stages to use as a launch pad.

That was over 35 years ago. I'm still speaking and, hopefully, still inspiring. I'm not rich and I'm not poor, but I am very happy, and I live in the world I chose because I knew that is where I wanted to be. I do what I love with the added bonus of giving back to all of those who helped me. I believe in paying it forward and that what goes around comes around. To inspire the next generation while respecting the one that gave me my opportunity continues to motivate my internal competition. Yes, I'm still competing with myself, refusing to ever become complacent, with the hope that all of you are the beneficiaries.

I told you all of that to ask you this: Do you think I would have made it as far as I have if I all I cared about were the gold medals and trophies and press clippings? I don't! Truth is, winning becomes boring, just like anything else if you do it long enough.

I know I got this far because I never lost sight of the fact that this is where I wanted to be. I was doing what it took, in my mind, to get here (i.e., succeeding in the sighted world), and that's what I challenge all of you to do.

Simple, right? So how do you do it?

Every new beginning comes from some other beginning's end.

—*Seneca (4 BC–65 AD)*

First, reread the chapter "Knowing Why." If you hope to experience any level of success in your life, I can't overemphasize the importance of knowing the WHY of your life. It's so important it demanded its own chapter.

Second, set your standards.

I have spent much of my career challenging individuals and audiences to elevate their world, to lift their performance, to make a positive, meaningful difference, not just in their own lives but in the lives of those around them.

I challenge everyone to take responsibility, to set standards of achievement and behavior, and to discipline themselves to maintain them. Once you have clearly established, in your mind, the standards below which you will never allow yourself to perform, then you start the incremental, step-by-step, process of getting marginally, tangibly better every day. The progress may seem insignificant some days, monumental on others, but the key is just to keep moving forward. You'll be amazed how quickly you rise to the top as you become a skillful practitioner of your craft.

Setting standards of achievement and behavior has always been my means of having a good life. It could, you might say, be the structure of the mental framework that has driven me to maintain my standard, regardless of the arena of competition. Surprisingly, to me anyway, the majority of people I meet don't seem to have the same interpretation. The most common question I am asked is not How do I live a good life? but How do I achieve greatness?

I always tell people that I don't know. I tell them that my standard is to be consistently *good*. Of course, if you are going to set a standard for yourself, you need a yardstick to measure yourself against. Here's mine.

I heard a talk many years ago that has stuck with me ever since. I forget if it was a minister or a sales manager. It might even have been another inspirational speaker I heard at a conference where I spoke. Regardless, it put the entire question of standards in perspective and it stayed with me. I'll paraphrase his comments and hopefully they will stay with you as well. He

You will see me the way you want to see me, but the way I see myself is what really counts.

had referenced the Book of Genesis as he compared God's opinion of himself with how we think of ourselves as humans. He said it this way:

> God created a tree and said it was good. Man invented the automobile and said it was amazing, stupendous, great. God created a rabbit and said that it was good. Man invented the refrigerator and said it was awesome, super, great. Well, the wheels fell off the car, and the fridge broke down, but the tree's still up and the rabbit's still running! The quality of God's work, *good.*

Now, if God didn't hold himself to a standard of great, what chance do you really think you have?

In my opinion, greatness, even for those we consider great, is too tough a standard to maintain. In fact, I don't believe it is a standard that is maintainable, let alone obtainable. We do great deeds, have great successes, see great results over time, but we do not live in a state of greatness. Great things are moments that happen, and greatness is the accumulation of multiple great moments during one's life or career. We don't live great lives. Albert Einstein summed it up best when he said, "You ask me if I keep a notebook to record my great ideas. I've only ever had one." One idea, but Einstein's legacy is one of greatness.

Great legacies, that's a different story. When someone aspires to greatness, this is what I believe they mean. The unfortunate reality is that most who aspire to greatness are living lives of mediocrity, waiting for a transformation that is never going to happen. The leap from mediocrity to greatness, whether it is a onetime event or a legacy, is just too far and totally unrealistic.

That is why I subscribe to the standard of *good.* Being consistently good, day in and day out, without exception, (which is what I mean by standard) is very hard work. It takes discipline, it takes personal growth, it takes intellectual growth, it takes follow-through, it takes the patience to do the right

You know what's weird? Day by day, nothing seems to change but pretty soon...everything's different.

—Bill Watterson

things and to do them the right way. It also takes consistency and dependability, not to mention a profound belief in yourself.

Being good is all about developing the proficiency, knowledge, and resources that enable you to apply your particular skills and expertise in a consistent and persistent manner. It is about being utterly dependable.

If you can achieve the standard of good, then you have accomplished something remarkable that goes beyond just the benefits of a wonderful life. You will have set yourself up for great moments to happen.

When you are good, you are ready to respond to opportunity. You can raise the bar in your life to take advantage of opportunities when they present themselves. The well-known quote suggests that luck is what occurs when preparation meets opportunity. In my experience, great achievement also occurs when preparation meets opportunity, but only if the prepared is good enough to raise the bar.

When you are good, you are also ready to respond to challenges, problems, and the unexpected. History seems full of far more examples of those who had "greatness thrust upon them" than of those who set out to achieve greatness and succeeded. When you maintain the standard of good, you will be ready to raise the bar when called on to deal with any obstacle that may rise before you, and often experience moments of greatness along the way.

The world of sports is full of examples of athletes having good careers who, in the face of seemingly insurmountable odds, have elevated their game and turned in a great performance that has gone down in history. The ones who did this more often are remembered as great, but even the greatest weren't great every night. In fact, their true character is more often remembered for how good they played when they were not at their best, how they were always good. Think of Michael Jordan or Cal Ripken or Wayne Gretzky or Gordie Howe or Jack Nicklaus. All utterly dependable and consistent, playing at a higher level than most, but not great every day.

When you're good at something, you'll tell everyone. When you're great at something, they'll tell you.

—Walter Payton

They were, however, far more capable of giving us moments of greatness because it wasn't too far to go from the standard they maintained.

The world of sports is a great example, but it is also a small and exceptional segment of our world. If you understand the example that Michael or Gordie or Jack represent, then you can transfer it to the business world. History is full of examples of those who, in the face of challenge or criticism or even failure, have answered the call to develop new procedures, products, programs, companies, and even industries that have produced great results. Do your research. You'll find that most of these people were good.

If you think about the world of medicine, you'll find the same story. Doctors, researchers, chemists, biologists, physicists, therapists, nurses, who, in the face of challenges, problems, emergencies, or just ongoing struggles, have found exceptional answers that have produced great results. You'll find that most of these people held themselves to the standard of good.

So, there is my philosophy on being great. Be good, day in and day out. Don't be afraid to raise the bar in your own life when you can, or when you have to, but never let your standard drop.

As you get better, and more proficient, don't be afraid to challenge yourself to maintain a higher and higher standard of good. It is the closest thing to a guarantee that you will never plateau. As you continue to evolve, always striving to stay on the leading edge, there will come a time when you stop looking to model the behavior of others because you will be the one setting the standard everyone else aspires to, and they will have begun modelling you. That's the epitome of "leading by example," and if you achieve that standard, there is nothing you can't achieve.

And if you truly want a great legacy, never lose sight of those words spoken by Vincent van Gogh, "Great things are done by a series of small things brought together."

One last dose of reality for you to consider. Your life is a competition, regardless of what you're doing or where you're doing it. Regardless of whether you consider yourself competitive or passive. Regardless of whether

---

When you're faced with a challenge, the profound belief in yourself will always prevail.

you have big ambitions or mild expectations. Regardless of whether you are happy earning a wage on an assembly line, selling securities, designing the next great cathedral, or occupying the CEO suite.

I'm not immune to this scrutiny either. After 35 years as an inspirational speaker, I'm still constantly being evaluated, on my message and against the last speaker they heard. You can't escape it.

What you do today is being measured against not only what you did yesterday but against what everybody else who does what you do did yesterday. It doesn't matter if you are competitive or passive, the world is evaluating you. That's the bad news.

The good news is that even if you don't want to compete, just striving to always be as good as you were yesterday without resisting the incremental improvements that are inevitable, ensures that you will always have the best of what you want, wherever you choose to be, and that is just the beginning. The rest is all under your control.

Here are some more pieces of kindling to throw on your competitive fire:

- Climb your own wall. You can learn from others and compete with them as a means of improving your skills and abilities, but as you climb the ladder of success, make sure that you are always recalibrating your trajectory so that when you get to the top, it is where you want to be.
- Maintain and improve. Establish the standard that reflects how you will live your life, even on your worst day, then work to get a little better every day.
- To me, hope is kindling. The more you have, the brighter the flame that burns inside you, but remember, you can't live on hope. Action throws the logs on the fire.
- Competition is your measurement against WHY you are competing in the first place.
- Success is a journey, not an event.

Competition is the spark that ignites the self-lit flame inside you.

- When your feet hit the floor in the morning, make sure you know what you're competing for, and WHY!
- Above all, commit to maintaining your bare minimum standard of good in your pursuit of all the activities on your way to your WHY.
- Action alone is not enough, but without action nothing else matters.

Be not afraid of greatness. Some are born great, some achieve greatness, and some have greatness thrust upon them.

—*William Shakespeare*

FIGHT PROCRASTINATION: DON'T PLAN TO BE SPONTANEOUS TOMORROW

I have some bad news for you. If you are waiting for the perfect time, the perfect mood, the perfect inspiration, or the perfect environment so you can get started, you need to know this. It isn't going to happen. The world doesn't wait for those who procrastinate. You can't just turn on creativity like a faucet.

You may have the "occasional" burst of Technicolor brilliance pass through your mind, but if your stars are not all perfectly aligned, the odds are that your spontaneous wisdom will ever come to fruition are virtually nil.

All too often this mind-set, the procrastinator's mind-set, governs our behavior, and so much opportunity and production is lost.

That's right, this is all about procrastination, otherwise defined as the art of keeping up with yesterday. There are many consequences to procrastinating and none of them are good. When you put things off, they grow larger and more challenging. Responsibilities don't diminish, they get bigger. Costs don't reduce, they increase. Resentment doesn't go away, it grows. Opportunities don't wait, they are taken by those who hustled. As Abraham Lincoln put it, "You cannot escape the responsibility of tomorrow by evading it today."

I understand that overcoming the habit of procrastination can be challenging, but the benefits are life changing. Procrastination creates stress and distraction and leads to, at best mediocrity, and at worst failure. Being

> **Only put off until tomorrow what you are willing to die having left undone.**
>
> —*Pablo Picasso*

proactive creates confidence, energy, and the mental clarity to capitalize on opportunity when it arises while still moving forward day after day. So, answer your emails the day you receive them, pay your bills before they are due, return your voice mail messages when you hear them, and be engaged in the pursuit of your goals and dreams every day.

Let me give you one example. A friend of mine is a writer, a very good writer in fact. I asked him one time where he finds the inspiration for the excellent work he produces, and his answer says so much. He told me, "I write for the garbage can." Yeah, I didn't understand either, so I asked him to explain. It turns out that his secret is to just write. He sits at his desk every day and grinds out content, most of which he claims goes straight to the garbage can, but because he is creating, he's engaged in the process, he is there to capture the genius when it occurs. Opportunity isn't lost and, he claims, he has far more good ideas when he is working than when he is waiting for spontaneous inspiration to come along someday. After all, someday can't be found on any calendar. Simply put, when he is in the zone and plying his trade, his Grey Zone can get focused and often produces moments of brilliance.

My point is this. If you have any goals, dreams, or desires, you need to get up and show up. You need to do what should be done, as it should be done, when it should be done, period, even if sometimes you are just going through the motions. You need to be active, in the game, engaging your conscious mind, and listening to your subconscious. That's how you make your own success. Keep in mind, showing up is the easiest part of the formula, but it's your focus once you get active that ultimately makes the difference.

So how do you overcome procrastination? Damned if I know. I gave you one example previously that works for one person, my friend the writer. Will the same strategy work for you? Maybe, maybe not. There are literally dozens, maybe hundreds of books with detailed step-by-step plans on how to overcome procrastination. There are thousands of videos on YouTube by speakers, consultants, teachers, and psychologists talking about how to overcome procrastination. Somewhere in that wealth of resources you can

If you give a procrastinator a good idea, what should you realistically expect in return? Absolutely nothing.

probably find a plan that works for you, or maybe you'll just have to come up with your own, but you have to get started.

I don't have that answer, but I will say this on the subject: Regardless of what strategy you adopt or rationale you choose to follow, there will always be two key elements present. Get started now and do a little bit every day. I'm not going to give you a step-by-step plan, rather, my intention is to help you rewire your hard drive—in other words, your mind.

The important point here is this: You must be aware of how procrastination is affecting your life and take action to deal with it.

I'm no different in this regard. I deal with procrastination every day. I have found my techniques and they work for me, but only because I decided to study procrastination. I didn't go back to school and get a PhD or anything that formal, but I did start to engage people on the subject. Almost everyone admitted to suffering from procrastination to some degree. As I learned more and more, from a wider and wider range of people, I began to get a picture in my mind of what was going on in theirs.

From the bankers to the stockbrokers to the doctors to the teachers to the grocery store managers to the taxi drivers, I began to formulate a consistent picture, which helped me find my techniques. Maybe knowing what I learned will help you find yours.

My first memorable experience with procrastination happened during my last year of middle school. My social studies teacher had decided that part of the lesson we needed to learn in his class that year was a little preparation for handling the responsibilities and freedoms that we would experience the following year in high school.

With that in mind, he decided that half our course credit would be based on one big essay. By big, I mean big for a 14-year-old kid who had never submitted anything longer than a five-page short story in English class. The assignment was to write a 10,000-word dissertation on one of several subjects that were popular at the time. We had a couple of weeks at the beginning of the year to set our topic, and once we informed the teacher, it was set.

When there is a hill to climb, don't think that waiting will make it smaller.

There was no more discussion about it. We were informed that we would be required to submit the final copy on the first Monday in June and aside from a note brailed on the corner of our daily homework assignments telling us how many days until it was due, it was never mentioned again.

Now, I had become quite proficient at staying current with my homework by then. Not because I was so disciplined or organized. No, I got my homework done every day because I had to have my teachers sign off that my work was complete. Without those signatures, I wouldn't be allowed to attend wrestling practice, which was the most important thing in my world, so I got the work done. Unfortunately, there was no yardstick by which to measure the essay, so it never came up. I had no enforcement to hold my feet to the fire and make sure I was working on it.

So, this is what happened to me. Wrestling practice took place every day, immediately after classes and it ended just in time for us to make it to the cafeteria for dinner. The rest of the day was ours, and, for most of us on the team, that is when we did our homework. It was a good system and considering I had approximately 160 school days to complete the essay, just a little bit of work every day would have made it easy, with plenty of time for rewrites and edits and second thoughts.

Simple right? Sure, but it didn't turn out to be that easy. There were choices to be made. Anybody know what I mean? Once the mandatory homework was finished, I had to ask myself, do I want to do a little extra homework, or do I want to raid the refrigerator in the home economics room? Do I want to do a little extra homework, or do I want to play tin-can hockey with my buddies? Do I want to do a little extra homework or sneak into the music room and jam on a piano? Did I want to do a little extra homework, or did I want to do my extra laps and crunches to keep my competitive advantage on the wrestling mat? And of course, because I'd been in class all day and had a full wrestling practice, and I'd done my homework, often the only real option was just to go to sleep. After all, there would always be time to get started on the essay tomorrow? Sound familiar?

The most consistent thing about doing nothing is the results.

Regardless, the essay always came second and by the time we were going home for Christmas vacation, I still hadn't written a word. No worries, I had two full weeks to catch up, and then I'd be more disciplined when I came back to school. Can you say *wishful thinking*?

Well, between hanging out with my buddies who I hadn't seen since the summer and visiting family and friends for Christmas dinner and to exchange gifts, I got a couple pages written. No worries, my buddies helped me devise a new plan, a better plan.

We had a wrestling tournament most Saturdays and then the coach gave us Sundays off. Well, since the coach's policy on homework meant that we were always current, my buddies and I devised a plan where I would write for a couple hours every Sunday. I still had 20 Sundays left before the due date, so it was going to be a breeze.

Then I discovered a new distraction. Girls. So now, if we weren't raiding the home economics room, or playing hockey, or practicing the piano, or working out, we could always sneak over to the girls' dorm and flirt with them, or more likely tease them, or play practical jokes on them. It was all totally innocent—we could never get into the dorm, we weren't that good. We were really too afraid to get close to a girl anyway (teasing them was more fun), and it was a lot more fun than writing a social studies paper.

By the time Easter came and went, I still had essentially nothing written. That wasn't good. When we came back after the four-day Easter weekend, wrestling turned serious. It was only a month before the nationals, and training became much more focused and intense. I didn't have to make choices every night after homework was done. I was too tired. I didn't even think of the essay.

I won the national championship that year and came back to school proud as I could be. The nationals were my signal that the school year was almost over, but not that year because on Monday when I received my homework assignment in social studies, my fingers happened to touch the corner of the page. It read, "Seven days to go."

Procrastination is the key ingredient in making sure that today isn't any better than yesterday.

All of a sudden, I was scared. Half my mark would depend on this essay, and I realized I hadn't even done my research. So, instead of enjoying the end of wrestling season, like the rest of my teammates, I now spent what used to be practice time in the library, furiously brailling out the notes I would need to refer to in order to write this essay. By Thursday I thought I had enough information, so I started writing. It was tough, not just because I was brailling, but because I really didn't have a structure in mind. I was literally shooting from the hip, with no time to edit.

I actually finished about 3:00 a.m. on the Monday that the essay was due. Then, after all that, I overslept and just barely got to class on time. I almost missed it, but I got it in.

A couple days later, a message was delivered to my room that my social studies teacher wanted to see me. I went to his classroom and he asked me to take a seat. I asked if everything was okay and he said, "Yes Craig, everything is fine, great in fact. I just asked you here because I wanted to tell you that your essay is the best I've ever seen in all the years I've been doing this exercise!"

I couldn't believe it. Then he burst out laughing, and said, "No Craig, I'm just kidding. This reads like you just finished it at 3:00 a.m. Monday morning."

In that moment, I realized that my teacher knew more about me than I gave him credit for. After I had picked my jaw up off the floor, I complimented him on his perceptivity and he asked if I had learned the lesson behind the essay. I told him I thought I did, but it would be many more years before the message finally sank in. Looking back, I am convinced that my grade never mattered. I truly believe that the lesson was more important than the essay. He was teaching us the pitfalls of falling behind in our work. His only mission was for us to understand the value of consistent, progressive behavior that propelled us in the direction of our ultimate goal.

I have found that in the minds of most admitted procrastinators, myself included, there were two competing voices, the rational, decision-making voice and the "we've still got time for a little fun" voice.

Most procrastinators are very busy doing things they don't need to do in order to avoid doing what they should do. Is that you?

Your rational, decision-making voice is always accessing your circumstances, your environment, your time frames, and your resources. It is the voice of reason. It is always asking, "What is the best use of my time right now?" It is the voice of opportunity that will always say, "This looks like a good chance to get some work done."

Your "still got time" voice is different. It is always accessing what options are available to you right now that would fun be to check out. It is a frenetic whirlwind of thoughts that comes at you fast from every direction, always saying, "Sure, we could get to work, but let's just check this out first," and most of us listen, ignoring the parental wisdom of our rational voice.

This is where the problem starts: Remember this famous quote: "Opportunity may knock just once. Temptation leans on the doorbell."

Well, when it comes to your "still got time" voice, it is more accurate to say, "Opportunity knocks just once, but temptation bangs and beats and pounds until it hammers down the door." I do think it's fair to say that most people want to be delivered from temptation, but unfortunately, they would like it to stay in touch.

You all know the scenario, even if you haven't heard the voices.

Your rational, decision-making voice tells you, "This would be a perfect time to get some work done."

Your "still got time" voice responds, "Sure, but first we should check out that webpage about CrossFit Athletic Standards because we might start going to the gym soon, and we need to check the fridge to see what new things might be there since we checked 30 minutes ago, and let's just watch one YouTube video to clear our minds and get inspired," and the next thing you know, you're into a YouTube vortex that starts with Freddie Mercury singing "Don't Stop Me Now" and is still going four hours later as you watch Simon berating contestants on *Britain's Got Talent* while you surf Google Earth to learn more about the differences between North and South Korea after you saw a weather map on MeteoEarth.

Procrastination is overcome by stepping on the first rung of your ladder.

You didn't get anything done, but it was a fun-filled, happy four hours that completely avoided the pain of hard work.

Now, except for your particular YouTube tours, this is not a unique scenario. We've all done some version. It might be as simple as deciding to mow the lawn when you should be making sales calls, but we have all chosen some simple, nonchallenging, short-term activity that provides some form of immediate pleasure or satisfaction over doing what we perceive to be the thankless, dull, unrewarding task called work.

It is unfortunate that opportunity is so soft-spoken and often comes disguised as hard work because the ultimate, although delayed, gratification is always so much more rewarding.

Doesn't matter, most procrastinators believe their redeemer will appear and they will save the day.

This is my favorite myth. This is the standard claim of most procrastinators that they work best under pressure, and as their deadlines draw closer, the small third voice of procrastination will wake up, and, like the Incredible Hulk, will burst on the scene with massive power, and supposedly inspiration, even if it is fear based. This voice is called panic, and since your "still got time" voice is scared to death of panic, when panic finally wakes up, the distraction of temptation will temporarily disappear, and the work will get done.

The work may get done, but history has proven, just as in my example, time after time, that rushed work, completed under stress and submitted at the last minute, is always inferior. It is true that waiting for panic to set in and producing under the demanding burden of a hard deadline converts delayed gratification to instant gratification, but on a scale of massively diminishing returns.

It's your choice whether you want to let your panic voice dictate the level of gratification you receive from your work, or not, but answer me this: What happens to you if there is no deadline?

When there is no deadline, procrastination starts to lose its charm. When you have no limits, when you have no reporting requirements, when you

Opportunity may knock only once, but temptation leans on the doorbell.

have no measurements with rewards or penalties, when you have nobody to answer to and no outward or immediate consequences, then there is no premise for the funny story. There is no myth about working better under pressure to fall back on.

You see, when I talk about procrastination in a speech or mention it in a blog or an interview, almost everybody can instantly relate. Almost everybody will admit to having had their own struggle with procrastination, but almost nobody has a funny deadline story.

Procrastination, in its most dangerous form, is that small, silent voice that holds you back from taking action toward something that you want to do but that you don't "have" to do.

It might be something entrepreneurial like starting your own business, becoming a sales agent, studying for a degree, just taking a course out of curiosity, losing weight, getting healthy, taking up a hobby, or moving to a new city.

This is the world of should've, could've, would've, but...

That one word, *but*, has caused more people to suffer more disappointment and regret and internal heartache than almost any other word in the English language. When you qualify your dreams, your plans, your alternatives with *but*, your focus changes. You stop thinking about what you have to gain, and you begin to worry about what you have to lose. You stop looking for solutions that would allow you to pursue your ambitions, or worse, you qualify your solutions with *but*...

And you procrastinate.

This is where I see the real danger of procrastination because it's not so obvious. It's not the simple, often lame decision to do something fun in the moment instead of the real work that you need to do or should do, or maybe even want to do. No, this is far more insidious because you choose to keep doing your work, you choose to continue to meet your responsibilities, you choose to keep paying your bills, working for the same paycheck, or staying in the same relationship.

What happens to you if there is no deadline?

And nobody knows it but you. It is not the obvious form of self-sabotage that is usually associated with procrastination. On the contrary, this becomes a slow-moving form of self-sacrifice that only you know about because only you know your true feelings.

Unfortunately, for many of us, this becomes that path we never escape. We never take the first step in that direction we really want to follow. The question you have to resolve in your mind is why? Or, Why not?

Why don't you take that step you dream about? What do you think is at risk? What might you have to sacrifice? What can you do to minimize the potential sacrifices? How can you find the courage to confront the consequences? And, god forbid, why don't you take a moment and think about what you have to gain instead of what you have to lose?

Why don't you take that step you dream about? Are you afraid you will have to work harder than you do now? Are you afraid it might be hard to live up to your current responsibilities while you work to change or improve, or expand your life? Why do you think it will be harder than the work you do now? I trust you're not afraid to enjoy the benefits of a little more success.

Let me ask you a better version of WHY? Why do you think you want to take that new step? What do you dream it could bring you? How will it make you feel? How will that be better for you, or for your loved ones? What is the ultimate goal you have for your life? Will the actions, the decisions, the steps, and the work you have been putting off take you there? Can you get there if you don't take action? Can you get there if you stay the current course? Is your lack of sacrifice worth it? When you can answer those questions, and stay focused on those answers, then you can overcome any *but* your imagination might throw in your way.

Sound good? Yeah, I thought so too the first time I wrote this, but the first time I gave this speech I left the stage with an emptiness. I felt like I stopped too soon, that something was missing, and I tossed and turned night after night, for an eternity, wrestling in my own mind to find that missing piece.

Procrastinating is like relying on the lotto for your retirement.

I wouldn't trade that time for anything. I thought of all kinds of ideas, several of which I wrote about, including:

- Don't just stand there
- It's not what happens to you
- Perception is reality
- Positive expectations
- Integrity
- Power of momentum—don't stop and start;
- keep moving forward
- Courage is a decision
- Is the rhythm of your life in balance?

But it wasn't until I woke with an epiphany that it came to me. That phrase is one that so many people know, yet so few have ever thought about, and I found it so profound. The simple phrase "Life is what happens while you're making other plans" called to me about all the people who die with their music still inside them, and I have come to realize that the saddest form of procrastination resides in those of us who don't know what it is that we aren't doing.

It is that sense that lives inside so many of us that "there must be more than this," but we don't know what it is. We know that we want something more, to do something significant, we want to make a greater impression on the world, or we just want to come home feeling like we gave the world the best we had, but the lives we lead just don't fill that void.

The procrastination here, if this is how you feel, is that life gets so busy that most, in fact almost all of us, never stop and take inventory of ourselves. We live in the world of routine. We don't ask ourselves what we can accomplish today. We don't ask ourselves what is possible today. We don't ask Why? or Why not? We don't even ask What? What would I really like to do with my life, or at least the next phase of it? What would I really like to do? Maybe How? How can I do that and make a contribution I'd be proud of?

There's no way I was born to just pay bills and die.

How can I do that and make a living? Or maybe, How can I do what I really like in a way that generates a living while I make a positive contribution that I can be proud of instead of just letting life pass me by? That is where your life starts to make a difference and where you stop having regrets!

Oh yeah, one last thing. Make sure, if you decide to take inventory of your mental toolbox and become who you really want to be, that it is really who you want to be. Your toolbox is filled with the God-given talents that will make your dreams reality, but you have to sharpen them, you have to polish them, you have to fertilize them. God has given you talent, but you have to turn that talent into skill if it is going to propel you to your purpose. The only way to convert talent into skill is to use it, and the only way to use it is to take action.

You don't have to make the next great discovery or build the next billion-dollar company, or—as one of my dear friends always says his true calling is—conquer the world (talk about pressure), you just have to be the person who satisfies you.

I have met day care workers who I am convinced do more good everyday than most politicians, and they're happy. That's someone to be envious of! I have met chefs who get more pleasure out of pleasing customers with their creations than anything else, and their customers get more pleasure from visiting their restaurants than almost any other option, a win-win if I ever heard of one. I've also met presidents who changed the world and still felt they could have done more, so don't let me talk down your dreams, just realize what is really your dream, then make it real.

If you can summon up the courage to take the first step, and you know it is the right journey for you, you can succeed.

No matter what stage or phase you're at, ask yourself, Is there something that I am putting off? Regardless of your circumstances, you can't change yesterday, and you are not smart enough to predict tomorrow, but you can make the most of where you are right now. Learn to live in the moment, be

> **You cannot escape the responsibility of tomorrow by evading it today.**
>
> —*Abraham Lincoln*

proud of where you are and where you can go with total awareness of where the moment is taking you right now. You can't let expectation derail the daydream that you plan to accomplish, rather, you need to revel in the experience of the moment without ever losing sight of where you want to go.

Get up and get going! After all, procrastination cannot resist the progressive, persistent activity of a mind and body that knows what it wants!

Here are some more pieces of kindling to help you defeat procrastination:

- A little delayed gratification can eliminate a mountain of stress in your life and improve the results expected of you, where you are right now. Do what you have to do, when you have to do it, with a plan to stay ahead, and you'll probably have more time for the fun and satisfaction that made you procrastinate in the past.
- If you have a dream, a higher ambition, a vision that you want to live, make sure you clearly understand why you want to make that real and never lose sight of that focus. It will lead you as far as you want to go. Remember, when your WHY is murky, your mind will always remain cloudy.
- If you feel like life is passing you by, that you have a calling greater than what you are living today, take the time to get inside your own head and discover the WHY and WHAT about yourself that will open your eyes to the life you want to lead. Then follow the second piece of kindling.
- Don't let your procrastination impede your inspiration for accumulation.
- Almost every opportunity you will ever encounter will be the result of someone else's procrastination. How many opportunities have you handed your competition through your own procrastination?
- If you let procrastination become a habit, will it eventually grow into a disease?

Tomorrow is often the busiest day of the week.

—Spanish Proverb

- Time only stands still in the mind of a procrastinator.
- Procrastination is the ability to withstand the urge to do anything productive.
- Stop procrastinating today! I promise there will be plenty of time for that later.

Laziness is nothing more than the habit of resting before you get tired.

—Jules Renard

THERE IS NEVER A TRAFFIC
JAM ON THE EXTRA MILE

There is no way to soft-pedal this message so get strapped in and let's go. You need to hear this!

How do you define success? There are more definitions, explanations, metaphors, allegories, and sayings than you can probably count. Beyond that there are more ways of interpreting, personalizing, visualizing, and recognizing success than there are definitions and metaphors.

The self-help industry dominates entire sections of the biggest bookstores with all the contributions of an endless variety of authors all offering their best-intentioned advice on how to help you succeed. YouTube is an endless treasure trove of videos offering inspiration and education, from every perspective imaginable, all designed to help you achieve everything you're capable of, or at least everything you want. Then there are entire subsets within the self-help community that want to guide you in appreciating your success.

After you've consumed all that wonderful information, there is still a community of motivational and inspirational authors, speakers, and teachers who do a wonderful job of keeping you focused and helping you find your strength and resolve as you continue along your own personal journey toward your definition of success, which they want you to revel in on your own terms.

I hope you have found the sliver of this fantastic and fascinating world that connects with your ambitions and supports your vision and expecta-

If you just do the bare minimum, you will always be stuck in traffic. Good luck getting to the extra mile.

tion of what success means to you. I hope you have that clear vision that inspires you to celebrate each achievement along your journey and powers you through the struggles between the celebrations.

I have spent 50 years immersed in that world. First as an athlete and ultimately transitioning to become a corporate goodwill ambassador and inspirational keynote speaker. Over that time, I've received many accolades for what other people perceive to be a remarkable amount of success, but that is only their perception.

My perception is that I have been able to build a very happy life that I share with my wonderful family, and I reached this point doing what I love. That has always been my vision of success. Over my journey, there were times when I did indeed feel very successful, and times when I was stressed out by the struggle to continue the pursuit. Much of this book is a reflection on that experience and a discussion from what I consider to be a rather unique perspective, which I hope will help keep your internal self-lit flame burning as you progress toward the realization of your vision.

I tell you all of this now, before I go any further, because I want you to understand that I am convinced that you can achieve anything you set your mind to do. I firmly believe, as it has been said so often, that whatever your mind can conceive, you can achieve. Of that, there is no doubt.

What I do not believe is that you are going to find a shortcut to your success, whatever it is. I'm not saying that there isn't tremendous value in learning to work smarter, in refining your techniques, your delivery, or your methodology. There is always a benefit from improvement, and you need to be consistently focused on refining that edge you are developing if you expect to gain any higher level of success, but there is no magic cannonball.

In 50 years of practicing, training, studying, and speaking about the subject of success, I've only ever found one consistent, common denominator that every person I have ever known who achieved a sustainable level of success that translated into happiness in their lives, and it was this: Success is the result of hard work. Period!

You can chart your own course. Just remember, there are no shortcuts. You can't take the easy road. It doesn't lead to the extra mile!

I'm talking about the kind of unyielding, challenging, heart-stopping, exhausting, exhilarating, sometimes depressing, always persistent, progressive, hard-charging hard work that leads to the constant and never-ending improvement that success demands. The kind of principled and uncompromising consistent effort that is fueled by enthusiasm and enlightenment for all elements of your personal and professional life that leaves everything on the field with no regrets, every day. Remember, this relentless pursuit of success is what gives you the resources to create a world of happiness for you and your loved ones. Your vision of success is almost certainly different from mine, but I am convinced that you didn't work hard enough to get here if your vision of happiness doesn't include reaping the rewards of your hard work. All I'm saying is that if you earned the means, you are allowed to enjoy them, but you are not allowed to become complacent. There is never an excuse for resting on your laurels.

Success is about making the commitment to be the best you can be and proving it every day because, if you're not moving forward in the direction of your goals and visions, then you're slipping backward. Time keeps moving. For all your hard work, you can only rent success. You can take a day off, but the world won't wait for you.

Notice also that I said hard work is the only consistent, common denominator of success. Hard work is no guarantee you'll succeed, but a lack of hard work is an almost certain guarantee of disappointment and frustration. In other words, being active doesn't mean progress, but a lack of activity, means a lack of productivity.

There is no shortcut, no Magic 8 Ball, no secret formula. There are only the accumulated and refined skills that you develop as a result of taking action to use the knowledge and lessons of your life. More importantly, it is the constant and never-ending improvement that results from the continual study and evaluation of your ongoing experience combined with your incessant pursuit of new and leading-edge knowledge that you apply to improve your performance, day after day, year after year.

Your journey to the extra mile is going to be mostly detours. Do you have the emotional resiliency to adjust your trajectory and stay on target?

Knowledge, though, is not enough. The continual acquisition of knowledge is essential, but it is the action you take applying that knowledge that generates the progress you need to ultimately see the results you desire. Knowledge is critical because it is the foundation of all wisdom. But, to claim wisdom is to understand that as solid as the principles of your wisdom may be, the world is an ever-changing orb that you must be able to adapt to, or else all your wisdom may just be a basket of diminishing returns.

Now, don't get me wrong, knowledge is critical, but all the knowledge in the world will get you nowhere if you don't have the skills to use it effectively. You may be blessed with talent, but talent is random and undependable, just as likely to shine as falter if it is not refined. It is only in putting that talent to work that you become skillful and dependable which, when combined with superior knowledge, leads to progress and success.

Then there are the intangible benefits that accrue when you get in action and do the work. These are abilities and resources that accumulate in your mental and physical toolboxes as you work toward the results that manifest in those events that you celebrate along your journey to success, and, understand this, success is a journey, not a destination.

My favorite definition of success goes like this: "Success is the progressive realization of worthwhile goals, while staying well adjusted." I'm also fond of the saying "There is never a traffic jam on the extra mile." Do you know why that is? Because most people never do the work necessary to get on the extra mile in the first place.

By the way, the extra mile is the promised land where you can utilize all the benefits of your time, effort, and energy to change your world, if not the world, and accomplish more than you ever imagined, without interference, even in your most enlightened moments. It's where the most finely tuned orchestra brings the music in your mind to life, and after all, if the world is playing your music, you need to get up and dance!

You are going to achieve your goals and set new goals and achieve them and set new ones and repeat the process, over and over and over. You think

I've never looked at my blindness as a handicap, rather, just a minor inconvenience.

that you know what success looks like now, or at least have a vision of what you want to achieve, but, as John Lennon famously sang, life is what happens while you're making other plans. You need to have your short-term goals. They will energize you day to day. You need to be focused on them, you need to pursue them relentlessly, and you need to study and practice and study and practice and study and practice if you ever hope to get on the extra mile and anywhere close to what you currently think is your ultimate dream. You also need to understand this: You study and practice relentlessly because it is very true that "he who sweats most in practice bleeds least in battle," but when you finally go to war, or work, you will start to learn lessons that you could never have understood in practice.

As Mark Twain put it, "If you grab a cat by its tail, you'll learn things that you couldn't learn any other way." Sure, you can study cats and watch YouTube videos of cats and talk to your cat-owning friends, but until you've actually held that cat's tail and experienced that frenetic fury firsthand, you just won't know the reality.

I'm not suggesting that you go grab a cat by its tail, but I am suggesting that you need to be immersed in the real-life experience of applying the knowledge you've gained and the skills you developed in preparation to react and succeed in any situation under any circumstance.

Real life is going to continually put you in situations and circumstances that you have no way of anticipating. You're going to leave the rarified and controlled world of study and practice and find yourself trying to apply yourself in an environment of stress and confusion and distraction and deadlines. There is going to be no time for analysis or consideration or methodology. You are not going to be able to follow the routine of practice. You're going to have to react and deliver with the knowledge that your actions will have consequences.

You know what I'm talking about. We've all been there. We all know what the first day on a new job feels like, but my message is that you do not want your life to be a never-ending recurrence of the first day on the job.

There's never a traffic jam on the extra mile because most people can't find their extra gear.

This is why success is a journey, not a destination. You need to take the trip, but don't forget, you need to enjoy it. You need to see and experience and learn from all the possible parameters that exist on route to your intended destination. You need to take the detours and find your own way back to the main road. Discover the additional knowledge and skill you'll need if you are going to make it to the top and stay there.

Is this making sense? You are going to spend your life pursuing your dreams, goals, and aspirations in a world where nobody else has an advance copy of your script or any care, concern, or consideration for your plans. That doesn't make them evil; it just means that you are going to have to deal with this uncertainty, more or less, for... ever!

You are not going to be an overnight success. If you really want to be somebody in this world, if you seriously want to accomplish all your plans, you are going to have to put in the time in addition to the work, but don't let that discourage you. It is the work that serves as the horsepower that takes you beyond the traffic jam, beyond the popular highway, on to the road less travelled, to eventually merge onto the extra mile. That's when you will finally be able to cruise with the elite and start learning lessons you can't conceive of, yet.

The work gives you the advantage you need to be at the top of your profession, at your level, every step of the way. If you've done the work as an apprentice before you're hired, you'll be better able to learn on the job and earn promotions. If you've applied yourself as an apprentice and mastered the on-the-job training because you never stopped practicing the essentials, you'll soon be an associate and then a partner and maybe even a principle someday. If that all happens, it's going to be because you have 20 years' experience as opposed to 1 years' experience 20 times. By the way, having 20 years' experience is my polite way of saying *becoming elite*.

This is where doing the work brings its biggest rewards.

Work happens in the day-to-day conscious world. Experience accumulates and grows in your Grey Zone. If you are consistently making the effort

Life is like a ten-speed bicycle. Most of us have gears we never use.

—*Charles M. Schulz*

to be the best you can be every day at whatever level you've achieved so far, you are accomplishing so much more than you are aware of.

All that input gathered from battling day after day on the front lines is being processed in your Grey Zone, 24/7 and being measured against the entire experience of your life. Over time, your success will begin to accelerate as your Grey Zone feeds the results of this never-ending study back to your conscious mind, at exactly the right time, in ways that will often surprise you.

Ultimately, this never-ending cycle of study and practice and work and process will lead to a realization that you possess—that rare and valuable thing commonly called wisdom.

So, let me revisit the subject of mental toughness and unpack what I mean by emptying your own personal tank. You must be willing to pay a price that your competition isn't willing to pay, and you can only do that by effectively refueling your self-lit flame. When you are filling your tank with productive knowledge, you're providing yourself with long-burning fuel that just might be your ultimate competitive advantage.

Athletics taught me to empty my tank mentally, and physically, by the end of every competition. Sitting in a locker room after a tournament with your tank half full didn't help you win, and you can't say, "I'd like to do it over again." This philosophy also transfers to the business arena. I honestly believe there is no greater feeling than coming home completely spent at the end of a competitive workweek. Remember that competition begins internally, and that ignites your Grey Zone to help you succeed in your personal battles, every day. How well you challenge yourself, day in and day out, will greatly determine how successful you become on your personal journey, as you climb your own mountain called life. That is the true power of a self-lit flame.

Just as I learned at the School for the Blind, almost 500 miles from home, there will not always be someone there to help you pick up the pieces and fight through your darkest hours. That is where my profound belief in myself originated and manifested itself into a tower of strength. I learned to be tough as nails from my very core, always believing and internalizing that I would

If you plan on merging onto the extra mile, you must have a personal roadmap that you can follow.

eventually prevail. That is the foundation of mental toughness, and without it, you will never merge onto the extra mile.

The most important ingredient in this process is that you must be willing and able to keep going even after you think your tank is empty. Trust me, just as I have done so many times in my life, you will be able to find the strength to persevere when you initially think you have nothing left to give. This is what separates your gusts of greatness from just simply being good. It all comes down to the strength of your resolve, your convictions and your willingness to pay the price, which will be measured by your sacrifice.

And one more word on the subject of wisdom. Wisdom is the manifestation of common sense, but you have to remember, common sense is rarely common practice. The word *common* is a total misnomer in this sense because common sense is the direct result of applying the rarest and most elusive qualities found in the most successful people. That would be the ability to think.

Wisdom is the accumulative result of all your years of work, practice, study, process, and improvement. Common sense is the result of being able to think through the application of all that accumulated wisdom while adapting to every unique set of circumstances in every conceivable state of a situation and demonstrating the behavior and producing the results that make you look like you have a magic prescription for every state of affairs.

We already know that magic answers, secret words, and enchanted formulas don't exist, but we all know of somebody who seems to have the secret.

What they have is the ability to think. Not react, think. Then act.

So, don't take this casually. Thinking is not common in any sense. Thinking, in the words of Henry Ford, is the hardest work there is, which is probably the reason so few engage in it.

Don't let that discourage you. Your secret to reaching the extra mile is your understanding that you will have to work harder than everyone else. Now you know that includes the hardest work of all, but the good news remains: The harder you work, the easier life gets, and if you work hard enough, long enough, you will appear to have the magic method, because…

You must be willing to pay a price that your competition isn't willing to pay.

Wisdom is the extra gear you earn over time, and that you can only earn over time, that ultimately gives you the ability to step on the clutch and merge onto the extra mile. That's why you do the work.

A Unique Example of Courage and Inspiration

When Brian Donaldson first approached me about writing another book, I hesitated, but not for long. Brian, a dear friend whose career long resided on the extra mile, is an example of success worth emulating. I decided to rely on his judgment, and he was in my ear and my head ever since, keeping me inspired. Then, he pushed my inspiration to yet another level. He revealed to me his battle with stage 4 cancer. I was shocked, but it was his positive demeanor that inspired me. I had perceived no change in his work ethic, his focus, or his continued success without letting his condition affect anybody he encountered. As I wrote this book, I watched as Brian treated stage 4 cancer like a minor inconvenience remaining a real-time example of how powerful one's inner strength truly can be. Unfortunately, as we were about to commence the first printing of this book, the cancer won. Thank you, Brian, for all your support and encouragement, not to mention the wonderful introduction you wrote for me. You were indeed a dear friend.

Here are some pieces of kindling, or in this case some logs, to help you accelerate your merger onto the extra mile:

- What does your extra mile look like? You are never going to drive on my extra mile. It is a beautiful, magnificent, fascinating place but it's not in your mind. It will never exist anywhere even remotely close to your most extraordinary orbit. You need to know what your extra mile looks like so that your Grey Zone can navigate the route to that

Nobody is going to appreciate all your hard work until you arrive on the extra mile. That's why you must celebrate your successes along the way.

ultimate lane change. You'll only get there when you own it. Get the vision in your mind's eye now and hang on until it's real.

- Take an inventory of your mental transmission. Do you have all the gears you need? Do you need to replace any? Do you need to tighten one or two? Are there some you've invested too much in that you really don't need? A well-maintained transmission gives you tremendous advantages.

- Balance is critical. What is the best use of your time right now? It might be to attend your daughter's recital or your son's Little League game. It might be to have dinner with your spouse. It might be to stop at the gym on your way to the office. It might be to ask forgiveness in advance from those who depend on you and go see that important client or work late and make sales calls. Remember, it all matters. You're not just building a brilliant career—you're building a great life!

- Think of your body as a brand-new car with your brain as the engine. Your engine will be powered by the fuel you put in your tank. What would happen if, every morning before you left for work, you scooped up a big handful of dirt and put that in your gas tank too? How long before that brand-new car fails to deliver top performance? The sand is the equivalent of negative information and energy being allowed into your brain. The question is, What diet are you feeding your mental engine?

- Speed bumps are inevitable on the road to the extra mile. Don't let them become mountains of doubt.

  "The fact that there's a highway to hell and only a stairway to heaven says a lot about anticipated traffic numbers."

- Which path do you think leads to your extra mile?
- The least appreciated ingredient in the acquisition of wisdom is consistency, which is the cornerstone of any sustainable success.
- The letter *P* in your mental transmission stands for procrastination and it propels you nowhere. Get in gear or get left behind.

Wisdom is the reward you get for a lifetime of listening when you would rather have talked.

—*Mark Twain*

YOUR PERCEPTION IS
YOUR REALITY

"Some painters transform the sun into a yellow spot, others transform a yellow spot into the sun."

— Pablo Picasso

The biggest challenge you face in your life is the fact that you are a human being. That means you are a complicated and ever-changing bundle of attitudes, knowledge, ideas, thoughts, dreams, goals, fears, strengths, and weaknesses that is under the control of a supercomputer that is 90 percent or more outside your control.

You are a completely unique and emotional machine that constantly absorbs and processes an incalculable amount of data and tries to make decisions and take actions based on how all that input is analyzed in your Grey Zone.

Your Grey Zone, despite its immense processing power, is hampered too. It gets twisted and turned around trying to absorb every element that exists anywhere remotely close to you, every second of your life while measuring all that information against every experience, lesson, and thought of your entire existence and trying to advise you what is real and how to deal with it.

All of this is going on under the surface while you deal with the day-to-day requirements of your life, with your Grey Zone only feeding you the information, analysis, and directions it thinks you need, when you think you need it.

Only you can decide what you think is reality.

With all of this going on inside your head all day, every day, every second in fact, how are you supposed to know what's real and what's not? The truth is, you can't. Only you can decide what you think is reality.

That's why I believe that your perception of yourself is your actual reality. It certainly was for me, and it manifested itself in my life in tremendous ways long before it was explained to me and in even greater ways since I gained a better understanding. I want to tell you my experience, but first I want to give you my understanding so that you can better appreciate my experience.

It was explained to me this way: As human beings we are all governed by what psychologists refer to as the self-concept, which, in simple language, is what you believe about yourself. The best way I've ever found to understand what that means, and how you can manage and maximize the power of your self-concept is to understand its three basic components.

The first thing you need to be aware of is that you have a self-image. Your self-image is very powerful, and you need to be aware of it. You need to question it. You need to understand it, and you need to evolve it.

Your self-image is defined as, Your perception of how well you see yourself performing a task, right now, today, in real time. The most important word in that definition is *perception*. Remember, this is *your* self-image. It is how well you believe you perform that task today, and that means it's right. More accurately, it is how well your Grey Zone tells you that you performed that task, right now, today, in real time, based on its comparison of you against every measurable byte of data it has accumulated over your lifetime.

I may not agree with your perception of how well you perform that task. I might think you do it better than you think you do, or I might see you as not being anywhere near as good as you think you are, but that doesn't matter. My Grey Zone is measuring you against a completely different database. Your self-image is yours. Your perception is your reality, at least for now.

It's also important that you understand that you have a self-image for absolutely everything you do or have ever done. You have a self-image for how well you do your job, how well you tie your shoes, how well you dress,

Knowing who you really are today is the first step in becoming who you really want to be tomorrow.

how well you drive, how good you are at making mac and cheese, how eloquently you write letters, how well you dance, how good you are at baseball, how nicely you cut the lawn, how well you take care of your garden, or even how well you have decorated your home. You have a self-image for absolutely everything you do, and they are all based on *your* perception.

Now, because your self-image is a perception generated by your Grey Zone based on the ever-accumulating body of information inside your head, together with your ongoing experiences and emotions, you have to also be aware that it is always changing. Sometimes it improves, sometimes not, but it is always in motion.

Your responsibility is to take charge and point it in the right direction. The place you want to direct it to is the second component of your self-concept. It's called your self-ideal.

Your self-ideal is defined as, Your perception of how you see yourself performing a task *perfectly*! Notice again, it is "your perception." It is how your Grey Zone believes a task should be performed and how it sees you performing at that level.

Now remember, again, that this is your unique vision of how the task should be performed in perfection. It is based on your Grey Zone's analysis of every iota of data from your entire life and tweaked by the intangibles of emotion, ambition, and faith. The most important thing to remember is that it is *your* self-ideal. It is not mine or your boss's or your spouse's or your teacher's or even your professor's. It is uniquely *yours*!

That's important because the only destination you can guide *your* self-image to is *your* self-ideal, and that is the objective.

That brings us to the third component of your self-concept. This component resides in the gap between your self-image and your self-ideal. It's called your self-esteem and it is defined, very simply, as, How you feel about yourself.

The greater the gap between your self-image and your self-ideal, the worse you feel. Conversely, and obviously, the closer your self-image comes to meeting your self-ideal, the better you feel about yourself. Your goal, as

Some of the biggest roadblocks in life are in your own mind. Treat the word *impossible* as nothing more than motivation.

the only means you have of consciously impacting your self-concept is to elevate your self-image to the level of your self-ideal, in a manner of progress that is meaningful to you.

In a manner meaningful to you! I can't overemphasize how important that is. You can't achieve anybody else's self-ideal, and you can't do it on anybody else's terms! It is absolutely imperative that you have a crystal clear and honest understanding of yourself and that you pursue your self-ideal in a manner that will be meaningful and inspiring to you.

Let me explain it this way, and I'll use your job as the example. If you were your own manager, the most effective thing you can do to grow your performance is to bring your self-image closer to your self-ideal though a series of progressive experiences that provide feedback in ways you find meaningful. You need to provide yourself with small, progressive success experiences on your own terms. You need to take the training that most effectively provides improvement on what you perceive to be your weaknesses. You need to gradually increase your levels of accountability to strengthen your confidence, in ways you find meaningful. You need to work on developing your own gifts to maximize your potential while keeping your eye on your goal.

If you were to manage yourself this way, it wouldn't be long before you would be promoting yourself, giving yourself more responsibility (and money) while creating new opportunities.

An interesting thing will happen as you manage yourself to your promotion. You'll start to sense that you are improving, coming closer and closer to your self-ideals, and you'll find yourself feeling better about yourself. Invariably, as you start to feel better about yourself, you'll start to do more of those tasks that made you feel good, and your progress, as well as your potential, will accelerate. You'll begin to feel as if you can accomplish anything you set your mind to do, and if you keep pursuing your self-ideals, you probably will.

I am a strong believer that mastering yourself is true power. It is the only thing over which you have total control, and if you do the work, it can empower you to do some very special things.

You lose your identity when you are striving to achieve someone else's vision. Continue to have the courage to be yourself.

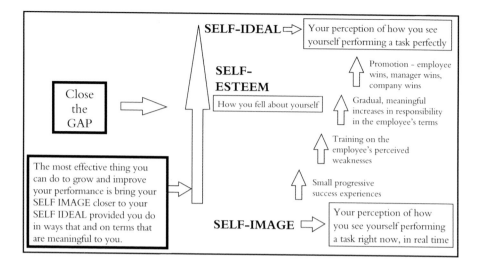

One of the best pieces of advice that I was ever given was, "Play the hand you've been dealt."

I've heard the message in numerous ways, but over the years I've come to realize that it was always the same message. I've heard it expressed as:

- Don't waste your time worrying about what you don't have.
- Don't pretend to be something you're not.
- Focus on what you have, not what you can't have.

What it has come to mean to me is this: We are all unique and have all been blessed with our own God-given gifts. Our responsibility is to develop those gifts to the best of our ability and not waste our time on false hopes and dreams, thinking *if only*.

Now, let me make one thing very clear. There is a difference between having gifts and being "gifted." You have gifts. We all do. We all have passions and abilities that, if we develop them, can lead to incredible things in our lives. The truth of the matter is that you must take responsibility to develop those gifts, or nothing will come of them. You are responsible.

You can't be everything to everybody, you're not that good, but you must be everything to yourself.

This advice, in a very direct manner, is another confirmation of the importance of knowing yourself. As Lao Tzu said, "Mastering others is strength. Mastering yourself is true power." In simple English, isn't that what playing the hand you were dealt is all about?

In a very practical sense, that is what has led to the success I have experienced in my life. I learned early that I had some qualities that were valuable to my desire for a "normal" life. I developed those qualities with a focus on my goal. Even at age eight or nine, I wasn't languishing in self-pity waiting for a miracle or dreaming about what life would be like if I could see. I thought I had found a means of achieving my goal doing something that was available to me.

The fact is that I was strong, durable, and energized. I craved physical activity, and someone in my life had the sense to recognize how that fit with wrestling. Once I was connected, I focused on developing those gifts of strength, durability, and energy so I could best take advantage of my opportunity. For me, that focus on developing the gifts I knew I possessed in that moment paid huge dividends and led to more opportunity.

Some of you are going to say, "Sure, but you got lucky. Somebody else thought you could wrestle, and it just worked out for you." For those of you who are thinking that way, there is another piece of advice I received just as often that I also want to share with you: "You make your own breaks and opportunities. You don't wait for the world to come to you on a silver platter." Remember, I saw an opportunity in wrestling that nobody else did. It wasn't handed to me. I had to make it happen for myself. I think I succeeded because I tried so hard to make the most of what I could do, without fretting over what I couldn't.

I may have been exposed to wrestling at an early age, but the people who saw my potential as a wrestler didn't see it as the opportunity I saw. They didn't do the sit-ups, push-ups, running, and practice. I did that work. They didn't see how wrestling could be my ticket home, my way out of that School for the Blind. Only I saw that. I played my hand and developed the gifts that allowed

I often enjoy having conversations with myself because I'm the only person I know who is always on my level.

me to become a winning wrestler because it was my best opportunity at the time. Finding a cure for blindness would have been a better solution to achieve my goal, but it wasn't an option. I played the hand I held at the time, with wrestling being my trump card, and it improved my life.

That's not the only example in my life of playing the hand I was dealt. Other trump cards became apparent when I saw an opportunity while serving as an honorary chairman of Wayne Gretzky's tennis tournament and recognized that my circumstances lined up perfectly to run a similar tennis tournament of my own. Why? Because I knew who I was, that I had a comfort factor with people who would let me pursue such a goal, and a passion for helping those less fortunate than I was. I was always looking for opportunities where I could capitalize on my personal strengths in a meaningful way that helped others in the process. This turned out to be one of the best examples of how I did that.

The same results came from living with Gordie Howe and learning where other cards in my hand had value, like getting on skis once and recognizing I had the physical dexterity to succeed, even though I needed to develop it. Similar results came from music, waterskiing, and public speaking. In every case you could say I got lucky, but I disagree. My eyes, or maybe I should say my ears, and imagination, have been opened to many opportunities over my lifetime. I have been able to take advantage of these because I have tried to develop my unique gifts, and I was ready for action when opportunity arose and had a deeply ingrained willingness to try. I attribute all the good things that have happened in my life to learning those few simple lessons. Let me repeat:

- Play the hand you were dealt.
- Don't waste your time worrying about what you don't have.
- Don't pretend to be something you're not.
- Develop your God-given gifts to the best of your ability.
- Make your own breaks and opportunities.

Vision is the art of seeing what is invisible to others.

—*Jonathan Swift*

- Always speak from the heart!
- Always be willing to try.

Notice I didn't try to become a great racecar driver. I did buy my own car, which I backed into several ditches, and I burned rubber in a friend's Ferrari a couple times in empty parking lots, but that was the limit of making that dream real. I also didn't pursue the dream of becoming a star hockey player, an expert marksman, a thoracic surgeon, or a dentist. All ideas that I would have loved to pursue but not possible in any meaningful way, considering the hand I'd been dealt. I stayed within myself, and the results speak for themselves.

What are the trump cards in your hand? What untapped asset do you possess that could change your life if you did tap into it? What are the God-given gifts that you should be developing? What are the opportunities around you that align with your assets? What great things could you make happen in your life if you took the action now to match your gifts to your circumstances? What are the gifts of your kids, or your grandkids—should you be starting to help them develop those now? How can you use your gifts to help them find theirs? You don't want to be one of those people we all know who say, "I should have, I would have, I could have."

If you don't want to be one of them, then start listening. Start asking. Your family knows what your strengths are, your friends know, your colleagues, too. I'm sure at your core, if you listen closely, so do you.

What opportunities are circulating in your life right now that you are not recognizing, or not seeing the connections to?

I urge you to start listening, watching, and feeling all the elements of your life. Take some time for self-reflection and pay attention to what your Inner Vision is saying to you. Develop your inner strength, learn to pull from it. Start learning and developing those gifts you possess that will allow you to make opportunity happen, to pursue your goals with passion and excel as you bring those goals into reality.

Your imagination is your preview of life's coming attractions.

—*Albert Einstein*

Soon, people will be saying you got lucky, too, but you'll know you made it happen for yourself. You have it within you. You have your own unique, personal dynamic, in the form of that special combination of gifts God gave you! Do you know what your gifts are? Have you fully developed your gifts? Are you even trying? Why don't you start now?

Assumption vs. Perception

A word of caution. Far too often people make assumptions based on their perceptions without giving any thought to ascertaining the facts. The result is almost exclusively the wrong conclusion because their perception was not remotely close to reality.

Recently, and for the umpteenth time yet again, I was changing planes in Atlanta. After having been seated and patiently waiting for the voice to come over the speakers, asking me to turn off my phone, I felt a tap on my shoulder. A reasonably friendly voice then commented that I seemed to be in his seat and asked for my boarding pass. Almost immediately, I heard a chuckle and seconds later the flight attendant was there.

Profuse apologies followed as she tried to explain to me that they just never assumed that a totally blind person, travelling by themselves, would ever be a Diamond Member on Delta, and they failed to notice my upgrade to first class. I jokingly replied, "Probably because no other blind person is as crazy as me," but I must admit I was slightly offended, and that is the risk you run when you prejudge without confirming your perceptions.

Many people, far more influential and more vulnerable, will cross your path throughout your life, with no preamble to warn you. They may be able to help you, or need your help, but you can only make a difference if you confirm that your perception is reality without falling victim to gambles of assumption.

If you are perceptive enough to see yourself in the same light as others do, you hold the keys to the world's perception of your reality.

Here are some pieces of kindling that, whether you believe it or not, are fueling your internal flame:

- Remember the words of Aristotle, "Knowing yourself is the beginning of all wisdom."
- Always be developing and improving your skills, knowledge, and abilities. If you pay continuous attention to your own growth and improvement, you'll be prepared for every new opportunity that comes your way while you maximize where you are right now.
- Don't confuse your gifts with your capabilities. You must maximize your gifts, completely exploit them to your ultimate advantage, but remember that you are capable of much more. Even the most gifted among us have had to develop the compensatory skills and learn the supporting knowledge to truly capitalize on our gifts.
- Understanding how others perceive you gives you the ultimate competitive advantage.
- The clutch in your mental transmission shifts you into overdrive when perception is perceived.
- Don't let someone else's perception interfere with your reality.

Change the way you see the world and the world you see will change.

Paul Newman

Tim Allen and Mario Andretti

Tim Allen

Mario Andretti

Michael Andretti

Joe Theismann

Evander Holyfield

Evander Holyfield

Don Cherry

Bobby Orr, 2016

Bobby Orr, 1980

Wayne Gretzky, 2016

Wayne Gretzky, 1980

Steven Tyler

Arnold Schwarzenegger

President George H. W. Bush

First Lady Nancy Reagan

President George W. Bush

Craig with George and Barbara Bush

Pope Benedict XVI (16th)

Alice Cooper

Aaron Lewis

Joe Thornton

Arne Sorenson (CEO of Marriott International)

Nido Qubein

1985 National Easter Seals Telethon with Pat
Boone and Donna Mills

Greg Norman

Mike Ditka

Jim McMahon

Red Berenson

Phil Esposito

Gordie Howe

Gordie Howe

Cito Gaston

Joe Carter

Roger Clemens

Carlos Delgado

Paul Coffey

151

Craig and Patti

Derek, Ashley, Morgan, Craig, and Patti in Edinburgh, Scotland 2019

Edinburgh, Scotland 2019

Venice, Italy 2019

Derek, Patti, Craig, Morgan, and Ashley 2018

Rome, Italy 2016

Monaco 2018

Derek, Patti, Craig, Morgan, and Ashley in Paris 2018

Dalton, Jack, and Amy December 2018

Tyler and Raven 2015

Dalton and Jack 2019

Tyler and Raven 2019

153

THE PRINCIPLE BEHIND PERFORMANCE

et's take a step back for a moment. Many of us are too often focused, sometimes even obsessed, with the idea of elevating our performance as a matter of success, achievement, or acquisition. We think of performance as hitting the game-winning home run, closing the sale, receiving a standing ovation, or otherwise overcoming the odds by delivering at a superior level in the moment.

I've resembled that comment my entire life, but I firmly believe that you can't sustain that approach to performance without a firm embodiment of the underlying principles that make the situational elevation of your performance consistently possible.

Think of this chapter as the basement, or the foundation, that you must have in place before you can build your house. If you lay the right foundation, you can build any house you desire, but without it, the whole house will eventually come crashing down.

Please take off any mental blinders you may be wearing and add this perspective to the fundamentals of your character, reputation, and integrity.

Performance is defined in the Oxford dictionary as:

- An act of presenting a play, concert, or other form of entertainment.
- An act of performing a dramatic role, song, or piece of music.
- A display of exaggerated behavior or a process involving a great deal of unnecessary time and effort; a fuss.

Don't let what you cannot do interfere with that you can do.

—*John Wooden*

- The action or process of performing a task or function.
- A task or operation seen in terms of how successfully it is performed as in *"pay increases are now being linked more closely to performance."*
- The capabilities of a machine, product, or vehicle.
- The extent to which an investment is profitable, especially in relation to other investments.

Have you noticed yet what all of these uses of the word *performance* have in common? They are all things that can be observed, and/or measured. I imagine that if you consider yourself a well-spoken person, you've probably used the word *performance* in all of these ways, which is terrific, but, from my perspective, the dictionary leaves out the most important example, definition, or connotation of the word *performance*.

Now, I don't blame Oxford, and Webster doesn't mention my definition either. I expect that is because most people, at least the ones I have met, think that performance is an event, or the specific measurement of a thing, like a car, a computer chip, or an investment fund.

I get all that, but it fails to even suggest the use of performance that I consider to be the most important of all.

It is this: Your life, your entire life, is a performance. People are always observing you. People are always measuring you. They are watching how you act and react. They're watching how you interact. They are watching how you deal with challenges. They are watching how you react to your successes, and your setbacks. They are watching how you express joy, happiness, empathy, anger, and love. They are watching how you deal with change. They are watching how you live up to your responsibilities, and they are watching how you help your fellow man.

They are watching all of this, and more. Wherever you go, whatever you do, you cannot escape the reality that the people you encounter in this world are always holding your performance up against a yardstick that their Grey Zone is using to draw conclusions about your character, your reputation, and your integrity, and everything matters.

People are always watching you. Give them the performance they deserve. *Walk your talk!*

Just as with tone, pace, volume, and inflection, your actions and behavior speak far louder than your words. Your actions and behavior define your character, reputation, and integrity. That's reality and there is no way you are ever going to escape it.

The challenge, therefore, is not to only accept it, but be aware of it and program yourself to act accordingly.

Yes, program yourself! You already know that you're too busy to take in and process everything that happens in your world every day. You're too focused on your job, the traffic, your workout, your hobbies and pastimes, or your children, family friends, and spouse—just to name a few of your daily distractions. And, never forget, you should be totally immersed in the moment with them.

I know I can't deal with all of that, and the rest of what happens in our lives that is just too voluminous to try and describe here, but the reality remains that we are always being observed and measured, as the performance of your life plays out. Remember, everything matters.

That's why you have to program yourself. That's why you have to achieve a state of mind, a consistently rock-solid mind-set where your Grey Zone is continually evaluating your actions and behavior and giving you the feedback you need to demonstrate the character, reputation, and integrity you want to be known for.

The thing to remember here is we're not talking about the measurement of success and failure. I know that gets measured too, and judged, but if your character, reputation, and integrity are solid, you can, and will be, respected even when you are perceived to have failed, or fallen short on occasion.

Character, reputation, and integrity are all about the subtle, intangible things that set the pillars of our community apart from the rest. It's about doing the right thing at the right time in the right way for the right reasons just because it's the right thing to do. It's about showing up even when you don't feel like it. It's about finishing what you started. It's about putting other people first. It's about being dependable and congruent, consistent in all areas

Your integrity lives in the heart of your performance, day in and day out, whether anyone is watching, or not!

of your life. It's about setting the example that others will follow because it makes the world a better place. It's about achieving a state of mind that is always aware of the right thing to do and acting accordingly.

I realize that there will still be events in your life where you will have to perform. For most of us, these events will not be high-profile, sometimes competitive, sometimes critical, do-or-die moments that raise the bar and challenge you to raise your standards and try to deliver great performances. No, for most of us, the events we will deal with are not so unique. I'm talking about your graduation ceremony, giving your wedding vows, simply accepting an award, being a master of ceremonies, or maybe just carving the Thanksgiving turkey. When your state of mind is programmed to maintain the highest levels of character, reputation, and integrity, you will rise to meet each performance in a manner that people respect and admire. The same will happen if your event pendulum should, unfortunately, swing the other way. Should an accident, unexpected problem, or injury occur, you will always be the one who can rise up and handle the responsibility calmly and effectively.

That's life, lived on an exceptional level, regardless of the level you achieve in your reality.

And isn't it true? Haven't you known very modest people who live happy, enviable, often exceptional lives without having achieved the trappings so often associated with success, let alone greatness. You respect them, not for what they have but for who they are. You would loan them money without a second thought because you know they'll pay it back. You have no worries about them taking care of your children or your house. You'd trust them with your very life because you know—they have lived it every day—that they are of the highest character, reputation, and integrity.

To embody all of this, you need to program yourself to have this constant current of character, reputation, and integrity running through the performance of your life. I totally respect and understand that you might, might have, or will never again, encounter opportunities, or crises, that will offer or

> **Character is performing the right thing at the right time in the right way for the right reasons just because it's the right thing to do.**

require you to raise the bar on your standard of performance to accomplish great things, overcome dangerous obstacles, or avoid catastrophe.

How you perform throughout your life is a baseline that runs hand in hand with your standards. If your actions and behaviors are conveying the highest levels of character, reputation, and integrity and you maintain a standard of always being good, you'll be ready. And that's where you have to be if you ever want to raise the bar and clear it. As so many champions have said over the years, if you stay ready, you don't have to get ready.

But even that isn't reactionary behavior. The ability to elevate your performance in the moment is a mental exercise that you have to be able to execute on demand, in order for you to respond. It's like Yogi Berra said about baseball, and this always puts a smile on my face, "Hitting is 90% physical, the other half is mental." Without the mental component, elevating your physical performance will be nearly impossible.

Here's another way to think about the performance of your life. The vast majority of businesspeople, executives, managers, and even coaches that I have known subscribe to the theory that they will always hire for attitude ahead of skill and experience. That's not to say that skill and experience aren't important, but even when they encounter the most skilled, perfectly educated, almost overqualified applicant, if they sense that this person is even a little bit of a jerk, they turn the application over and move on to the next candidate. If they can't find a candidate with the skills, education, and experience they are looking for, together with an attitude that they sense will make a positive contribution to their company, they always hire the right attitude and provide the necessary training. They simply won't hire someone they perceive might not be a positive influence on their team.

More importantly, it's how they complete this evaluation process that tells the real story. They will read résumés, check school transcripts, test the applicant's skills, do the regular psych evaluations, and call the applicant's references, but the ultimate determination will be made by observation. It's made by watching the applicant's behavior. It's made by watching the applicant's

Performance doesn't care what stage or phase you're at in life. It just demonstrates your integrity. Remember, everything matters.

interactions. It's made by watching the reactions of others to the applicant. Everything they need to know about the applicant's attitude and potential impact on the existing team of employees they will be joining can be, and usually is, made by accessing the applicant's behavior.

That means for most employers, how you perform the smallest tasks to the most significant; how you treat the strangers, family members, clients, and superiors you encounter; how you conduct yourself when you think nobody's watching; how you treat waitstaff and salespeople; and even how you react to traffic are better indicators of how you'll succeed in and benefit their company than all your skills, education, and experience combined.

That doesn't mean that all your skills, education, and experience aren't important. However you choose to define success, you are going to have to have the skills, education, and experience necessary to deliver your boss's expectations on their level. After all, your boss is your number one customer, regardless of your profession. To meet, and exceed, their requirements is the key to any definition of success so I strongly support being the most skillful, knowledgeable, and effective employee you can be, but you also must understand this: If your behavior does not demonstrate a consistent picture of solid character, respectable reputation, and enviable integrity, everything in your life will be harder than it needs to be and less rewarding, on your terms, because you will be constantly battling against yourself.

You're going to face more than enough battles in your life. A battle with yourself shouldn't be one of them.

Here are some more pieces of kindling to further focus your perception of your performance in real time!

- Imagine that your entire world is a stage, and everyone is watching, judging, and scrutinizing the performance of your life. From the most trivial to the most monumental, your behavior is the most demonstrative element of how the world judges your character, reputation, and integrity. Make sure you're Oscar worthy.

Life has stages, phases, and standards. If your standards do not waiver, you'll shine regardless of the stage or phase.

- The performance of your life must be genuine. Any attempt at acting out your life instead of genuinely living it will always ring false and tarnish your character, reputation, and integrity rather than enhance it.
- Performance is the culmination of your time, effort, and energy focused on the right things in the right way and harnessed to fly in unison to positively impact everyone and everything you ever encounter.
- The ability to perform is not an art, it is a hunger and a passion that you cultivate into an irresistible force.
- At the core of every great life performance is the refusal to compromise your standards for convenience.
- You are not going to live your life in a vacuum. That means that unless you choose to live as a hermit in a cave on the side of some remote mountain in the Philippines, you are going to spend your life interacting with other people. More than any other factor, your character, reputation, and integrity are going to be defined by how you treat those people, and everybody can, and will, observe and comment on that treatment.
- You will earn more in this lifetime, in every respect, by helping others achieve their goals than you ever will by being focused on yours. The reputation for how you treat others will proliferate far beyond your local sphere and will be returned to you in exponential abundance, either positively or negatively. How you cultivate that reputation is determined by the performance of your life.
- The reward of performing with integrity is a good night's sleep.

No matter how educated, talented, rich, or cool you believe you are, how you treat people ultimately tells all. Integrity is paramount.

COMMUNICATION IS EVERYTHING

Looking back, I would have to say that the most important skill I have developed in my life, in terms of my success as an athlete, as a business consultant, as a keynote inspirational speaker, as a friend, as a father, and as a husband is the ability to communicate.

I would go so far as to say that the most important skill for anybody, in terms of their current and future success, is the ability to communicate. I say that not knowing if you work as a bricklayer, a brain surgeon, or anything else. I say that not knowing if you are blind, deaf, healthy, handicapped—or as I describe myself, just having a minor inconvenience—old, young, tall, or short. The statement simply applies. Period.

Let me explain what I mean by the skill of communication. Communication, in my experience, is your ability to be effectively understood. Please do not confuse that with your ability to be heard. That is something you already have. What you need to ask yourself is whether or not the person hearing you is understanding your message. More importantly, are they receiving your message in terms and in a manner that they can comprehend and utilize effectively, on their own terms, at their own level?

If not, you are wasting your time. Always remember, as I have said elsewhere in this book, a confused mind always says no.

If you have read any of my stories, then by now you know that I tend to be a focused, bottom-line kind of guy. I like to be around people, I prefer working with others to working alone. I love to laugh and joke, but when there is a job that needs to be done, I like to get to the point and take care

Don't confuse the ability to be understood with the ability to be heard.

of business. When I am in my preferred environment, dealing with other people like me, with my values and my priorities, this is how I behave and how I communicate.

If you are similar to me in your natural behavior, you will probably think I am a great communicator, you'll get my message right away, understand me, and together we will produce the result we want. Isn't that why we are talking in the first place?

The challenge, as has become far too obvious to me over the years, is that not everybody is like me. Not everybody wants, needs, appreciates, understands, or can respond to a direct, straight-from-the-hip, matter-of fact-style of bottom-line communication. You have to be able to adapt your style. Your message doesn't have to change, but the way you interact must change if you want to be successful in dealing with other people.

You can't adapt unless you have a very good understanding of yourself first. Have you ever taken the time to really think about how you do things, how you communicate ideas, instructions, and requests? What do you value in communication from others? How do you like to be treated? When you are treated this way are you more likely to respond favorably? Will you better understand what is expected of you or what is being told to you if it is told in a manner that you respect?

Don't you think the same is true of everybody else? Absolutely, it is. So please make it a mission to develop a deep and sincere understanding of who you are. It will make you better in everything, particularly how you communicate.

Once you realize this, and start to understand your tendencies, you also start to become aware of the differences, and similarities, between you and everyone around you. You will start to notice that people speak at different paces, in different tones, that their focus and priorities within your message are different, that their pace and tone will change depending on how you

> **I have learned people will forget what you said, people will forget what you did, but people will never forget how you made them feel.**
>
> —Maya Angelou

engage them and what you are talking about. One person will focus on the people in your message, the next will want all the minor details, the next just major facts. This is where the skill of communication starts.

When you learn to recognize the differences and then adapt how (notice I didn't say what), you're connecting with others, you will notice that you become infinitely more effective.

Why is this? It is because everybody, including you and me, do things for their own reasons, not yours or mine. When you can communicate your ideas, thoughts, instructions, requests, or demands so that the person you are dealing with can find their own reason to act on, appreciate, or even care about what you are saying, the probability that both of you get a satisfactory result from your communication increases exponentially.

Here's another way to think about it. When I meet someone who speaks to me in a direct manner, someone who delivers the important facts quickly or gets to their question without beating around the bush, I find that I tend to pay attention right away. If they give me the respect of listening to my answer in full without interrupting and then respond in a considered manner that shows they actually listened to what I said, I'll start to get engaged in the conversation. Often a sense of rapport will develop. If it continues for several minutes, I will start to develop a sense of respect for this person. After all, they think just like I do, they must be very intelligent and well intentioned. That is where seeds of all good relationships start to germinate.

Here's the wild card. At that early stage I honestly have no idea if that person is actually like me at all. A good communicator, if they care about delivering their message effectively, will take a moment, although often we only have a second, and gain at least a cursory indication of the characteristics of who they are about to talk to. Then they adapt. If they want to talk to me, not that I'm particularly special, they most likely have something to say or ask that is important enough that they would want to be sure I "get" the message. By talking to me in a manner that appeals to my style, the odds of being "effectively understood" are dramatically improved.

Communication is how I talk to you. Conversation is how we talk to each other.

This is all good, for me. They communicated with me in the way I appreciate and, I assume, we had a successful first meeting. Now, what if, the next time we talk, I'm reaching out to share some new information, ask a favor, or get an answer and I simply accept that they are just like me, because that was how they gave me information. I could ruin the entire relationship right there if I'm not perceptive enough to assess them and gain at least a cursory indication of their characteristics and tendencies too.

I've learned over the years that not only is everybody not like me, but the hard truth for me is that, according to studies in behavior that have been shared with me, over 80 percent of people don't match my core characteristics. The scarier number, at least the way I see it, is that even if your core characteristics match the largest of the four basic human behavior patterns, you're still only consistent with 40 percent of the population.

Think about that. The best-case scenario of you connecting with someone who naturally appreciates your usual style is less than one in two. When I realized that even the best case still means that every other person you meet won't completely appreciate your way of connecting to them, it became abundantly clear to me that I needed to learn not just what to say but how to connect because simply being heard is not enough.

That's what George Bernard Shaw meant by his famous quote, "The single biggest problem in communication is the illusion that it has taken place." In other words, just because you thought you expressed yourself brilliantly doesn't always mean you did.

I want to reiterate here that I'm not talking about creative writing. You do not have to be a brilliant author like Hemmingway or a fabulous speaker like John F. Kennedy. You don't have to be inspiring. What I want to talk about is being effective. Being understood.

Being understood starts with "how people hear you." That's where you start to differentiate yourself from just being heard to being listened to. Believe it or not, there are elements of how you communicate that are far

You can have brilliant ideas, but if you can't get them across, your ideas won't get you anywhere.

—Lee Iacocca

more important than the words you say. Let's face it, if nobody is listening to your words you could command the world's greatest vocabulary and it would not matter one iota.

Communication is all about tone, pace, volume, and inflection. Those are the variables that you need to control in order to connect with somebody on their terms. Those are the variables that will cause a person's ears to perk up. Those are the variables that will cause someone to stop and take notice. Those are the variables that will cause someone to say, "Yeah, I get that," or to respond with a question because you've got their interest. Those are the variables that will get someone to listen to you.

One of the distinct advantages of being totally blind when I communicate with someone is that I can't interpret their body language. I am dependent on their tone, pace, volume, and inflection to understand their style. That's why I am so passionate about the message of this chapter. I know everyone is taught to make and maintain eye contact when you talk to someone, but I am convinced you'd understand so much more if you closed your eyes and really listened to the nuances. On second thought, that might be kinda weird though, if not outright dangerous.

If you haven't figured it out by now, I am an enthusiastic fan of effective communication. Stay with me through the next few pages as I share the lessons I've learned, both technical and anecdotal, that I have used to try and be as effective a communicator as I can.

Many will also claim that body language is a key element of effective communication. I don't consider myself qualified to talk about the interpretation of body language, after all, I've never seen body language, and I certainly can't hear it. I do, however, believe that using your own body language can enhance your message, and I'll get to that, but for me, body language is expressed in a person's tone, pace, volume, and inflection. Let me explain.

I firmly believe that most people can "hear" a smile in your voice. I've heard many managers tell their people to smile when they are on the phone

The single biggest problem in communication is the illusion that it has taken place.

—George Bernard Shaw

167 FIND YOUR FLAME

with customers because it will improve the experience, even though the customer can't see them. Even in my own experience I know that when I'm on the phone, which is a huge part of my life, that when I smile my mood improves and so does my conversation. It's intuitive, a subconscious thing that you can control through your body language, but it does improve your tone, even if you don't know how you're doing it. You can always control what you did. And remember, an insincere smile always beats a sincere frown. It's a choice you control, and that will make you a better communicator.

And it's not only effective on the phone. In my experience, when I check into a hotel, usually at one of the numerous Marriott brands and as often as 160 to 170 times a year, I can always tell when the front desk clerk has a smile on their face, and I appreciate it, especially after a day where I may have been on two or three connecting flights to reach the site of a speech in smaller town America. Now, this is the real power of the smile. I had been told many years ago that Marriott actually teaches their staff about the power of the smile in their employee orientation. Knowing that, I decided I would become a member of the Marriott Rewards Program, and on March 9th, 2014, I celebrated my 25th anniversary as a Marriott customer, where, by my calculation, I have spent over one-third of the nights of my adult life. What does that tell you about the power of a smile and its ability to build relationships and loyalty? If you're building a business, that's something for you to think about.

In fact, and please forgive me if I sound like an overt champion of Marriott because I know many of you have had similar experiences with other great hotel companies, but I need to tell you that this culture runs throughout the Marriott organization. A few years ago, I had the pleasure of meeting with Arne Sorenson, at the time, the chief executive officer of Marriott International. From the moment I shook his hand I could hear the smile in his voice. He walks the talk that his organization teaches, and he now leads the largest hotel company in the world, with more than 1.1 million rooms under management. What does that tell you about building relationships and loyalty?

Words are free. It's how you use them that may cost you.

That's why I've told audiences for years that they need to always let their smile change the world, but they should never let the world change their smile.

The power of the smile is just one example, but think about this for a second: Do you think someone perceives that you are passionate or excited about your message if you're leaning back in your chair with your feet up? Hell no! If you want people to perceive passion in your tone, get up and move around. Get your blood flowing.

Do you think someone perceives a seriousness you want to convey if your body is in a relaxed posture? No! Even if people can't see you, if you sit up, lean forward on your desk, maybe even drop your elbows on your knees while you're talking, people will take notice. It changes your tone.

If you want to have a relaxed, easygoing discussion, then lean back, relax, put your feet up, or if you're in the office, maybe keep your feet on the floor. It will help create the disarming tone you're looking for.

That's what I mean when I say that your own body language can enhance your message, but it is still tone, pace, volume, and inflection that get people to listen to you.

Once they're listening to you, whoever they are, that's when communication begins. Then, if you're paying attention, you might even be able to elevate your communication into a conversation.

For now, let's just focus on being understood.

We need to get serious for a moment. If this is going to make sense, I need to step back at this point and share my understanding of tone, pace, volume, and inflection. It is imperative that you understand what those terms mean to me if the rest of this chapter is going to have any meaning whatsoever.

WHAT DO I MEAN BY TONE?

Tone is what conveys our sincerity. It is the element of our message that people respond to regardless of what we're saying. When your tone is not

The ability to see beyond your excuses will allow you to find your clear vision. The ability to clearly express your vision will get you there.

consistent with your words, you are likely to receive a response that feels totally inconsistent with your message.

Your words might express the most positive message, but if you express them in a bitter or unfriendly tone, you may provoke a harsh or angry response. Your initial reaction would be shock as you find the reaction to be unfair, but if you could replay your delivery, you would most likely find that you got the reaction you deserved. You see, your tone is almost always genuine, regardless of what you are trying to say.

It comes from your Grey Zone, which rarely lies. This is because most of us have a hard time recognizing our own feelings, especially the negative ones, while we are feeling them. So if someone accuses you of being in a bad mood, indifferent, or even condescending, you need to hear them out, because they're probably right.

The same is true when you get that sense about somebody else while they're talking to you. To communicate effectively, it is imperative that your tone is congruent with your message. If not, your message will either not be listened to or it will be misunderstood or taken as insincere. None of these results can be considered effective. That's the entire meaning of the common saying, "We need to set the tone."

WHAT IS PACE?

Pace is how we convey our emotion and how we control our listeners' emotions. When you're happy or excited, you are more likely to speak at a faster pace, sometimes in an elevated pitch, as your energy bubbles up into your message. This type of speaking is often contagious. It will grab others' attention and draw them to your message because your positive emotions are so clearly on display.

The same is true when you're more serious or sad. Your pace will slow, and your pitch will drop. In this case you are more likely to elicit sympathy, or concern, but your emotions will still be discernable.

How can you effectively express your tone, pace, volume and inflection in 140 characters?

The good news is that if you're paying attention, you'll find that your pace is much easier to control than your tone. If you don't pay attention, your pace will still come from your Grey Zone, but if you know the reaction you want your words to create, it is easy to match your pace to your desired result and generate the expected outcome.

WHAT IS VOLUME?

For the skillful communicator, volume is a tool that can be used to create emphasis, suspense, intrigue, and even urgency. Volume is not just about being loud; sometimes that is totally counterproductive. I know, in my own experience, that people often raise their voice with me to compensate. It doesn't help. After they're done, I usually have to tell them that they are playing to the wrong sense. My hearing is actually quite acute.

Being loud can be effective in grabbing attention. It can be effective in creating an exclamation point if you need to punctuate a point you are trying to make, but not as a means of explaining anything. And on the topic of being loud, there is a distinct difference between yelling and being powerful. A powerful voice is under control, a yelling voice is not. It's like the difference between screaming and singing. No screamer ever sold a million albums. In fact, they probably never even sold one.

And when it comes to being taken seriously, a projected whisper is usually far more effective than the loud, emphatic, point-punctuating presentation. The whisper draws people close, and they hang on to every word out of fear of missing something. You'll never let that happen, but it doesn't hurt sometimes to let them feel that way.

WHAT IS INFLECTION?

Inflection is the natural rise and fall in the pitch of your voice during normal conversation. Without inflection, you are just blasé, and you'll never

Why do people speak louder to me when they find out I'm blind? They're using the wrong tool to fix the wrong problem but, if the only tool you have is a hammer, I suppose all your problems look like nails.

hold anyone's attention for long with a purely monotone delivery. Let your inflections flow, and you'll naturally reflect interest and seriousness.

WHAT IS PAUSE?

I can't wrap up my explanations without giving honorable mention to pause. Pauses are powerful. Pauses mean silence for a few seconds, and set up skillfully, they can provoke thought in a listener, emphasize a point you've just made, or grab your audience's attention before a significant message. You can also use a well-placed pause to convey confidence, command, or even emphasis. And for the truly skillful, a pause can even be hilarious, but that's on a PhD scale. I'll stick to being effective for now.

Any questions? Good, now we can get to the cool stuff.

If the goal of communication is to be effectively understood, I still contend that the evolution is to turn communication into conversations.

Communication is defined as the ability to be effectively understood. It is accomplished by effectively using the tools we have discussed to connect with another individual on their terms in order for your message to be meaningful to them on a level they can understand and use.

This means that together with learning to use your tools, you must learn to recognize the core characteristics of who you're communicating with and adapt your message by managing your tools.

Recognizing that most of the people you will meet in your life are not exactly like you, let me give you some clues to use your tools more effectively.

When I was a young man first entering the business world, I was told that there are basically four types of people that you will encounter. I've learned since that the study of types, styles, personalities, behaviors, and attitudes goes far deeper, but, in my experience, if you understand the four basic types, you can improve the effectiveness of your communication dramatically. Here is how it was explained to me.

A smart person knows what to say, a wise person knows whether to say it or not.

- **There are the detail people.** They tend to be softer spoken, analytical, and cautious. They seem to know all the rules and are inclined to obey them. They will always have questions, and if they find too many holes in your message you may lose their interest quickly. They also tend to be introverted and take a long time to warm up on the personal front. My approach when I sense this style is, in the words of Joe Friday, "Just the facts ma'am, just the facts."

- **There are the supportive people.** This group's interests are more aligned with the people connected to any question, task, or objective. They don't tend to take the lead, preferring the status quo. When confronted with change, they are not early adapters, preferring the tried and true, but with an open mind. They are more inclined to offer support and be part of the team. They are good listeners. My sense with this group is that they are guided by the saying, "If you don't hurt my feelings, I won't hurt yours." I also believe that if you do hurt their feelings, they probably still won't hurt yours, but you are just likely to lose their support.

- **There are the people people.** These are the outgoing, wear their heart on their sleeve, enthusiastic, optimistic, persuasive, social crowd. They put people first, listen to their feelings, abhor details, and tend to trust everyone until given a reason not to. They are the most verbal group, preferring to work with other people than alone. They prefer to solve problems through conversation rather than analysis. They have a definite glass half-full view of the world and live by the motto, "Everybody is just a friend I haven't met yet."

- **There are the driven people.** This group is all about results. They tend to be outgoing, prefer to work with and through others, but they don't like to waste their time. While they are outgoing, they tend to be thinkers. They will listen to their gut instincts, but they will put task first, feelings second. They prefer communication to be specific.

The difference between mere management and leadership is communication.

—Winston Churchill

Tell them what they need to know but don't tell them everything you know. If you missed a detail they need, they'll tell you without making it personal. The underlying motto here is, "Git-r-done!"

Already, I know some of you reading this are thinking about where you can get more details about these four types, and some of you already feel like you have too much information. That's where the opportunity lies. Assuming, you've already figured out which category you belong to, and if you can identify which basic style the person you are meeting with belongs to, you can adapt and give them what they need, full of details or just headlines, blue sky visions or simple outlines.

So, how does this translate into reality? Here are a few examples.

You're going to a meeting with Fred, who was, for many years, the controller at my best friend's company. That means that Fred was responsible for the money, the books, the financial statements, and the tax returns. (You should already be getting a sense of Fred's style.)

Here's what happens when you arrive for your meeting with Fred. You'll approach Pat at reception and announce that you're there to meet Mr. Watkin. Pat will offer you a seat in reception, ask if you'd like a coffee, and then call Fred to announce you've arrived. When he's ready, Pat will lead you down the hall to Fred's office. She'll knock on the door, which is almost always closed, and then escort you in. (Are you getting any more clues yet?) She'll introduce you, and Fred will stand up, reach across his desk, which is huge by the way, offer you a seat, and sit back down.

Now you're seated across from him with that desk as a barrier, preventing you from getting too close, or too "personal." Don't get me wrong, he's a very nice, friendly man, but, if you've clued in by now, he's also a detail guy. You might become his friend, but you're not his friend yet.

If you need more clues, take a quick glance around the room. I'm told that his bookshelves are full of tax journal and manuals. The magazines on the coffee table are *Popular Mechanics, Consumer Reports,* and *The Economist.* Not a single copy of *People Magazine* even in his area code.

Some talk to you in their free time and some free their time to talk to you, learn the difference.

There is also a picture of Fred and his wife playing golf.

With all this information at your disposal, let me ask you the important question, how do you start your conversation with Fred?

Do you ask him about that picture of him and his wife, or comment that you're a golfer too? NO! That's too personal, you already know you're not his friend yet.

You need to get right down to business. Tell him why you're there and begin to present your case, in detail, or at least with enough detail to show you know your facts. Then let him engage you, through his questions, and let the rapport develop while staying on point. By the time you're finished, the seeds of a friendship may well be growing, but, more importantly, you will have had your best chance for success in your meeting. Perhaps, on your way out the door, you mention that you're a golfer too. If he smiles, you know you've made a connection.

Now, let me give you the alternative: Let's say you're coming for a meeting with Charlie, who is the VP of public relations. In effect, he arranged for the company's free programs to be delivered at schools and colleges throughout the region and around the country. Here's what happens when you come for this meeting.

You approach Pat at reception and tell her you're there to see Mr. Barker. She'll pick up her phone, call Charlie, tell him you've arrived, and before she can even get up from her desk, he's halfway down the hall to meet you. He'll greet you with an enthusiastic handshake, thank Pat, and offer—insist actually—to take you out for a coffee.

On the way to the coffee shop he'll be asking about the traffic, if you had any trouble finding the office, the weather, and anything else that might have piqued his interest that day. He'll order coffee, say hello to the staff (he seems to know everybody), and invite you to take a seat, usually in a couple of wing chairs with no more than a low coffee table between you.

Kind words can be short and easy to speak, but their echoes are truly endless.

—Mother Teresa

Absolutely no barriers or resistance. You'll feel like his best friend before you even sit down. Do you sense the difference? Obvious, isn't it?

So, let me ask you the all-important question one more time. With all this information at your disposal, how do you start your conversation with Charlie?

Truth is, it's already started, but do you ever get right down to business and start presenting facts and figures? NO! He'll be looking out the window and thinking about his next meeting before you know it. Ask him about the company or some other open-ended question and let him talk. He'll bring you in and you'll talk about business during a bigger discussion. He'll be more interested in the concepts than the details so be prepared to paint mental pictures.

But know this, if you connect effectively, Charlie will become your champion at the company, and that is always a great result.

One last thing, as you become more effective at adapting your message to connect with Fred or Charlie or anyone else you ever talk to from now on, you will start to notice a unique benefit that results from having made the connection. The other party will, gradually, start to reflect some of your style as well. It's an effect called mirroring, and when they begin to respond in a manner that is connecting with you, that's when communication elevates itself to conversation.

Throughout my entire professional career, I have been working toward my master's degree in the use of tone, pace, volume, and inflection as an inspirational speaker, with the occasional effective pause, and working even harder to earn my PhD in adapting during one-on-one communication. I still haven't earned either degree, but the pursuit has taken me further than I ever imagined I would go. If you are confident enough to close your eyes and listen, I am certain you can go even further too.

Here are some more pieces of kindling to help you better understand each other:

- Being effectively understood is the first key to being an effective manager, account executive, businessperson, friend, spouse, or child. Remember that a confused mind always says no, does nothing, or does it wrong.

Raising effective communication to the level of engaged conversation is like elevating calculus from mathematics to art.

- Effective communication leads to conversation. Effective conversations lead to positive relationships. Positive relationships are the foundation of stable and growing businesses.

- You now have knowledge that I'm sure 80 percent or more of the population never learns. This means that you now have a responsibility. You can never again say, "He didn't get it," or "She didn't understand me." It's not their fault, it's your delivery! By extension, you can never again claim that you failed to connect with someone. If you have taken the time to understand your own style, you can extract the information you need, or lead someone into giving it to you, using the same techniques you would use to connect with them.

- Communication is how I talk to you; conversation is how we talk to each other.

- When I first meet someone, it never crosses my mind what that person looks like. I don't care about what color hair or skin they have, what clothes they're wearing, how tall or short they are, if they're thin or overweight. What I care about is what they say and how they say it because that is what I need to connect with. That's what reveals their inner beauty and gives me clues to who they really are, on the inside.

- Like it or not, when a sighted person meets someone new, more often than not, they have drawn a conclusion about the other person without having heard or considered a single word the other person has to say. I've always thought, if sighted people could temporarily put a blindfold, or mental blinders, on, perhaps we would not be so judgmental of others when we first meet. We would truly connect with the real person inside.

- I hear you; I feel you; I understand you. Your inner beauty touches me. That's the potential of communication.

- Putting on your mental blinders will allow you to connect with everyone's Inner Beauty, which leads to almost total inclusion regardless of race, religion, creed or financial status.

In life, it's important to know when to stop arguing with people and simply let them be wrong.

BUILDING MEANINGFUL RELATIONSHIPS

Life is a cobweb of human relationships. It's a collection of intermingled experiences that have evolved as you interact in loving relationships, friendship relationships, and business relationships.

A satisfying life has, at its core, a handful of highly rewarding personal relationships that inspire you emotionally and give you your reason for living.

A successful life is a vast network of connections that bring you all you want in life because you've made the effort to cultivate relationships that allow you to tell those people what they need, and why, before they realize it themselves, because you understand them so well. So well that they send everyone they know to you because they appreciate how you take care of them.

Life is a nonstop series of interactions with other people ranging from connections that last a lifetime to passages that may last no more than a sentence. You're human. If you intend to live in this world and experience all it has to offer, or even just enjoy the small sliver you have decided to occupy, you are sooner or later going to have to interact with other people.

The quality of your life and your success will ultimately depend on your ability to handle those interactions and your skill at evolving those interactions into mutually beneficial relationships.

That's right. The quality of your life and the level of success you achieve are totally dependent on your skill at developing your relationships.

If you want to know somebody or are forced to know somebody and you want that connection to be a satisfying and rewarding experience, short or long term, you have to make the effort to develop your connection with that person to the level that meets your hopes, expectations, or needs.

An effective relationship is not 50/50. It's 100 percent both ways.

I know that sounds harsh and transactional, but it is the truth. You both are essentially creatures of self-preservation and self-interest, but you are both, at least at first meeting, also hopelessly ignorant. That's not a bad thing, it's just reality.

The good news is that you can grow your relationships, if you are willing to pay attention, be proactive, and evolve the skill. The simple truth is that people are attracted to people who treat them in a manner consistent with their needs and preferences. They are attracted to people who communicate with them in a manner that they can understand, appreciate, and follow through on. They are attracted to people who treat them in a style that connects to the core characteristics of their natural behavior, even when they don't know what those characteristics are themselves.

The bad news is that quality relationships, like everything else in life, takes work and time. There is better news, however. If you are willing to learn, and refine the skill of evolving your relationships, they will take you further than you ever imagined with less exertion than you think, if you make the effort first.

The effort starts with your ability to be effectively understood. Regardless of whether you're dealing with your spouse, your best friend, a long-term acquaintance, or a brand-new contact, you are going to be far more effective if they understand your message on their terms.

That is the first essential element to establishing a level of respect. After all, if you can connect with a person and be understood, regardless of your message, then, in their minds, you must think just like them, and that makes you smart. Truth is, it just makes you effective, but if you have a worthwhile message that you need the other person to hear because it is in their best interest, then being effective is an honorable thing.

Being effective means you need to become a student of human behavior. You need to observe how people do things, what pace and tone they speak with, what they prioritize, what they react to, and how. What makes them smile, what makes them pause, what makes them angry?

A good relationship is totally predicated on understanding, and that is your responsibility. A great relationship is founded on trust, and that's a mutual responsibility.

Then you need to adjust. Please note that I did not say *change*, just adjust. You need to adjust the delivery of your message and your interaction to be consistent with the characteristics of the person you are dealing with. You need to do this because a confused mind will always say no, do nothing, or get it wrong, and that is a waste of your time, and theirs, assuming you have a worthwhile message to share.

That's where it starts. That's where you gain enough respect to elevate the connection from expressing a message to the give-and-take of actual communication. Communication is good, but it doesn't mean that your responsibility in evolving this relationship is over. Quite the contrary, this is where it starts.

If you can establish enough respect to ignite earnest communication, now you have the added responsibility of making the effort to understand them, regardless of their style of communication or how much their style deviates from your own. Remember, they don't know you yet, and you haven't had time to train them, so you need to adapt your listening as well as your delivery if want your communication to be effective. I'm assuming that you are only communicating because you have a worthwhile objective you wish to accomplish. If not, ignore the previous two pages.

Now, if you've established communication, we have something valuable. The next evolution comes in your ability to respond to them, answer their questions, soothe their concerns, quell their emotions, raise their spirits, excite their vision, and guide them to the best decisions and conclusions for them in a way that they find meaningful, inspiring, and trustworthy. Done well, communication at this level means that you will also be able to learn more, gain valuable and honest answers to your questions, and reach a level of mutual understanding that will become the foundation of an equally beneficial, long-term relationship.

Don't forget to pay attention to the intangible, often silent communication as well. Your words will always be critical, but just as often, your body language will speak volumes, assuming you can see it. You need to learn how, especially in your close personal relationships, to make intuitive connections that will be appreciated far more than what you say.

If you want a great business, build a team of great friendships and let them make your vision greater than you imagined.

Most importantly, you must always be mindful of the congruency of your communication. If your face, body, pace, tone, volume, inflection, and words do not all convey the same message at the same time, your message will always be suspect.

Can you do that? Of course, you can! Remember, communication is a skill. That means it can be learned, and whatever can be learned can be perfected through practice and patience.

If you want a life, and career, of great relationships, take responsibility and develop your skill, but don't stop there.

It's a great feeling when you establish communication, but if you want a lifetime relationship that rewards you personally, and professionally, without the constant conscious effort of assessment and adjustment, you want to take the entire experience to another level. Stay with me because a little more work on your part will mean a lifetime of rewards for both of you.

Effective communication establishes respect, which is the foundation of all relationships, but it will be your actions that establish trust. You must be a master of what you say, but it is infinitely more important that you walk your talk.

If you say you are going to deliver anything, from a letter to a construction crew, make sure it is there when you said it will be there. Give your words respect.

If you book an appointment, be on time. In fact, be early, never leave any doubt because if you're not early, you're late. Give your words respect.

If you offer to perform a task, do it early in the manner the other person expects, and if it is something you will be doing regularly, never stop working to do it in a manner that continues to exceed expectations. Give your words respect.

If they ask you for a favor, exceed their hopes. Give your words respect.

If you borrow your friend's car, return it with a full tank of gas. Give your friend respect.

An honest relationship is built on trust and integrity, which requires unwavering belief in each other.

If you tell you someone you'll call them back, call them, and do it expeditiously! Show some integrity! (This is one of my pet peeves, by the way.)

If you take on a responsibility always deliver more than promised, sooner than promised, and be proactive enough to take action before you're asked. Give your words respect.

Why should anyone respect you, or do business with you, if you don't show respect for yourself?

Eventually, you want to become so close to your spouse, your family, your friends, or your clients that you can give them what they need, or want, the way they need or want it, before they even know they need or want it.

When you have reached that level, you'll have a great relationship. Not only that, but a few additional benefits will have accrued along the way, if you've been paying attention. You see, great relationships are a lot of work, but they are not one-way streets! Only half the work is learning to adapt to your spouse, family, friend, or client. The other half, which happens almost automatically, is training your spouse, family, friend, or client to adapt to you. It just requires patience and awareness.

Don't be shy about acknowledging when someone goes out of their way for you. They'll appreciate it and your relationship will improve, again and again. PhDs refer to this as merging to the middle. The practitioners refer to this as co-cooperating. That's all too technical for me, I just know it works.

As you continue to meet, and exceed, the expectations of your spouse, family, friends, and clients, you will evolve to yet another level. I call this one commitment. By the time your relationship has reached the level of commitment, you'll notice that:

- Your communication has become simpler. You're not consciously working to adapt your message to their unique style and your understanding of them takes less work. It's what I think of as elevating communication to conversation. By now, you can relax, your Grey Zone has taken the wheel.
- They will become just as aware of your style and requirements. You'll start to be pleasantly surprised as they begin to respond to you, in

Never look down on anyone unless you are admiring their shoes.

terms of both communication and action, in the manner that you prefer without you having to constantly adapt.
- They will begin to anticipate you and even respond to you, sometimes before you ask, as they become aware of your needs and routines, so long as you continue to proactively respond to theirs.

Can you sense where all this is going? If you build quality relationships with all the benefits and attributes that will evolve, you will eventually achieve the ultimate level. I call that loyalty. Every iconic business has been built on loyalty.

That is the amazing place where you know that as long as you continue to walk your talk, as long as you live up to your end of the bargain and live your life with rock-solid integrity, your back is covered.

You can live your life, rest assured, knowing:

- That your spouse will always be there for you and that your happiness will always be a priority.
- That your kids will always respect you, be proud of you, and make you proud of them.
- That your friends will always be there when you need them, will always show up when you invite them, and will always include you in ways that make you feel special.
- That your clients will always respect you and follow your advice.
- That your clients will always come to you with problems, and opportunities, without considering the competition because they know you have it covered.
- That your clients will send you all their friends and associates who need your service.
- That your industry and community will respect you because your integrity and reputation will speak loudly and positively.
- That you will be able to achieve everything you want in your life because you are helping so many achieve everything they want in theirs.

A repeat sale means you have a relationship. Don't take it for granted while searching for new business.

Now, as so often is the case, I told you all of that to tell you this: The benefit of learning to build and maintain meaningful relationships is a major material benefit that will ultimately be overtaken by your Grey Zone, if you never give up! If you make the focus of your career to serve the people, all the people, with whom you plan to interact and depend on, it will become second nature. That doesn't mean that you stop paying attention, because if you don't use it, you'll lose it. Your sense of effort will seem to diminish over time while the benefits will continue to accelerate at an ever-increasing speed. And always remember, there is no speed limit on the extra mile!

Here are several more pieces of kindling to help your relationships evolve:

- "You can make more friends and acquire more clients in two months by becoming interested in other people than you can in two years by trying to get people interested in you." —*Dale Carnegie*
- People do business with people because they choose to, not because they have to. We can always find others doing the same thing or selling the same product. It's the personal connection that makes the difference.
- The cornerstone of a great business is relationships. The cornerstone of a great life is friendships.
- Leaders manifest relationships by demonstrating what they expect without expectation.
- Effective communication establishes respect, which is the foundation of all relationships, but it will be your actions that establish trust. You must be a master of what you say, but it is infinitely more important that you walk your talk.
- A satisfying life has, at its core, a handful of highly rewarding personal relationships that inspire you emotionally and give you your reason for living.

We make a living by what we get. We make a life by what we give.

—*Winston Churchill*

- When relationships grow for all the right reasons, they can last for a lifetime and everybody wins.
- When building a new business, your ability to earn and sustain the trust of new clients is critical. The ability to earn referrals is priceless.

We've been friends for so long, I can't remember which one of us is the bad influence.

LEADERSHIP

Leadership is just a series of signposts on the continuous journey of a successful life. Don't get caught up reading your own headlines—they don't mean anything. You earn the reputation of being a leader, but you can't assume it. You will always have to work for it! There is no time to rest. If you can't check your ego at the door, you will always be fighting an uphill battle!

The leaders who have impressed me the most over the course of my career were the ones who seemed most engaged in the moment when they were with me. The tone and pace of their voice, together with the insightfulness of their comments and questions, told me that they were totally in that moment, yet they always conveyed a greater presence that made me want to ask them more and deeper questions because I sensed they had answers that would open my mind in ways that couldn't help but make me better. They were never about ego, they simple raised everyone around them, like the tide raises all boats, and if you ever let your ego grow so large that you compare yourself to the tide, you're not a leader, you're just over your skis.

I believe that leadership, in its simplest form, is the inspiration of one individual to help one other individual to raise their place in this world even just one level. This applies even to parents, teachers, coaches, clergy, politicians, and any other person in a perceived position of leadership. The simple recognition of what your example represents, and acting accordingly, is often the greatest demonstration of leadership that our society experiences, and hopefully benefits from.

Leadership is behavior, not position.

WHEN I TALK TO MANAGERS I GET THE FEELING THAT THEY ARE IMPORTANT.

WHEN I TALK TO LEADERS I GET THE FEELING THAT I AM IMPORTANT.

We are not all capable, or destined, to assume the level of responsibility that was beset on someone as historically significant as Winston Churchill, but we are all capable of assuming the level of responsibility required to elevate the lives in our own immediate circle.

Leadership has always seemed to me to be the simplest, yet possibly the most misunderstood, requirement of those who truly desire to be successful. Being a good leader—remember good is your minimum standard—should be the natural result of everything you have ever tried to learn, practice, believe, develop, and embody throughout your life. It is, in fact, the personification of your entire experience of life, delivered effortlessly with grace, eloquence, and effort in an example that everyone around you feels compelled to follow, if not emulate.

Leaders live their lives with a passion that is personified. Their world is an admirable demonstration of every quality the rest of us should desire to embody in our behavior to inspire those who follow us. This is the ultimate expression of the age-old saying, "What you do speaks so loud I can't hear what you're saying." If you want to make a positive difference in this world, you better decide what your actions are saying. That's what people follow.

A leader's talent is not to create opportunity for you, but to elevate your vision until you see your own.

That doesn't mean you leave your leadership to chance. You need to inspect the behaviors, actions, and results of those who allegedly are following you, then adapt your behavior to help them correct for their results. Lead by positive example. Teach but don't criticize. Inspire but don't give false hope. The truly capable will follow your lead, and your success will be enhanced by how high you help them elevate their own ambitions.

One more thing: If you intend to be a leader, be worthy of being followed. Before you go any further, stop and take a look in your "mirror of self-reflection." What do you see? Would you follow yourself?

Success is the reality that you resemble when all of your accumulated hard work reaches a point where you make everything look easy. It is also the first place where I sense that all the aspiring leaders I meet get it wrong. I said that leaders make it look easy, but reaching that level wasn't. Like everything else, possessing the qualities and skills of a great leader, let alone being able to generate worthwhile results, takes a lot of hard work, period. There is no way around that.

You can't decide that you are going to study a course or two on leadership and expect that you can graduate into being a leader. It is true that the best leaders have amazing skill sets that we can all aspire to, but they didn't learn them in a book or a class or by watching a bunch of videos. They learned them by becoming the best they could at every other component of success and compiling more than enough practice at applying that collective body of knowledge and experience in a progressive program of self-management that resulted in the proverbial 20 years' experience versus one year of experience 20 times. Compiling your 20 years' experience is how you pay for your ticket to merge onto the extra mile.

Now, if you don't have 20 years, or don't want to wait 20 years, then you need to up your intensity. You may have noticed that good things don't actually come to those who wait. Good things come to those who work their donkey off, relentlessly, and never stop learning. If you aspire to achieving levels of leadership, know that you still need to do the work. Make up your

A candle loses nothing by lighting another candle.

—*James Keller*

mind to be the first to arrive at work every day and be the last to leave. Make up your mind to accept, or apply for, every iota of additional responsibility you can assume and then deliver, for the knowledge, the experience, and the recognition. The only way to shorten the curve is to outwork the competition, and once you get there, don't stop, just because you're in the lead. Remember, the competition hasn't quit.

Intensity, and focus on improvement, with practice, can dramatically shorten the curve. That is not a shortcut. It simply means that you have to be a person of action and be prepared for more *action* than you've experienced before, instead of reaction. By *action* I mean work. You decide.

I didn't just magically figure this out. I spent more than 18 years as a corporate goodwill ambassador for Edward Jones, the investment company. My responsibility was the development of positive brand recognition and a positive corporate culture.

I came to realize this early in my business career when I found myself spending so much time in the world of financial advisors struggling to develop a rapport with them. After some soul-searching conversations, I came to realize what was missing. If I wanted to connect with them, and connect them to the company, I needed to learn how to think like them, I needed to learn what they already knew, and I needed to adapt that knowledge to my style if I was going to have credibility with them. That, to me, meant I needed my Series 7 license. That is the license needed to be a stockbroker. To receive it, you must complete a 250-question, six-hour exam, which I had to take orally.

Problem was, I needed it now. I needed 10 years of experience and personal growth, and I needed it in 10 weeks. Even more daunting was the reality that it started with my obtaining a license no other totally blind person had ever held, or at least so I was told, up to that time.

That is when the real lesson of winning the US Blind Snow-Skiing Championship hit me.

There is no limit to the amount of good you can do if you don't care who gets the credit.

— *Ronald Reagan*

I went from being a novice skier to a national champion in four months. If I could do that on the slopes, why couldn't I develop the knowledge base and understanding of the skills to be a successful financial advisor in the same amount of time?

Think about that. How did I catch up to the field to be able to win in Alta? The competition, the group I wanted to be equal to, had anywhere from 10 to 20 years' skiing experience. With the skiing season averaging maybe 20 weeks a year and most skiing one or two days a week, on the weekends, that would be approximately 200 to 300 days or 800 to 1,200 hours, if my competition skied aggressively.

If that was their body of work, then I should have thought of myself as having 10 years' experience also. When I hit the top of the hill in Alta I had been skiing every day for four months, averaging six to eight hours a day on my skis, being mentored by a successful coach. That's 120 days at, say seven hours a day, or 840 hours of actual skiing experience. When you add two to three hours a day of mental preparation and visualization, all compressed into four months, you have a substantial body of work that produced tremendous results.

Now, I do believe there is one more reason why I was able to accomplish so much in such little time. I started with a specific goal crystalized in my mind. I had a reason why I was doing all this, and I measured myself against that goal every day. Was I getting closer? What did I learn today? How did I improve? Was the improvement enough? There was no casual experience. Everything was measured, and everything had a reason.

With that mind set, I think my experience accelerated me beyond skiers with many years on the slope. I had to get better, and the better I got the more I wanted to do, and the more I did the better I got. As a result, I am certain I skied more in four months than most people did in 10 years. Not only that, but I learned and improved as a matter of routine, not just residue from simple time and repetition.

If you don't know where you are going, you might wind up somewhere else.

—*Yogi Berra*

Once I understood the reasons behind my skiing success, I was able to transfer that mind-set to my Series 7. I completed the training and obtained my license in two and a half months. There are no Braille training manuals for the Series 7. My course of study was to tote around 88 hours of training material on cassette tapes. The leadership of Edward Jones actually had to make special arrangements for those tapes to be recorded, and I have always been thankful that they went the extra mile for me. I listened to and memorized the material while I maintained my full travel and speaking schedule. I was assigned a coach from the training department, and I continually challenged her, not only to ensure I understood the material from a licensing standpoint, but I challenged her about how it applied to the work of the financial advisor. I related that to my training and experience in communication and relationships (my equivalent to the sit-ups and push-ups that prepared me for wrestling) and soon was asking much better questions of the financial advisors I worked with. I became exponentially more effective at immersing them positively into the culture and fabric of the company. The results for all of us, the financial advisors, the company, and me were tremendous. So good, in fact, that I remained with the company for 18 years, and I'm still a limited partner to this day. In fact, I remain a proud, entrenched member of the Edward Jones family, and I'm still asked to speak to thousands of members of the Edward Jones world every year.

Why did I tell you all of this? Because it is vital for you to understand that the application of the knowledge gained from very hard work produces substantial results. It's not just going through the motions of the work, but the quality of the work that ultimately makes the difference. The work required by your circumstances is unique, and you must figure out what that is. You must also take charge of the variables if urgency matters to you. Totally submerge yourself if necessary but you must do the work. Nothing great is accomplished without it.

Here's the reality. The miracle edge is your experience. The miracle edge is learning from your experience and applying those lessons in a never-ending

Leaders have 20 years of experience. Managers have one year of experience, 20 times.

program of self-evaluation and improvement until you reach the point where it appears you know the secrets and have the magic techniques that make success look easy. The shortcuts that everybody seems to be looking for actually come in small incremental gains in skill, knowledge, and awareness that accumulate to become a great advantage. At the same time, if you didn't do the work necessary to have the knowledge, strength, or energy needed to create the residue necessary for such a self-improvement program, you will always be frustrated.

Why work so hard?

Because leaders must have the book smarts, usually knowing their business better than all their subordinates. They must have the intangible skills, knowing how to deal with individuals, groups, and communities in ways that bring focus, enthusiasm, and cooperation.

They must have the intangible skills. They must know what you learn by "grabbing a cat by its tail." They must have the insight that only massive practical experience can provide.

They must have confidence to entrust their knowledge to good people. They must know how to manifest their knowledge, experience, and insights across vast numbers of people to accomplish amazing things.

Most importantly, they must walk their talk. They must represent exactly what they expect and leave no doubt in any mind that they deserve your loyalty and respect. They might have the position of leadership, but the real question is, Are people willing to follow them? True leaders know the difference.

Simply put, leaders live and breathe their character, reputation, and integrity on a level most of us can only aspire to and hope to emulate.

They can do all of this because they have put in the time, effort, and energy (i.e., sacrifice) that it takes to acquire that one quality that separates the haves from the almost haves. That quality is wisdom.

Having said all that, let me ask you, How does leadership, real leadership, manifest itself in everyday life? Let's face it, that is where most of us live. We may be deluged with stories and images of absolute leaders day in and

---

If you're not passionate about how you deliver your message, why should I believe you care?

day out, but that is not reality for most of us. Most of us are not presidents of countries or CEOs of multinational corporations. Most of us are dealing with our team at work, our class at school, our clientele, our PTA, or our neighborhood improvement association. Interestingly, succeeding as a leader, at any level, tends to manifest itself exactly the same way, and it isn't something you can study. It is something you become.

THE BEST BOSS

The most common place that most of us encounter leadership is on the job. With that in mind, I want you to take a second and think about the best boss you ever worked for. More specifically, think about what it was that made this person the best.

What characteristics did they demonstrate, how did they act, what was it that you remember about them that brings them to mind right now? Go ahead and take a second or two and make a list.

I was first confronted with this question while sitting in a workshop with a group of 20 or more businesspeople and managers. By the time we were done, not only had we each made our own list, but our trainer had assembled a class list of more than 45 characteristics. I have seen this exercise performed countless times since, in classes comprised of all manner of participants, from senior executives to entry-level factory workers. Interestingly, the list always turned out to be essentially the same. I have even seen classes of high school seniors do this exercise, just changing the focus from best boss to best teacher. Guess what? The list never changed.

If you actually took the time to create your own list, it would include some of these terms:

Patient
Understanding
Disciplined
Honest

Weak leaders hire inferior people; great leaders hire superior people and inspire the potential.

Sincere

Caring

Funny

Tough

Organized

Thoughtful

Creative, welcomed input

Direct, to the point

Compassionate

Had my back

Supportive

Easygoing

Encouraging

Likeable

Led by example

Walked their talk

Hardworking

Believable

Trustworthy

Loyal

See, I told you, the list never changes and neither does the lesson it teaches. To understand that lesson, I want you to ask yourself one question: For every item on the list, is that item a skill or an attitude?

If you were honest with yourself, you have to admit that every item on this list, and I'm sure any items you may have that aren't listed previously, is an attitude. Even if you want to suggest that something as abstract as organized is a skill, I would counter that by arguing that it is, at best, a soft skill based on attitude. After all, if you don't want to be organized, you won't be, no matter how much organizational training you may have. But, when you deliberate on the issue of skills, that is a moot point at best.

Leaders don't have to tell you they're a leader. You'll know it, or they're not.

Consider this: If this is the best boss you have ever worked for, then it is reasonable for me to believe that they have achieved some success and a recognized level of leadership. They have gained the necessary education, developed the ability, and demonstrated that they can perform a specific task or deliver a specific result well enough to have earned the right to a more responsible position and the benefits that go with it. If that is the case, answer me this, why is it that nobody ever identifies a single, hard, specific skill that this person must have in order to have reached their current level of success?

Why doesn't anybody ever say:

- He writes fabulous code.
- He writes fabulous letters with great sentence structure.
- She is an excellent mathematician.
- He is a master machinist.
- She could conjugate a verb like nobody's business.
- She is a brilliant analyst.

Why? Because if they hadn't connected with you effectively, on your terms, they never would have been able to teach you what they knew or lead you to produce what they required of you. That connection was manifested through their attitude, particularly the attitude that touched you the right way. Remember, leadership is behavior, not position, and behavior is the best example of attitude any of us can demonstrate. Even more interesting, look at the range of attitudes. Some people liked a manager who was funny, others appreciated patience while still others needed discipline, or directness. People are different, and the best managers, and leaders, invariably can connect with different people, different ways, as I have said so often.

The best leaders, managers, and bosses, not to mention the best teachers and professors, connected with their people and students in ways that made it possible for them to deliver the results that they had to produce on terms that gave the individual a personal sense of satisfaction in their work. Essentially, they created an environment where their people look forward to coming to

Great leaders don't tell you what to do—they show you how it's done. Simply stated, they walk their talk.

work and strive to meet or exceed what is expected of them while having some fun along the way.

Do your people look forward to working for you? Do they go home feeling successful in their own right, or do they just look forward to going home? How much easier would it be for you to achieve what is required of you if they did? Did you empower them to believe in their own vision?

Remember, responsible corporate leadership is focused on the development of new, insightful, and creative leaders. Assuming you resemble that statement, your future is dependent on your ability to bring even more talented leaders behind you. Great leaders surround themselves with talent and propel them to even greater levels. Be a leader who is humble enough to let the prodigies rise, and everything you desire will be yours.

Are you up to seizing the moment? Can you take your opportunities beyond your potential?

Here are some powerful pieces of kindling to elevate you to the world of leadership:

- Leadership is just a title. You determine what it represents.
- You might have a position of leadership, but the real question is, Are people willing to follow you?
- Leadership is the demonstrative embodiment of a lifetime of knowledge, experience, and compassion, focused on the success of everyone who depends on you!
- The ultimate compliment is when everything you do and everything you accomplish makes the people around you better.
- Great leaders empower you to achieve your personal goals for your mutual benefit.
- Leaders have a vision beyond your vision and the ability to elevate your sights to find yourself a higher place in the bigger plan.
- Esteemed leaders earned their position by being the smartest person in the room. They earn their success by surrounding themselves with the next generation of the smartest people in the room.

In leadership, character is more important than strategy.

- If you're the smartest person in the room, and you're not the boss, find another room.
- Respected leaders are perceived to be at the top, but they never look down on anyone, except to admire their shoes.
- Leaders don't set the standards; they personify their own standards and then hire people who can exceed them.
- Leaders should not just give the example, they should be the example
- Leaders don't have to demand greatness, they inspire it.
- The most effective leaders check their ego at the door.

Leadership is the art of getting someone else to do something you want done because he wants to do it.

—*Dwight D. Eisenhower*

NO EXCUSES: DON'T ASK FOR DIRECTIONS IF YOU'RE NOT GOING TO START THE CAR!

At the tender age of two, I lost what most of you consider, consciously or subconsciously, the single greatest asset a human being possesses. (After all, don't most of you consider a picture to be worth a thousand words?) I have no idea what that picture looks like. I totally lost my eyesight when I was two years old. So many perceived my suffering as a major tragedy, but in my experience, I have never looked at my blindness as a handicap, rather, just a minor inconvenience. We will all be faced with life's minor inconveniences, it's what you do about them that counts.

I find it is hard to accept shallow and hollow excuses.

There is always an excuse that can be made. Always a reason to delay, change, or reschedule, but none of them are ever acceptable. There always will be an excuse, a justification, or a rationalization that can be made, but this is nothing more than the trap of the viable excuse derailing your plans, responsibilities, and obligations. If you are not going to perform, respond or even simply show up. It doesn't matter what the excuse is, it's still just an excuse, viable or otherwise.

For example, my principle has always been that if I need to reschedule a meeting, I move it forward in my calendar. I refuse to make people who have committed to me wait on my circumstances. After all, my challenges are not their problems, but my respect for their time will make me exceptional

Success occurs when consistency collides with optimism because optimism doesn't accept excuses.

in their experience, and that is priceless to me. How many of your competitors think like that?

Even worse, if you find yourself leading with an excuse, you are creating a self-imposed mental block, barrier, or wall before you even get started. You are rarely confronted with circumstances where you should consider making an excuse. Find a way to get it done and learn the lesson necessary to ensure that you aren't confronted with that situation again. Beyond everything else, don't let your excuse be somebody else. Don't blame somebody else when you fail to deliver. Take responsibility for your mistakes. If you're in management, take responsibility for your team. Take responsibility for your results. Never lead with an excuse!

And remember, success is not final, and failure is not fatal. It's the courage to continue that counts, and you can only continue if you show up. If you don't show up, any excuse will do.

Now, taking responsibility does not mean that failure is not an option. Quite the contrary, I am a firm believer that failure is a necessity. I have long followed the philosophy of coach John Wooden who professed throughout his amazingly successful career, "You can lose sometimes when you outscore somebody and you can win sometimes when you are outscored."

The inescapable truth is that the most successful people in the history of the world had a history of failing far more than they succeeded. I've discussed numerous sports examples throughout this book, and let me share one last example before we transition to the real world.

It always amazes me how the statistics of baseball resemble real life and have so many lessons to teach us. There is a place for everyone in baseball. It doesn't matter if you're 5'7" or 6'6", there is a role, and a need, for you in baseball. You don't need to suffer from a pituitary disorder to excel on a baseball diamond. There is opportunity for everyone, and the statistics of the game prove that.

One of those lessons that always resonated with me is so supportive of the rationale for being optimistic. You already know my thoughts on maintaining

Nothing will be more detrimental to your future than the trap of the viable excuse.

a positive attitude, but let's look at baseball to understand how vital your positive attitude is. A good career as an individual in America's pastime means that you succeed, as a batter, one in every four times you had an at bat. The greatest career on record only achieved a .367 lifetime batting average. Most Hall of Famers didn't even achieve .300. That means greatness is achieved if you fail 7 or more times out of every 10 times you try. Can you find the strength to be optimistic against those odds? If you need a little rationale, consider this quote from Babe Ruth, "Every strikeout just brings me one at bat closer to my next home run."

That is the mind-set of a Hall of Famer. One of the most successful Hall of Famers, but even the typical Hall of Famer, had a batting average of less than .300. That, in simple language, means that to reach the Hall of Fame, they needed to remain optimistic even knowing that they would succeed less than 30 percent of the time. How often do you think they would have succeeded if they let the least little bit of pessimism into their mind?

Now that may be the challenge you face individually every day, but there is another reality, which Sparky Andersen, a Hall of Fame manager, always focused on. You have to know that you are going to lose one third of all your games, but you are also going to win one third of all your games. Your success will be determined by how many of the remaining games you win. In other words, winning the World Series isn't about winning every game, it's about being good enough to win more often than you lose in the games that make the difference. You win the majority of those games when consistency collides with optimism.

Just to get a little perspective, remember, if you persist long enough only getting on base 3 times out of every 10 times you go to bat, you're in the Hall of Fame. If you are presenting to Hall of Fame prospects and you succeed 3 times out of 10, what will your life look life? Imagine, if you succeed 3 times out of 10 with your Hall of Fame prospects, how would that affect your success in your mainline career?

When you lead with an excuse don't expect anyone to follow you.

We can change the arena, but the reality persists. We all can be members of the Hall of Fame.

The point is this. You are going to fail. That is alright if you gave the greatest effort you could, and if you learned from your failure and tried again. If you showed up and gave your all, you don't need any excuses. But, like I said, if you didn't make the effort, any excuse will do. You will never reach your full potential by accepting excuses, especially your own. Like Benjamin Franklin said, "He that is good at making excuses is seldom good for anything else."

Sports is a fine metaphor to illustrate my message, but the truth is that even if you are the best in your game, the odds that you are pursuing a career in professional sports are zero. Think about it. The most plentiful position in North American professional sports is a pitcher in Major League Baseball. That means there are roughly 320 positions available to a population of over 330,000,000 Americans, and when you consider the number of players in the majors from Japan, the Dominican Republic, Cuba, and Puerto Rico, not to mention Venezuela, Mexico, or Canada, the odds of you even getting a chance are slim to none. Even if you do get there, the odds of making the Hall of Fame are less than zero.

I don't say this to discourage you. I say this because I want you to know that the best examples of how a philosophy of showing up and giving your all (i.e., my definition of *no excuses*) come from the world of real life, achieved by ordinary people, admittedly, doing extraordinary things, but, if they can do it, *you can do it*. I did, and I'm as ordinary as anybody!

It would have been so easy, early in my life, to use my blindness as an excuse why not to. I refused to then and I continue to refuse to now.

Consider these examples from outside the world of sports:

Thomas Edison made more than 1,000 unsuccessful attempts at inventing the light bulb. Did he make excuses? Not on your life! When asked about his perceived failure, he replied, "I didn't fail 1,000 times, I successfully identified 1,000 ways that didn't work." He also said, "Great success is built on frustration,

I'd rather make the attempt and fail than make an excuse and not try at all.

failure, even catastrophe." He was good, and a few times ascended to great, because he showed up and never quit!

Colonel Harland Sanders, founder of Kentucky Fried Chicken, is legendary for approaching 1,009 prospects who rejected him before he ever found the first restaurant owner who agreed to license his fried chicken recipe. I'm willing to bet that every single person who reads this book has tasted, and probably loved, Colonel Sanders's chicken, but how many of you would have faced 1,009 rejections to have a chance at success? That's a lot more failure than 7 out of 10 at bats. I think his philosophy of life says it all, or at least comes very close: "I've only had two rules. Do all you can and do it the best you can. It's the only way you can ever get that feeling of accomplishing something." He also said, "One has to remember that every failure can be a steppingstone to something better."

Need another example, consider Frank Bettger. After a brief baseball career that came to an end due to injury in the early 1900s (what did I tell you?), Frank went to work for the Fidelity Mutual Life Insurance Company in Philadelphia. He struggled at first, and after only 10 months he was seriously considering quitting to become a bill collector. Then, one Saturday morning he overheard his branch manager giving a talk to a bunch of senior agents and was inspired to try a little longer after hearing his manager tell the group, "Sales is the easiest job in the world when you work it hard, and the hardest job in the world if you try to work it easy." He resolved to start working it hard. He set a minimum standard of 25 appointments a week and committed to a program of learning, both about insurance and sales skills. His closing average at the time was one in twenty-seven appointments, and it never got better than one in three, but if you do the math, those are Hall of Fame numbers, and Frank was the number one salesperson nationwide for Fidelity Mutual five times over the next 20 years. You try winning five batting championships.

These people were tremendous successes in our world, the real, everyday world, but it came as much as a result of the effort as it did their knowledge, skills, or luck. Truth is they made their own luck by applying their

Don't be victimized by your own, self-imposed, mental roadblocks.

knowledge and developing their skill by being willing to fail more often than most people are willing to try, by a huge factor in most cases, and they are not unique. How many elections did Abraham Lincoln lose before being elected president of the United States? If you don't know the story, look it up, you'll be astounded. And if you keep searching, you'll find thousands more examples.

Bottom line is that hard work always beats talent when talent doesn't work, and as I've already told you, talent is fleeting and doesn't become skill unless you work it hard. It all comes back to the simplest cliché, "The harder I work, the luckier I get!" and the first thing about hard work is to show up, put your game face on, and empty the tank!

Now, as I said earlier, one more time, showing up to anything is the easy part of the equation. It's how you apply yourself once you get there that ultimately makes the difference. Let's face it, if you're not in the game, you don't have any chance at all. A dog with a note in its mouth will be more successful if it just shows the note to enough people.

If you have any interest in being a success at anything, you need to re-solve it in your heart because your head won't do it if your heart isn't into it. You have to resolve that you are willing to push your failure rate to the limit without taking it personally; that you are going to increase the quality of your failures if you ever hope to achieve the "feeling of accomplishing something." Something significant anyway.

The same goes for the problems you are dealing with day-to-day as you wage your personal war to achieve your reasons WHY! Today your major worries might be putting food on the table or paying the Visa bill or keeping the lights turned on, and I guarantee you that if you have a sincere talk with the leaders in your company, you'll find out many of them faced the same worries when they started out. That's reality, but I also promise you that the problems they deal with on a day-to-day basis now are much different. They put the worries about the mortgage and the car payment behind them a long time ago and have progressed to solving, or contributing to the solution of problems, far bigger than their own personal needs. Your challenges, or

An excuse gives you a reason to do nothing.

problems, and the responsibilities attached need to grow if you intend to succeed. Your failure rate has to remain high, not because you didn't get better but because you took on greater challenges as your skill and character grew.

Let's talk about character for a minute. You are always going to have a reputation, and your reputation is what you are perceived to be. Your character is what you are. Character is far more important than reputation so if you want to be perceived as what you really are, *walk your talk!*

Here's one more quote from Thomas Edison that puts it all in perspective. He famously said, "Vision without execution is hallucination!" I assume that you are not hallucinogenic.

Here are some more pieces of kindling to douse the flame that fuels your excuses:

- An excuse is nothing more than the pathetic rationalization to justify the decision to fail before you even try.
- Nothing stifles growth more than an excuse. Excuses are like weeds, left unchecked they will overwhelm you. Excuses will always be there for you, opportunity won't!
- Excuses are the self-talk of failure. So many people spend more time thinking up reasons why they can't do something than they spend trying to do it, and those who lead with an excuse are justifying their failure without giving success a chance.
- Those of you who are inclined to make excuses are simply rationalizing, justifying, and giving fuel to your habit of procrastination.
- If you're going to make excuses, stop being creative. If you're not going to do anything, any excuse will do.
- Making an excuse today is like writing a prescription for failure tomorrow.
- Excuses are your personal kryptonite. As soon as you utter one, your power to achieve is gone.

Is it an excuse or just a minor inconvenience? What's the difference?

ACTION SAYS IT ALL

To paraphrase my mother's philosophy, it's not what you know, it's what you do with it that counts. Knowledge is not power; knowledge is only potential power. Action is power!

Beyond that, remember, any action is better than no action. That's the danger of procrastination. No action produces no results.

We all know of somebody with an alphabet of letters behind their name and the apparent talent to be whatever they choose but they continue to grow older in relative obscurity, working in modest, safe but mediocre middle management somewhere, with seemingly nothing left to do but put in the time until they retire while less refined colleagues with inferior education and substandard talents are passing them, left and right, on career paths that are producing much greater success and satisfaction.

Why is this happening? One simple reason: Hard work will always win when talent doesn't do the work. The work is the action!

The greatest differentiating factor between successful people and everyone else is that successful people take action.

That's where the power comes from. That's where the difference between "book smarts" and "street smarts" becomes reality, and it is that reality that generates the experience you need if you are ever going to be a leader.

It's that experience which, if you're paying attention, leads to choosing more effective courses of action as you progress toward the top of the mountain. It also teaches what additional knowledge you need to continue to improve.

All your excuses and negative energy never inspired anyone, especially yourself.

Without the experience that taking action brings, your talent will never evolve into the skill you need to scale the mountain, and you'll spend your life struggling in the foothills.

Now, don't get me wrong. I'm not saying that taking action alone will ensure your success. So far, all I'm saying is that any action is better than no action, but if you are going to make the conscious decision to get into gear and make something of your life, yourself, and your career, then it is an incalculably tremendous benefit to gather, embody, apply, and master all the knowledge you can.

You can't go out in the world after reading this book and say that Craig told you that you don't have to study because if you are a person of action, you are going to succeed. It's quite the contrary.

If you plan on succeeding, in any profession, then you are going to need to know your business, whatever it is, from the technical and factual to the practical and intangible, better than anyone in your field if you expect to experience any respectable level of success. More important, if you intend to maintain that success, you are going to have to keep your knowledge on the leading edge because every day you don't grow, you recede.

You have to do this, but what I'm telling you in this chapter is that all that knowledge will only ever be good enough to get you to level three on a one to ten scale of success if you don't take action and apply that knowledge. Once you get in action, you'll learn to refine your decisions and focus your actions, but first you have to do something.

This book, assuming you read all the pages leading up to this point, has increased your knowledge. It may be additional information on subjects you're already familiar with or have already studied in some detail. In some cases, the knowledge provided in this book may offer completely new perspectives on topics you've been aware of or it may have awakened something in your Grey Zone and refueled your inner flame. In some cases, the knowledge is a completely new take on a completely new subject.

**Practice and hard work are just the dress rehearsal.
Success comes if you can deliver in the moment.**

The important thing is this. On those subjects that resonate with you, those knowledge areas that, if applied to your life, can be realistically expected to bring positive benefits to you, you need to go back and take ownership of the knowledge.

You need to do that across the spectrum because as much as it will be your actions and attitude that determine your success, it will be the combination of the quality and quantity of knowledge together with how effectively you apply it in the process of your life's journey that will ultimately determine the altitude you achieve.

What do you do now?

You continue your process and get on with the journey. Your routine should be the process of applying in practice an ever-increasing body of knowledge and a continuous, well-rounded experience of personal, professional, and intellectual growth that considers all aspects of your life, and it happens something like this.

Being a person of action, your next objective is to take the knowledge you've just acquired and make it such a part of who you are that you begin to benefit from it without having to think about it. This is what people more educated than me refer to as the transition from conscious incompetent to unconscious competent. It's what I think of as imbedding the knowledge you've just acquired so deep in your Grey Zone that it becomes a dependable part of natural behavior, which rises to the occasion when needed and makes those momentary gusts from good to great possible.

So, let's pick a chapter and get busy. I suggest you start with the chapter that resonated with you the most. That's the one that would dominate your conversation if you had to describe this book to someone else. If you're not sure, I suggest you start with "Knowing Why." That's the one that resonates most with me, and I promise you it will serve as a great launching pad as we start your journey to the top of your mountain.

Notice I said, "your mountain." We're going talk about the process of you ascending to the summit of your personal mountain of achievement.

When inspiration is fueled by action and impossible becomes your motivation, a world of opportunity will quickly become your stage.

This is about you achieving your vision of a successful life and career on your terms. It's about the slopes and cliffs and plateaus and summits that are what your self-concept, or preferably, your self-ideal, perceives as what it will take to succeed and what the look and feel will be as you come closer and closer.

The process can't be based on anybody else's perceptions, it has to be yours. Let's face it, I can't teach you to climb my mountain, and I have no idea what your mountain looks like—nobody knows. I don't know how big or steep it is, but you know, and if you can't see it now, ask your Grey Zone, it definitely knows. Truth is, I've actually never seen a mountain, but I've certainly skied down enough of them to understand, and what I can do is help you think through what it's going to take to climb yours, especially when you encounter the inevitable detours!

Once you've chosen a chapter, it's time to commit to a program of total immersion. Reread the chapter, Read it out loud. Record it and play it in the background while you're doing other things. Put on your headset and let your recording play when you're sleeping. And, most importantly, visualize, visualize, visualize. You want to own the material, you want to embody it, bury it so deep in your Grey Zone that it takes root and starts to grow.

You also want to start climbing your mountain. You want to start applying the knowledge right away, make some mistakes, get frustrated, and try it again. Succeed and celebrate and try it again. Start up the first slope and just climb. At first, you'll be picking your steps carefully as you think your way through the terrain. Before long, you'll be making your decisions faster and breathing easier. Next thing you know, you'll be taking in the scenery and appreciating the view as you effortlessly proceed up the slope. Then it will happen.

You'll have what I call "the dream." It may happen when you're sleeping, or it may be a daydream, but a time will come when your Grey Zone plays back all you've learned and all you've done, almost like a signal that it understands. Like a signal that you've arrived.

How quickly, or slowly, you reach "the dream" will depend entirely on how intensely you pursue the process. Just like when I trained for the US Blind National Snow-Skiing Championships, it was the intensity of training

Action is just a word until you give it purpose, passion, and meaning.

that gave me 10 years' experience in only four months and gave my Grey Zone the power to elevate my game when I needed to.

Reaching "the dream" will often feel like you've reached a plateau, but you've really just completed a stage of your climb. You will know in that moment that your process of intense immersion is no longer necessary, and you can relax into a program of periodic review, as long as you keep applying what you've learned because, if you don't use it, you'll lose it.

Reaching "the dream" also means it's time to make a decision. Most people at this point are thinking that decision is "which chapter's next?" but that's too narrow of a thought process for me.

After reaching a plateau, I think we should all take time to appreciate where we are and how far we've come. It's time to look out and appreciate the majesty of our place on the mountain, marvel at how small and distant our starting place seems as we look down that slope we just ascended, and appreciate and be inspired by how high the peaks around us are and how far we can still climb.

You should take a personal inventory and notice how much stronger you feel, how much confidence you've developed, and how the trappings on this plateau have improved from the trappings around you where you started. It's time for a celebration, a long weekend, or a trip to the beach. Spoil yourself for a moment or two because there will be plenty more work to do when you get back.

As you take your breather and appreciate yourself and your achievement, you should also be asking, What is the best use of my time right now?

You've become stronger in the process of completing this stage of your climb, but you should always be aware of the cost you paid to get this far, and often the debts you should repay, not to mention how you recharge your internal battery for the next stage of your ascension up your mountain?

When I reach one of these remarkable stages in my life, I find myself taking a half-step back and asking, What is the best use of my time right now?

How quickly, or slowly, you reach "the dream" will depend entirely on how intensely you pursue the process.

Is it:

- spoiling my wife Patti with dinner, a show, or a weekend just catching up on whatever chores I might be behind on because I was busy?
- spending some quality time with one, or all, of my kids—Derek, Ashley, and Morgan—and giving back to them for all the love and encouragement they always give me? Of course, I'm talking about the gang still at home.
- taking all of them on vacation, so we can all recharge?
- calling our oldest son Dalton up in Canada, just to catch up, or checking in with Raven to see what's going on in her life?
- going into my office and making business calls to ensure I can continue to meet my responsibilities when I start the next climb?

Or is it:

- jumping into the next phase of my constant and never-ending process of self-development and choosing whether I am going to climb the slope to my left or scale the cliff wall in front of me depending, of course, on which chapter you dive into next?

A word of caution here. Intensity and focus are the keys to progress, both in your personal, never-ending process of self-development and in your career, and is going to result in sacrifices along the journey, made both by you and those who love and depend on you. When you arrive at one of those remarkable places on your journey that I think of as plateaus on my mountain, I strongly encourage you to be grateful and pay back all the love, support, and understanding you received during your pursuit. And take a wide-angle view of where that support and understanding may have come from. Remember your colleagues, friends, clients, teachers, mentors, and competitors because very few of us ever make it on our own.

So, the next time you're being consumed by a sales contest, the overtime needed to meet a production deadline, or, in my case, the grueling travel

People are happier when they balance what they have in their lives.

schedule of a three-month speaking tour, remember who made it possible and show them the gratitude they deserve when you reach one of those milestones, when your Grey Zone says you made it.

I know from my life experience that 90 percent of my ability is the result of taking action and failing most of the time. I simply persisted until the failures became small enough to convert them to success because I never stopped learning as I continually tested myself. I honestly think the secret of success is the process of improving the quality of your failures because, as Lee Iacocca put it, stickability is 90 percent ability. Can you say *persistence?*

Now, pick a chapter and get busy with it.

Here's a bunch of kindling. Get into gear and throw it on your internal flame:

- Just because you might be on the right track doesn't mean you're going to succeed. If you're not in action, you're going to get run over. You have to keep moving forward.
- You can't get to the extra mile if you're living your life in neutral.
- Any action is better than no action, but the proper action would be even better, all things considered.
- Nothing is accomplished in business until someone makes the first move. Action is power. What are you waiting for?
- If you're not in action, you're in reaction. Action is offense, reaction is defense, but the best defense is a great offense. Take action!
- Most highly successful people are willing to fail more than most people are willing to try. Oxford defines *try* as "make an attempt or effort to do something." Making an effort requires action.
- You can't consistently deliver a high level of performance unless you have a laser-like focus, a mountain of sacrifice, and a heart full of passion.

When your actions contradict your words, your words don't mean anything.

HAPPINESS

In 2013, in *Craig MacFarlane Hasn't Heard of You Either*, I included a short essay titled "Happiness Is a Choice." That has been my view of happiness throughout my life, because there are just too many reasons to be unhappy if you let yourself dwell on them.

I wake up with a smile on my face every morning, regardless of my circumstances, my stress, my challenges. I know I have to deal with them, but I don't have to be unhappy about them, and I think my message is getting through, at least to the people I care about most.

How else can you explain the quote that our daughter came up with all by herself, when she was only 12 years old?

Over the years, I have made a point of collecting as many quotes and expressions as I could as I try to make my point and crystalize my philosophy because so many people don't get it. If you ever find your happiness having a challenging day, come back and visit the quotes on the bottom of these pages.

I once heard a very prominent surgeon speak at an insurance agent's convention where I was also scheduled to appear. He gave a brilliant speech about the dangers of hypertension, heart disease, and the symptoms of a stroke, which were usually sudden death, but he primarily focused on the impact of lifestyle and the health of your heart. After a rousing, and hilarious

People have been searching for the key to happiness when there never was a lock.

—Morgan MacFarlane

45 minutes, he wrapped up with two rules that you need to follow to have a healthy heart and a happy life:

Rule 1: Don't sweat the small stuff.
Rule 2: IT'S ALL SMALL STUFF!

I hope that resonates with you because I can't think of two truer statements that I've ever heard.

Think about it for a second. If a world-class surgeon can go on stage and tell the top 1,000 life insurance agents in North America that you can decide that it's all small stuff, isn't the choice to be happy a small decision by comparison?

The reality is that everything can be resolved. Virtually nothing in the everyday world that most of us live in is dangerous, or consequential enough, that we should let it steal our happiness, but the vast majority of us, or at least the vast majority of people I encounter, see everything from catastrophe to simple pitfalls everywhere, when all that really exists are problems, most of which can be solved simply by taking some action.

If you deal with your problems while they are still small, then you never really have problems, and dealing with small problems is always better than dealing with big problems, but for most of us, our primary form of action is reaction. Reaction is almost always too late. You react because you have a problem, and the slower you react, the bigger your problem becomes. Do you think that would change if you were proactive instead of reactive?

It has been my experience that problems, challenges, and setbacks are rarely spontaneous events. They leave clues before they finally take hold. They develop patterns that you can recognize. They come at you from a distance where you can see them approaching and, even if you can't see them, you'll sense their approach. Knowing you have the benefit of anticipation, or what I think of as the growth curve of most problems, doesn't it make

Happiness is turning success into significance.

sense, doesn't it behoove you, to be proactive and deal with your problems before they exist? Maybe you can't always see them in advance, but I know you can always be prepared to react in the moment and diminish the impact of a problem without pain, stress, or struggle.

You are always going to have problems and challenges in your life. You need to accept that right now. That doesn't mean you have to accept always being stressed, scared, or apprehensive, or walk around like you're on egg-shells all the time.

Quite the contrary, it means you have to take charge. You have to take action. You have to determine that you will put your small, resolvable stuff behind you and build routines for dealing with the minor, recurring small stuff that we call life.

This is critical if you have plans for a successful career running alongside your happy life. If you can deal with the small stuff, it will free you up to create the bigger, more consequential, better quality, self-inflicted kinds of problems that come from pursuing the extra mile. In other words, don't let the speed bumps of everyday life turn into a mountain of doubt. You'll just knock your mental transmission out of gear before you even get started.

The problems you should be dealing with in your life are the ones where you can make a difference, contribute to the greater good of your family, your community, and your career. They are the type of problems where you see the opportunity to use the knowledge, skill, experience, and wisdom that you are acquiring every day for causes greater than yourself. That's when you can truly move from personal reaction to societal proaction because your personal world will be under effective management. Why is that?

Happiness is a state. So, if you're not feeling happy, change your state. If you're wise, or at least have a little common sense (but be aware that common sense is rarely common practice), you'll study yourself when you are in a happy state and when you're in a sad state. You'll perform your own metamorphosis and convert your physical state.

Happiness resides not in possessions and not in gold. Happiness dwells in the soul.

—*Democritus (+/– 400 BC)*

Let's face it, you know what state you are usually in when your happy. Learn how to re-create that state, that body language, those external sensations that always make you happy and dispel your sadness by choice, not by chance.

Seriously, I have never been more convinced that happiness is a choice. You know how to plant seeds in your Grey Zone. Are you planting happiness seeds? You know the power of a smile. Are you smiling? Even your Grey Zone responds to a smile, any smile! Is your body language unhappy? Take charge of yourself, move, sit up, act like you're happy! Even your Grey Zone can be deceived by sad body language. Is your metabolism sluggish? Then get up and move, stimulate your system and get your blood flowing. Stimulate some adrenaline because you can't be sad when that stuff is flowing, And if all else fails, drink a Starbucks.

This is the point: Everything I just told you to do is a choice. You can take charge of your state and make whatever adjustments you need to keep the happy juices flowing. I suggest you don't question it, just do it. It will change your life. At the very least it will put you in control and give you a fighting chance.

The same thing applies to your focus. Now, without getting all Pollyannaish, I know you are going to have to deal with problems, some minor, some not so much, but they can all be dealt with. They are not the end of the world, or anything remotely close, unless you let yourself believe that, but I give you too much credit.

You need to learn to visualize the images, feel the emotions, smell the smells, taste the tastes, and hear the sounds, all available from your Grey Zone by the way, that you saw, felt, smelled, tasted, and heard when you were spectacularly happy, and decide to call up those sensations and focus yourself there whenever sadness threatens, because in the blink of an eye, you can be happy again, if you make the right choices.

What I'm trying to say is that happiness is not a destination, it's a way of life. Remember, I told you that the journey of success is the progressive realization of worthwhile goals, while staying well-adjusted. Guess what the

Happiness is not a destination, it's a way of life.

first word is if you look for a synonym to *well-adjusted*? It's *happiness*! Is this resonating yet? Happiness is a necessary, in fact, critical component of any success you have any intention of experiencing, let alone maintaining. So, deal with it, if you want to be successful, you're going to have to enjoy it.

By the same token, you have to be very wary of building a house of cards. Sure, some superficial, frivolous fun resulting from a few lucky hands that you played can be enjoyable, for a moment, but houses of cards have a way of collapsing on themselves, unless you build the right foundation over the course of your journey. I'm not saying you can't have one, just don't ignore the other, or soon you won't have either, and having both begins with a focus on your four pillars of happiness.

My four pillars of happiness are faith, family, community, and career.

I was asked once if I'm a man of faith. I responded that the sun came up this morning and I don't know of anyone who did anything to make it happen. That is proof to me that there is a greater power somewhere, and I have faith that it will continue to provide me a world to live in and opportunities for health, wealth, and happiness. My mom made sure I grew up in a strong Christian household, and it has been a pillar of strength to me throughout my life.

Faith, in my mind, is the knowledge that there are forces larger than what we can see, feel, or hear that are at work in our lives and can exponentially accelerate the achievement of our ambitions in life, in terms of both scope and time, if we continue to do the right things the right way for the right reasons, with passion, as we pursue a worthwhile purpose. It's like seeing the light with your heart when all you can see with your eyes is darkness.

Most often, when faith has an effective place in your mental machinery, it manifests itself as that calm, small voice deep down inside that tells you to keep going, that you're on the right path and that it's going to work out. It's the navigator that tells you, if you'll listen, to make the small course corrections on your journey that keep you on target for the conclusion to your mission. It is also the coach in your Grey Zone that pushes you to get back up

**A chair with three legs can't stand. Happiness has four pillars.
Do the math.**

when you get knocked down by the inevitable setbacks you will encounter on your journey. It's the voice of reason that tells you to stay down when you've done all you can.

It resides somewhere outside your control and has a secure means of back-channel communication directly to your Grey Zone that allows it to provide exactly the message you need, when you need it, if you have the confidence to listen to your Grey Zone. You could say it's like WiFi. It's invisible but has the power to connect you to what you need.

Your faith, or your belief in yourself, is the antidote for doubt, but it will only be the cure for short periods unless you nurture it, feed it, and listen to it. People often tell me that faith is great but it won't last. I tell them that neither does bathing, that's why you need to do something about it every day. If you don't regularly oil your mental machinery, sooner or later, it's going to seize up, so nourish your spiritual engine and reap the rewards.

When your faith is right, then you can take the proverbial leap, confident that your faith will make your purpose reality while you work your butt off, because it still all depends on you. Is your faith right? It is a critical cornerstone of your long-term happiness so if it isn't right, I suggest you make it so.

Faith may well be the sextant that feeds the navigational information to my happiness compass, but it is my family that is my pillar of strength. They are my source of motivation and my inspiration. Being human, they are also a source of frustration and exasperation, too, but much like I expect yours is, I tell people my family is like fudge, mostly sweet with a little nuttiness to make it interesting.

The truth is I'd do anything for my family and often find myself making sacrifices and going to extreme lengths just to be with them, to take care of their needs and give them every minute I can in return for the inspiration and love they give me.

I have always thought it was a valuable gauge of a person's character to observe what lengths they will go to and what sacrifices they will make in the name of their family. It has never failed to tell me about a person's integrity,

Faith is like Wi-Fi, it's invisible but it has the power to connect you to what you need.

and it always comes through in little things that other people most likely never notice, but I do because family is my priority.

It's not my purpose to talk about others here, so let me use my life, once again, as the example. I trust you have figured it out by now that I travel, a lot! I log over 150,000 air miles a year and have been doing so for more than 30 years. That means that I spend at least a third of my Monday to Friday nights in hotel rooms, alone, away from my family. At least it used to be that way until my children were born. Since then it is more like half of my Monday to Thursday nights, and during my busiest times, often entire weeks are spent away from home.

That was fine when I was a younger man, sometimes it was fun, and it certainly was profitable, but when my oldest son was born, a man I consider to be very wise, my father, told me that children spell love T-I-M-E. It was his way of telling me that I needed to change my routine and find a way to get home as much as I could and maximize my time with him.

From that day, 30 years ago, I have never stayed away on a Friday night, unless it was absolutely unavoidable. I am committed, at least to myself, that I always fly home on Friday, even taking the red-eye and sleeping on the plane if necessary because it is my priority that I am home, awake, and waiting in the kitchen when the kids wake up Saturday morning. That's my equivalent of going the extra mile even if they are air miles.

Sometimes I'm only there for 36 hours, taking another red-eye Sunday night to be on time for a lunchtime speech on Monday, but the results have been tremendous. I am very proud of the connection I have with Dalton, Raven, Derek, Ashley, and Morgan. Our bond has become so strong that we have become a synergistic circle of strength for each other, each providing love and inspiration to the others in unlimited and unconditional abundance.

Of course, the foundation of all this happiness is my wife Patti. She's the love of my life and the indispensable intangible that makes every element of our family work. I will do anything for any of them and make it my ultimate priority that the five of us are together as much as humanly possible.

**Silence is golden. Unless you have kids.
Then silence is suspicious.**

I openly acknowledge that I am the face of our family to the world, but if the happiness, and resulting success, of us as a family was dependent on a pretty face, I wouldn't even qualify for fifth place. That's the truth, but even more truthful is the fact that we succeed because of the glue that holds us together and holds us up, 24/7, without question, or compromise.

The success of our family is dependent on, and the result of, the prettiest face in the household, my wife Patti. Patti is the quintessential cornerstone. She is tireless and selfless in her support of the efforts, ambitions, and needs of the rest of us, while seeming to never ask for anything in return, except the best from each of us. She is the uncompromising yardstick that measures all of us against our potential while gently pushing us all at the same time, holding us to a level of responsibility that, while tacitly implied, is clearly understood.

There is no doubt in any of our minds what is expected of us, and we have complete confidence that we will receive all the support and encouragement we deserve. She is always there, and not one of us, in any way, would ever want to disappoint her.

That's not to say she's the dragon lady of the family. Far from it. She doesn't demand, she inspires. She doesn't criticize, she consults, and often consoles. She doesn't hurt your feelings, she uplifts your spirit, all with an unwavering, firm hand on the rudder of the family. She may lead us from behind the scenes, but she is clearly the leader, and the results go far beyond Dalton's burgeoning success and independence.

Growing up, Dalton enjoyed playing hockey and now has evolved into an MMA fighter where he remains undefeated. He loves the outdoors and has a keen interest in hunting, fishing, cutting wood, and really anything physical. You could say he's our Paul Bunyan. Dalton lives on a farm in northern Ontario with his wife, Amy, and his awesome son, Jack. Of course, I had to say it that way, he's our grandson.

MMA fighting remains Dalton's passion, but following a path similar to his father's, he is transitioning into the business world where I believe he has

If you want to bring happiness to the world, go home and love your family.

—*Mother Teresa*

found his niche in life and is a highly successful corporate financial consultant. His future looks very bright.

Raven is the caregiver of the family. Her lifestyle and her career clearly demonstrate her passion for helping and caring for others. She is an accomplished level 1 trauma nurse in Texas where she lives with her husband, Tyler, and her numerous pets, all of whom she loves to spoil. In keeping with the family tradition, she also has an athletic background and was a very successful gymnast and cheerleader. Today she enjoys staying fit by working out. We all have so many laughs and a ton of fun whenever Raven comes to visit us.

Derek is a standout academic and, at the time of this writing, is about to begin studying finance at Butler University. I don't tell you that just to brag, although I wouldn't blame any parent for being proud of their child for such an achievement, but also to tell you that his success is my loss. As much as I'm proud of Derek's scholastic accomplishments to date, I'm more impressed with his sense of responsibility as he follows his mother's example. In the past couple of years, Derek has become my right-hand man when I'm in town. He drives me to my appointments, helps me with my correspondence, and is otherwise always there when I need a helping hand, without ever complaining. Butler is only a few miles from home, but when he leaves for college, I am going to miss him tremendously. Of course, Ashley now has her driver's license, so a new chapter may be about to begin.

In addition to becoming a licensed driver, Ashley is making a reputation for herself as the free spirit of the household, and the compassionate environmentalist of the family. I can't say yet if this will be the focus of any future career, but it is so very engaging to watch how she cares for and dotes on her brother and sister, and her mother, not to mention our two cats, Coconut and Mittens. Her most endearing qualities come through in her ability to entertain me with the creative theories she shares about her pets as she encourages me to pet her hamster and her hedgehog while she describes her numerous species of colorful pet fish. Her latest project as I

Kindness is the language that the deaf can hear and the blind can see.

—*Mark Twain*

write this is to name my best friend's 12 Black Labrador puppies. My friend tells me they are so similar, he can't tell one from the other, but Ashley tells me she'll name them all and will always know which one is which. I have no doubt she's right about that.

Morgan is yet another story. She is the physical fitness fanatic of the household and, at times, seems determined to keep me in shape as well. That's good because I have come to realize that if I intend to enjoy my role as a father, I am not going to be able to relax in my La-Z-Boy and enjoy soundtracks, audiobooks, and great conversations for at least another decade. These days I am much more likely to be in the basement with Morgan doing calisthenics, crunches, and often the latest millennial fitness craze that is trending on YouTube, and that's only when she doesn't take me out to jump on the trampoline with her. I must profess that I cannot do a tenth of the acrobatics that she can, but we do have a ton of fun and I am so inspired by her belief that I can do it all. I could never deny her the laughs she must get from watching me try.

And that is the keyword about the happiness of our family. Every one of us is always willing to try. We are not afraid to try, and sometimes fail. We understand that trying to achieve anything and failing is better than never trying to accomplish anything and succeeding. It's not always easy, but we know if we fail, there will be a soft landing and a new launching pad to try again.

How do we know that? Because we have Patti!

I've also noticed a transition over the years regarding my red-eye experience. In the beginning, I did it to give the kids time. I did it to show them through my actions the expression of love that words just can't express. I know they got the message from how they treat me today, but, interestingly, even though they are now teenagers, or millennials to speak in the vernacular of 2019, I'm still doing it. They are old enough, aware enough, and mature enough to know that Dad loves them and that he travels to support them, and he pays their tuition and keeps a roof over their head and food on the table by

> **Happiness lies in the joy of achievement and the thrill of creative effort.**
>
> —*Franklin D. Roosevelt*

doing what he does when he's away from home. They have the perspective to cut me a little slack and let me get some rest over a short weekend to and from the West Coast (or some other faraway destination where I might be speaking), but I still catch the red-eye. I'm still there in the kitchen, with my coffee, listening to the news, when they finally get up (it is one universally consistent reality of the human condition that nothing can sleep longer than a teenager) and come down for breakfast. They are always happy to see me and me them, but I have come to realize that I am now in that kitchen for my own inspiration as much as to express my love for them. Honestly, my family inspires me, they really do! I feel so blessed.

There is no greater feeling in the world. It is what I live for, and I will never let anything get in its way.

I know I seem a bit obsessive about my home life, and it's a healthy obsession (or so I tell myself), but in my world, family goes beyond the biological ties that we choose to create and nurture. They are the kindling and the fuel that keeps my tank full. In my opinion, or at least in my world, there is an extended family that I call my friends.

Friends are the family that you choose for yourself. In many ways, that makes them an even greater indication of your character. I love my family, unconditionally, and always will, but I did not have the opportunity to select them. I have the opportunity to mentor them, to educate them, to lead them, and to love them. I have the responsibility to mold them and help them become the best they can be, and I indulge in the right to be proud of them, but I didn't get to choose them.

My friends, on the other hand, were fully formed when I met them. The decision to let them become part of my life was totally up to me as was just how much of a part of my life they ultimately became.

Friends come in far more categories than family. There are the hand-shaking acquaintances you nod at or give a wave to when you pass them on the street. There are the people with mutual interests who you hang out with at your child's concert or baseball game but rarely if ever see each other in

Let your smile change the world, but don't let the world change your smile.

any other setting. There are the people you do business with who you have known long enough that they feel like friends even though you really know nothing about each other. There are the people you work with, who probably know you better, but never see you outside of work or work-related events. There are others, many others, who we all know casually, enough to call them friends, but who we never get close to.

Then there is the inner circle. The rare, not blood-related human being, who you connect with on an almost spiritual level that makes them as much or more like an actual relative. The friends of your inner circle, and I hope you are lucky enough to have at least a few of them in your life, are the people you hold close because they parallel you, they resemble and embody the same values, traits, characteristics, preferences, and priorities that you do. You are as similar as overlapping dinner plates, and that leads to chemistry that is magical.

These are the people you keep in your life for no other reason than they are your friends, your best friends. You would do anything for them, and they would do anything for you, no questions asked. They will always have your back, and you theirs. You defend them without question and come to their rescue because you know they would come to yours.

These are the choices that set you apart. How you raise your family distinguishes you. How you love, respect, and care for your spouse compliments you. Who your friends are and how their character reflects on your judgment confirms you.

Let's face it, you could have great kids despite being a total idiot. It happens. Your spouse might just stay with you and defend the fact that you're a degenerate because they feel sorry for you or they are too desperate to believe anyone else would ever take them. You might support members of your family because you don't think they have a hope without you, and the outside world might never know because you didn't get to choose them. Let's face it, the strongest are those who win battles the rest of us know nothing about.

Your friends tell the world all about your judgment and your appreciation of character. It not only speaks volumes to the rest of the world about

There is family, there are friends, and there are friends that become family.

who and what you are, but when badly chosen, can devastate your reputation and your life.

I have felt this way my entire life, but it was confirmed to me in crystal clear terms in my late forties when I heard my best friend tell a story during a speech. He was talking about trying to pull himself up and get a career started coming out of high school. His family wasn't poor, but they didn't have college tuition money either. He decided to try and become a police cadet and pursue his degree through the force's ongoing education program, hoping to graduate and gain some experience by the time his pension vested, before he was 40 years old.

His worry was that several of his cousins had criminal records and he feared that might cast aspersions on him. He tells how he brought it up with the interviewing officer, and it was that officer's answer that says everything about how your choice of friends can impact your life. The officer told my friend, "We don't worry too much about your blood relatives, you didn't choose them. We worry about who you choose as friends because they are the family you choose for yourself."

I don't tell you this to suggest that you only choose friends who can benefit you in some way. You'll have plenty of mutually beneficial friendships on that level that will never get into the inner circle, and don't have to.

The inner circle brings more joy and happiness and camaraderie than any transaction of any type ever will. The friends in your inner circle will be the ones you laugh with, and at, cry with, and celebrate with. They will be the ones that define you, lift you up, or hold you back.

They are also the ones you'll sacrifice for, without hesitation or worry for yourself, only because they need you. They are the ones that you will go the extra mile for, period. Let me give you an example.

Picture this, it's the middle of the night, not that I can tell the difference, but I was fast asleep, in yet another hotel room, this time in Detroit, Michigan, when my cell phone starts to ring. Initially thinking, what the heck, I

Don't let someone who gave up on their dreams, talk you out of going after yours.

shook off my sleep, found my phone, and was surprised when the voice on the other end was my best friend, calling me on Skype from an Internet café in the Philippines. I was expecting that one of my children had a high fever or was, in some other way, unwell. I didn't expect the call to be anyone other than Patti, not at that hour. And the truth is, I don't think anyone else other than my best buddy on earth would make that call, but I could tell right away he was in trouble. I knew he had gone on an extended vacation after having gone through some very tough times back home in Canada, but even I was shocked by what he told me.

He told me he had been ambushed getting out of a tricycle taxi, whatever that means, and his backpack, with his wallet, credit cards, debit card, and cash had been taken. His passport was locked in the safe in his hotel, thank god, and he could walk back, (he told me later it was only 14 miles), but he had no money, no access to money, no bus fare back to Manila, and I was the only family he had left, blood relative or not. I didn't hesitate, this was my brother.

I didn't stop to ask how, or where, or what had he been thinking. This wasn't the time to ask. I told him to hang up and call me in an hour. I pulled on some pants and headed for the lobby where I had the desk clerk grab me a taxi (because I can't book my own Uber on my flip phone), and I headed out into the night in a city I had never been in during a snowstorm to find a 24-hour Western Union. I didn't even ask him if he had the money for another call, I just sent him what he needed.

Now, remember, I'm totally blind. I didn't have a clue where I was going or who I was going with, but this was more important.

To make a long story short, he was able to get the money I sent and return to Manila, where he resolved the lost credit cards and caught a plane home. Now, you might be asking yourself why I did what so many of my acquaintances tell me was a reckless, if not risky, act. For only one reason, because I know he would have done it for me.

This man is the best person on this planet that I know of with whom I don't share DNA. This man has championed my causes, my character, and

Families are like fudge, mostly sweet with lots of nuts.

me in ways and on levels that have made us both better men, and our entire extended circle has benefitted.

Do you have friends in your world who you can say that about? You should have, because you need them. Life is too challenging to stay the course alone.

A word of caution here, about rationalization. You all know my stance on no excuses. I have no use for them. I'll accept an admittance of failure from someone who has left it all on the floor, on the diamond, in the boardroom, or in the office, but I don't have any time for excuses. Let me tell you why.

If you are inclined to rely on excuses, you can rationalize an excuse for anything, and I think that here, I win over 98 percent of all the rationalized excuses I've ever heard.

Consider this. Human beings are visual beings. Heck, even I preach the power of visualization, and I can't and have never seen anything that I can remember. But there are visions I dearly wish I could know.

I have never seen my wife. I have never seen my children. I have never seen a smile light up their face or watched them celebrate a magic moment. I have never looked into my wife's eyes and felt that emotion that you simply can't experience any other way. And the horrible part is that the fact that I cannot see does not diminish my desire to see everything that you want to see. If anyone could justify an excuse to not be happy, at least at times, I think I qualify to be a champion in that category, but I refuse.

That would be selfish, and no doubt diminish the happiness and beauty I wish I could see. The world doesn't deserve a sad Craig MacFarlane for such selfish reasons, and I refuse to let it see one.

The point here is, if I can choose to always be happy and find ways to make it so, you can, too, and you deserve to be happy just as much as everyone around you. Make the choice.

The third pillar of happiness in my world is what I call community, but not in the geopolitical sense. I do believe that you should be proud of where you live and try, as you should in all areas of your life, to make it a better

Play the hand you've been dealt. Don't worry about the gifts you don't have. Appreciate and develop the ones you do.

place for all concerned. That doesn't mean I think everyone should run for political office, become mayor, or join the local PTA or Neighborhood Improvement Association, unless that's truly your thing. On the contrary, I don't think about improving where I live from the standpoint of writing bylaws and building recreation centers or attracting more jobs to town. Not that it isn't important, just that it is more of a management function. I think of improving where I live from the perspective that nothing improves your property value more than a good neighbor.

That's the spirit of community that matters to me. Being a good neighbor, but on a more metaphorical level. It's about lending a helping hand, giving of yourself in both big and small ways that might do anything from simply putting a smile on a stranger's face to changing someone's life.

The truth of human existence is that unless you choose to live like a hermit, hidden away in a dark, dank cave, isolated on the side of a remote mountain, you are going to interact with others. It is unavoidable. In fact, it's essential. We are, at our core, social creatures who crave loving companionship and interaction on a perpetual, if not ever-present basis. If it wasn't such a vital part of who and what we are, why is solitary confinement considered the most severe form of incarceration?

I contend that if human interaction is such an essential element of living our lives, that interaction should, on the whole, make the majority of people you meet a little happier for having known you.

It is also about multiplying that little bit of happiness, like ripples in a pond. We can all make small, positive contributions to the community of people we encounter, regardless of how local, or far-flung, they may be, and it is the accumulation of those little things, however seemingly unrelated they may be, that ultimately changes and improves the world we all share together.

The fact is that you just don't know. I might have restated something in this book that I heard 20 years ago, and even if I can't remember who said it to me, or where, the beauty is that the message can travel from there, to me,

You can't make everybody happy. You aren't a jar of Nutella.
(For our daughter, Morgan)

to you, to a friend of yours, and to that friend's son or daughter, who carries it forward a decade before sharing it as a random thought that inspires a total stranger to do something brilliant, because a tiny piece of inspiration was transmitted through a generation of strangers with only the goal of creating a second of happiness.

That's why everything matters, even if it all seems totally disconnected. It all contributes positively to, or diminishes from, the greater good. I choose to be a positive contributor and I know that I am happier because of it. I can only hope that I have made some others happier along the way.

It is also about the selflessness of being a positive catalyst. By that I mean we should give and do, on whatever level we can, because it is the right thing at the right time, without calculating what's in it for us or expecting an immediate return. It's a matter of principle that will pay its dividends to others and ultimately back to you at the right time and, I suspect, from sources totally unrelated.

After all, haven't you had the pleasure of sitting in the shade of a big old tree on a hot sunny day, just because someone, years before, had the good sense to plant an acorn in that exact place where you were going to be, two generations later, when the sun was going to be so hot? It works like that.

That leads me to my fourth pillar of happiness—career. What kind of tree does your career resemble? One that inspires you to climb as far as you can go, or one that just encourages you to sit on a branch and endure the slow, almost imperceptible ascent that takes years if not decades to appreciate. If your career tree doesn't inspire you to climb, you might as well spend your life watching paint dry. It will bring about the same level of happiness.

I firmly believe that you need a significant measure of career happiness in your life if you want any hope of assembling your four pillars into a solid structure.

Please note, I wrote *career happiness*, not success. I've known many failures, in the conventional sense, who were much happier than their

> **Have you ever considered that there are two ways to get to the top of an oak tree? You can sit on the acorn, or you can climb to the top! I suggest you start climbing.**

spectacularly successful colleagues because their careers, or more often jobs, provided a plethora of elements that combined to make them enjoyable while delivering just enough to keep the wolf away from the door.

If you have found a way in this life to be doing what you love and love what you do, then you probably have more career happiness, freedom, and success than most. You no doubt have all the conventional trappings of success, and enjoy them, because you earned them doing something particularly satisfying to you. I commend you because most people in your position had to make that happen for themselves. Few of us are blessed with it. Unfortunately, for those on the outside looking in, all they see is the money that comes with significant success, and too often develop the belief that career happiness and success is dependent on generating significant financial wealth.

In my experience, that couldn't be further from the truth. That's not to say that money isn't important. It is essential, in fact. The vast majority of us just have the formula backward, and it messes up our sense of career happiness. An abundance of money is not a guarantee of career happiness, but a lack of money is an almost certain guarantee of career sadness.

Let me put it another way, from the standpoint of the inspirational speaker. In my study of factors that inspire superior performance from employees, money is not on the list. When money reaches the level where it is no longer a concern, it loses its power to inspire. For the vast majority of us, when our income is sufficient to keep us in the lifestyle we have chosen, with a few bonuses every now and then, along with the peace of mind that we can rely on our paycheck, money stops being an inspirational motivator. Sure, there is a small segment of the human condition that is motivated by the money they earn, but even for them money eventually becomes primarily just a way of keeping score.

The truth about money and career happiness is this: A lack of money is guaranteed to demotivate employee performance, and a demotivated

---

The culture of a workplace—an organization's values, norms and practices—has a huge impact on our happiness and success.

—*Adam Grant, Wharton School of Business*

employee is not likely to be deriving career happiness from any other element of their job either. So, I grant you, money is an essential element of career happiness, but only to the extent that you don't have to worry about money.

And if you really do not want to worry about money, then do the right things for the right reasons. Isn't that the essence of customer-centric selling, or if you prefer, client-centric selling? If you want your clients to take care of you, if you want opportunity to find you, with all the commensurate rewards, including money, then stop worrying about the money and worry about doing the right thing.

When you are focused on your client's needs and priorities without concern for yourself, then you will provide them with the best product, service, advice, or guidance strictly based on their best interest, and that is like throwing a stone in a pond. The ripples will multiply, and the repeat business, referrals, and rewards will grow beyond anything your imagination can conceive. But, it's your choice. You can focus on maximizing your commission today, and only today, or you can focus on the relationship and maximize your commissions for a lifetime.

Beyond that, career happiness is about the accumulated little things that comprise your day on the job. It's about the people you work with, your pride in what you produce, or provide, your enjoyment of, and proficiency at, the tasks you perform. It's about your confidence that your employer will support you. It's about making a positive difference in other people's lives. It's about looking forward to going to work just as much as you look forward to coming home. It's about appreciating the good things, big and small, and having such an abundance that that's almost all you see.

For some of us, many of us in fact, when you are able to appreciate all that is good in your job, or career, it can be enough to carry you a long way, like riding the limb of a strong and growing tree, and if you're happy, that is often enough. Enjoy the ride.

It is neither wealth nor splendor but tranquility and occupation that gives you happiness.

President Thomas Jefferson

For the rest of you who suffer from the restlessness of unbridled ambition, I suggest you start climbing and make sure you appreciate all the good things around you on every limb. Pursue your dreams, but remember, your career happiness will lie in the little things along the way.

Here are some more pieces of kindling to keep you happy:

- Remember, someone else is happier right now with less than you have. Never fail to appreciate all the good things in your life because there are always people less fortunate than you.
- A chair with three legs cannot stand. Happiness has four pillars. Do the math.
- The best feeling of happiness is when you're happy because you made someone else happy. Be a candle of happiness. After all, a candle loses nothing by lighting another.
- Happiness is the oil in your engine that keeps all the other aspects of your life running smoothly.
- You can't achieve someone else's happiness. Make sure you're striving for what makes you happy. It's your life.
- Make a conscious effort to start each day in a positive state of mind. Regardless of how you feel when you wake up, you have the power to take control and choose to be in a good mood, if not outright happy. When you learn to do this, your self-lit flame will carry your good mood throughout the day.
- Remember, tomorrow is not today.

Every man is guilty of all the good he did not do.
—*Voltaire (1694–1778)*

AMBITION LIVES IN THE MOMENT

*The lion is
Most handsome
When Looking for food*

Here we are.

The penultimate chapter. I'm impressed that you've come this far. It is my understanding that most people are lucky to finish the first page, let alone the first chapter, if they even bother to pick up a book at all.

It also tells me about your character. It tells me that you have goals and aspirations. It tells me that you are willing to invest in yourself to continue making progress on your journey of success and accomplishment. It tells me you have ambition.

I will never let anyone turn down my ambition because someone else is uncomfortable with the volume.

For that I commend you. Everything you have read in this book was offered with exactly that in mind, and I promise if you apply the message of this book on a consistent and persistent basis, you will realize tangible and significant progress in your pursuit of purpose.

However, I also need to tell you that everything you've read since you first picked up this book was nothing more than an introduction to the most important question I've ever asked:

WHAT IS THE BEST USE OF YOUR TIME RIGHT NOW?

That's where having a great life begins and ends! All you have is time, and how you invest it is everything when it comes to the health, wealth, and happiness that you experience on this earth.

So, what is the best use of your time right now? Only you can answer that question, and I hope you ask yourself that question often. I also hope you hear yourself correctly! Notice the question does not ask, What is the most profitable, fun, or relaxing use of your time right now? The question is, What is the *best* use of your time right now? That holds you to a higher level of integrity and responsibility because it requires you to walk your talk, live up to your word, do what you say, and say what you do!

Here's the point: At this time in my life, my reason WHY is to help you build a great life, not just a great career. My reason WHY is to help you realize riches beyond just money and the things you buy with it. My reason WHY is to help you reach a place beyond monetary wealth where you can experience true happiness and not just success because you're going to be remembered for what you gave, not what you made.

That means you need to apply this last, but all-important lesson. It is, at the same time, the hardest, and the simplest, thing you will ever attempt, but you must master it, or you will never truly arrive.

What is this all-important lesson?

He who sacrifices his conscience to ambition burns a picture to obtain the ashes.

—Proverb

Simply this: Wherever you are, whatever you're doing, whomever you're doing it with, commit to the moment. Be there. Don't let the outside in. Don't let the outside noise cloud your thought process. Don't divide your attention. Don't dream your life. Live your life! Employ the power of now!

The power of now is all about character and reputation. It is about doing what you said you're going to do, when you said you're going to do it, as you should do it, and, this is the important part, with the people you committed yourself to and to the exclusion of outside distractions and influences.

It is about making a first impression for the second time, and the third. It is about giving proper respect, not just showing it but giving it, without exception.

If you don't, your credibility, which in my opinion is far more important than your reputation, will be damaged, and that is damage you cannot recover.

Here is how it manifests in my life: When one of my children has a concert, game, or doctor's appointment, and I'm not away for business, it is my responsibility to be there for them. More importantly, it is my responsibility to be in that moment with them, to experience it fully and revel in the afterglow, with them and for them. That is what it takes for them to know I really care and that my words are real.

You have to walk your talk. Sure, it is admirable if you make the time to attend, but if you spend that time returning text messages, taking calls, and checking your voice mail, odds are you will miss the highlights of the event, and that will be the message you send. If you don't want your words to always be perceived as hollow, be there, plugged in to the moment.

Nothing will ever bring greater benefit or happiness. Remember, kids spell love T-I-M-E but hollow T-I-M-E speaks even louder than not being there at all. Don't be there just in body, be there in spirit. Don't just be a shadow; be fully in the moment.

Here's another example: In the course of my business travels, when I fly into a city for yet another speaking engagement, I am very often chauffeured

The very substance of the ambitious is merely the shadow of a dream.

—*William Shakespeare*

by one of the conference organizers who was almost always instrumental in booking my appearance. I owe it to this person, during that time, to give them my full attention. I could easily get rapt up with my phone—it rings all day—but what kind of signal would that send to my host about my attitude toward them? What would that do to my chances of a repeat appearance? And what about the opportunity cost? What opportunities might I miss out on if I don't pay the appropriate attention and show some respect? I could miss out on developing a profitable and meaningful relationship for the sake of taking a phone call I could easily return two hours later. And then there is the invaluable insight I could gain about their company that I'm going to be speaking to, or for. Is that worth not letting a call go to voice mail? And what would that say about my communication skills?

How about during a face-to-face meeting or sales presentation? How do you think that person who has taken the time, and often made an effort, to be face-to-face with you feels when you interrupt your time with them to prioritize someone who just picked up the phone? I guarantee the odds of you accomplishing the objective and the dynamic of the meeting just changed, and not in your favor.

Wherever you are, whatever you're doing, be in that moment, and remember the moment is rarely about you! Life lasts a long time and you'll have all the time you need to respond to voice mail, email, texts, tweets, and chats. If you learn how to use your technology, you might even be able to gain an advantage and demonstrate the strength of your integrity by changing your greeting or using your auto responders to tell people when you'll get back to them if they'll be so kind as to leave you a message, but, of course, make sure you do what you say you're going to do. Not only will it demonstrate your integrity, but it will enhance your reputation and teach your contacts how to communicate most effectively with you.

Please understand, this is critical, if not to your success, most certainly to your happiness. As I said, life lasts a long time, so you can plan and manage, but moments are fleeting. Miss the moment, and the memory, along with

A person's worth is no greater than their ambitions executed with integrity and respect for every life they touch.

the trust factor, your credibility, reputation, integrity, and even happiness are gone. Miss too many moments and even life might pass you by.

What I'm trying to say is that I want you to *live your life*! Live it with passion, energy, enthusiasm. Be 100 percent in every moment, give it all away and watch it come back tenfold. Life is all about the moments.

Don't get caught in the worn-out cliché that life is a juggling act. I've never met anyone who could juggle any better than I can, because most people can't. If you stop for a second and imagine juggling with your eyes closed, you'll understand just how disastrous that approach to life could be.

I subscribe to the alternative to the juggling act. I believe in practicing what I call *managed priorities*, with a sense of balance. Everyone you've allowed into your life, particularly your inner circle, is always going to want a piece of you. Sometimes they want a few minutes and sometimes they need hours, or days. You need to be there for all of them, but not in bits and pieces. You can't, as I perceive juggling does, give a little bit of yourself to everyone who needs you, relies on you, or just loves you. You need to give them the time they need, when they need it, while taking care of your responsibilities. Listen to your Grey Zone when it tells you that somebody, not something, is "the best use of your time right now," and always be aware of those people who are a waste of your time. Nobody has the right to take advantage of you.

Then, be there. Always give 100 percent of yourself. Life is not a 50/50 deal. You can only take responsibility for what you deliver. If it isn't returned, learn the lesson. You'll be happier in the moment, and 10 times happier down the road.

So, now you know the secret. Living your life is your responsibility. I can assure you that if you step up to be counted, the quality of your contribution will be rewarded in ways only your Grey Zone can perceive right now. Go live your life.

> **Ambition is a lust that is never quenched but grows more inflamed and madder by enjoyment.**
>
> —*Thomas Otway 1652–1685*

Here's some pieces of kindling to propel you toward your dreams:

- Action is the differentiator that separates successful people from everyone else.
- Life is not a juggling act. Make a difference in people's lives, don't just entertain them.
- Make life's moments your priority because you don't want to miss the special ones while you're making other plans.
- Remember, the power of now is all about character and reputation. It is about doing what you said you're going to do, when you said you're going to do it, as you should do it, and—this is the important part—with the people you committed yourself to and to the exclusion of outside distractions and influences.
- Athletics taught me a valuable lesson: how crucial it really is to perform in the moment.
- Ambition is the spark that fires the pistons in your internal engine. Without it you can't propel yourself forward toward your dreams.

Your future relies on the ambition that stirs your soul and your conviction will inspire your sacrifice. Together, they accelerate your purpose.

SADDLE UP!

In some ways, we live in a very cruel world because there is so much window dressing camouflaging the real messages that we need to see, hear, and understand. I've tried to go beyond that window dressing in this book and open the windows on the principles, philosophies, and beliefs that have let me enjoy an extremely satisfying life.

I thought it was important to share this message because too often I only have the opportunity, as an inspirational keynote speaker with a very unique story, to create a moment or two of inspiration when there is so much more to tell.

I firmly believe in the need for sources of inspiration, and you should have many, but I am also a realist. I know, from years in the battle, that inspiration is not enough. Sometimes inspirational messages make it all seem too easy, so I want to end this book by being very clear.

There is absolutely no doubt that you can achieve everything you want in your life, in this world. Getting there is simple concept, but it will not be easy. Life is hard! It is a cruel and unforgiving place that will slap you down if you give it even half a chance.

That's the bad news!

The good news is that you can slap back. You were born with the strength, stamina, resiliency, resolve, courage, intestinal fortitude, and discipline needed to slap life right back, to get up every time life knocks you down, and to persist in the face of seemingly overwhelming odds, if you just choose to use the resources you already possess.

Inspiration does exist, but it must find you working.

—Pablo Picasso

Now, again, that sounds too easy because you need to develop your resources. You need to exercise them. You need to show up and fight with everything you've got. When the battle is over, go dress your wounds, strap on your gear, and fight again.

Everything I've told you in this book has been designed to give you the resources to pick yourself up and return to the fight, as many times as it takes to reach your extra mile. You now know the value of developing your talents and elevating them to skills.

You now know the value of hard work and repetition, in perfection as much as possible, to be prepared for battle.

You now know the value of the battle itself and that metaphorical bloodshed under real conditions will strengthen you faster than anything else, but only if you are prepared. Battle without preparation can be devastating, but you don't have to take that chance.

You now know the value of living in the moment and the power of *now*. Your accomplishments are going to require a mountain of passion and sacrifice, so don't waste the moments you will regret missing by being somewhere else in your mind.

You now know that you are going to make sacrifices to achieve your ambitions. You are going to take the hits, suffer the rejections, embarrassments, and frustrations that will come with striving for more than what is being offered to you if you just "go along."

The real question is, Are you brave enough to get up and try every time life knocks you down? You need to develop a powerful passion to overcome the obstacles and challenges that are right in front of you, because you'll need that strength and those skills to overcome the obstacles and challenges that lay beyond what you can see now. Ultimately, it is all about getting up one more time than you get knocked down. Do you have the strength?

Yes, that's my point. Regardless of how much you achieve, it is never going to get any easier, at least not if you intend to keep what you've

---

Everyone wants to tell you what to do and what's good for you. They don't want answers; they want you to believe theirs.

—Socrates

achieved. As a wise man once said, "The more successful you become, the more expensive happiness gets."

So, a final heads-up as you venture forth in pursuit of your dreams, goals, and aspirations. Purpose and passion are the vehicle and engine that you need to reach your ultimate destination, but sacrifice, along with its first cousins, action, courage, and discipline, are the fuel that will get you there.

Action is the manifestation of your "inner vision." Without action, nothing happens—absolutely nothing—but I understand that taking action isn't always easy. Easy to say, sure, simple to conceive, yes, but in the face of uncertainty, easy to do, heck no!

Action requires courage. Action may be the manifestation of your inner vision, but the courage to act is what will make your inner vision your reality. The good news is that as mental muscles go, courage is one of the fastest to develop and one of the most dependable as it grows. Here's your dichotomy: The food that makes courage grow fastest is action.

I'm not saying this to be a wise guy. I'm serious. Action taken in the heat of battle, which could be anything from making sales calls to changing diapers, will reinforce your belief in yourself faster than anything else. At the same time, nothing will dissipate your fears faster than being under fire, especially if you did the work in practice.

All of that is very true, but this is where the rubber meets the road, metaphorically speaking. Yes, action conquers fear, and courage fuels action, but if you are expecting that if you just subject yourself to a steady diet of inspirational messages while focusing on your goals, that some magic psychological cocktail of action and courage is going to stir itself up in your Grey Zone, I have bad news for you.

The key to taking action and reaping the benefits to your sense of courage, and self-respect, comes from listening to sacrifice's third cousin, discipline or, more importantly, self-discipline.

Self-discipline means that you do what needs to be done, when it needs to be done, as it should be done, whether you like it or not!

The best place to measure how good you really are is in the heat of competition.

And that's it. Every other message in this book was shared to give you the resources, tools, techniques, strategies, visions, perceptions, and even parables that you will need to keep yourself inspired enough to be a slave to the sacrifice and self-discipline you are going to need to build, live, and enjoy a happy and satisfying life.

I don't know how many sit-ups, push-ups, or chin-ups you are going to have to do to achieve your next goal.

I don't know how many laps you are going to have to run to be ready to win your next race.

I don't know how many phone calls you will need to make to secure the ultimate grand marshal for your next event.

I don't know how many runs down the mountain you'll need to make to win a national championship.

I don't know how many alligators you'll have to ski past to be a world champion.

I don't know how many times you'll have to rehearse your speech to be good enough to get paid to give it.

I don't know how often you'll have to show up early and stay late.

I don't know how often you'll have to play injured, mentally or physically.

I have no idea how many times you'll fail in front of your colleagues. I do know they'll respect your effort more than your result.

I don't know how many times you'll visualize yourself performing a task perfectly before you do it under fire for the first time, but I know your first time won't be perfect.

I don't know how many times you will have to taste your own hunger before your sacrifice begins to feed you.

I don't know how long you'll hide behind procrastination and excuses before you finally summon up that iota of courage you need to take the action that puts all the excuses behind you.

I don't know how long you will plod along punching the clock until you push yourself to do what is needed and not just what is required.

Self-discipline begins with the mastery of your thoughts. If you can't control what you think, you can't control what you do.

I don't know how many diapers you'll have to change before both you and your child don't dread the experience.

I don't know how long it will be before your rearview mirror stops being the anchor that is preventing you from merging onto your extra mile.

I don't know how long it will take for you to find the courage to always be yourself, but I do know you can't be anyone better.

I don't know how long it will take for your self-ideal to convince your self-image to listen to you Grey Zone and start doing what you need to do instead of what you've been doing.

I don't know if you'll have the awareness to adapt your practice as times change, even though your Grey Zone will be telling you to evolve. That's the manifestation of 20 years' experience over one year's experience 20 times. Can you say *wisdom*?

I don't know if you will have the temerity to recalibrate your WHY as many times as it takes to keep going.

What I know is that if you seriously want to achieve anything, you'll have an honest conversation with your Grey Zone. Your Grey Zone keeps no secrets, but your conscious mind is your source of judgment. If you listen to your Grey Zone, you'll do whatever it takes, as often as it takes, as perfectly as you can, until you've accomplished everything you set out to achieve. Don't rationalize, you're not that smart, none of us are.

You are going to climb your ladder of success in your conscious mind, but not necessarily under conscious control, and that brings me to my ladder and rope analogy.

When you climb your ladder of success, even the bottom rung gives you a foundation to push toward the next rung on the ladder. The next rung may be inches away, or an arm's length away, or an imaginary leap, but all within your grasp and within your control, if you listen to your Grey Zone.

The truth is that all of the above is real, depending on your character. Being on the bottom rung of your success ladder is better than hanging on to the end of a rope, expecting others to pull you up.

I don't know how many times you will have to taste your own hunger before your sacrifice begins to feed you.

Once your feet leave the ground, you are totally dependent on those at the other end of the rope. I admit, a rope can be climbed, but the strength and training required before you confront that rope is greater than most of us ever develop, while even the bottom rung of your ladder gives you complete control to deliver your next move, right now, in the moment, in your real world.

It is imperative that you establish your foothold on that first rung of your ladder and use it to propel you to success, again and again and again.

Nothing will ever earn you more respect than showing up, which takes the real courage, but once you're there, if you don't perform, you've wasted everyone's time including those who were counting on you.

Please, don't waste time.

Here are some final pieces of kindling to ensure that your pilot light never goes out and your internal flame will always be ready to propel you:

- Live life to the fullest because you only get to live it once. This is not a dress rehearsal.
- "Change is the law of life. And those who look only to the past or present are certain to miss the future." —*John F. Kennedy*
- Life is too short to wake up in the morning with regrets. So, love the people who treat you right, forgive the ones who don't, and believe that everything happens for a reason. If you get a chance, take it. If it changes your life, let it. Nobody said it would be easy, they just promised it would be worth it.
- "People grow through experience if they meet life honestly and courageously. This is how character is built." —*Eleanor Roosevelt*
- Your life will be a cinematic, big-screen release for every critic watching to critique, and these days, with social media being what it is, most of them will. The creation of this portrayal is beyond your control, automatically and continuously produced by your thoughts

Life is a series of moments, enjoy each one, don't worry about what's next, always live in the moment.

and actions. Be grateful that those are under your control because that is your only opportunity to direct the performance.

- Ultimately, your legacy will not be noteworthy for the material wealth you left behind but for how you used your success and wisdom to enhance others not so fortunate as you.
- Never allow waiting to become a habit. Live your dreams and take risks. Life is happening now.
- Your legacy will carry on through the actions of other people if you take the time to plant the right seeds in those people while you're still here.
- Be grateful for all the unsung heroes that have touched and impacted your life in a positive way. You may have created your own breaks and opportunities, but you didn't achieve your success without the support of others.
- "You cannot push anyone up a ladder unless he is willing to climb a little." —*Andrew Carnegie*
- The hardest thing to overcome in the pursuit of a successful life is inertia.

Being on the bottom rung of your success ladder is better than hanging on to the end of a rope, expecting others to pull you up.

A FEW FINAL RANDOM PIECES
OF BRILLIANCE

- The reward from a life of continuous learning is that the competition never has a chance to catch up.
- It's impossible to forget what you don't remember.
- Sowing seeds of happiness wherever you go is like planting a garden and watching it grow.
- People will know where you have been, but only you will know where you can go.
- Ambition without mental toughness equals failure.
- You can't fail if you never tried, but you won't succeed if you never tried to fail.
- People follow leaders who demonstrate an overwhelming passion for the future.
- If all you have is a hammer, then all your problems look like nails.
- How can you fuel a flame that doesn't exist?
- Failure is the inescapable reality of success.
- Productive daydreaming is the process of understanding yourself.
- If you gained more value from looking in your rearview mirror, it would be bigger than your windshield.
- Develop the skill to throw the light switch up, even in your darkest hour.

The hardest thing to overcome in pursuit of a successful life is inertia.

- We all know someone who is not happy unless they are unhappy.
- Understand that you will have to invest yourself in ways that will never emotionally pay you back.
- When you're working toward something that stirs your passions, you won't have to be pushed, the vision will pull you.
- Inner vision sees the potential that is illuminated by the self-lit flame that exists in all of us.
- Inner vision will show you your ultimate potential if you are just brave enough to look.
- People can't drive you crazy if you never give them the keys.
- The best place to measure how good you really are is in the heat of competition.
- Practice and hard work are just the rehearsal. Success comes if you can deliver in the moment.
- I'd rather be standing on the bottom rung of a ladder than holding on to the end of a rope.
- Procrastination has no limits. You can fail to do as much as you want.
- The most consistent thing about doing nothing is the results.
- If you don't have time to do it right, when will you have time to do it over?
- How much could you accomplish if you put as much energy into doing work as you do avoiding it?
- Your vehicle to your extra mile is your mind. What octane rating is the fuel you're putting in your vehicle?
- You can't consistently deliver a high level of performance unless you have a mountain of sacrifice and a heart full of passion.
- The decisions we make at the intersections we encounter in life will greatly determine who we become tomorrow and on down the road.
- Your dreams may begin on the dark side of the morning, but they come to life when your feet hit the floor.

If you listen to others who try to set the odds for you, how can you ever hope to reach your full potential?

- Some of the biggest roadblocks in life are in your own mind. Treat the word *impossible* as nothing more than motivation.
- The status quo is like concrete, the longer it stays there the harder it gets, and making changes becomes more difficult.
- Live generously, your happiness depends on it.
- In leadership, character is more important than strategy.
- You can't achieve my happiness. Make sure you're focused on your own.
- You can't get to the extra mile if you're living your life in neutral.

Life is not measured by the number of breaths we take, but by the moments that take our breath away.

—*Patti MacFarlane's kitchen wall*

THE KINDLING SUMMARY

Sustain your internal flame with this perpetual kindling.

PURPOSE, PASSION, AND SACRIFICE: SUCCESS BEGINS WITH A SELF-LIT FLAME

- Have a clear vision of how your purpose will look when you arrive and absolutely understand WHY you want to get there.
- Make whatever sacrifice is necessary to keep your passion burning brilliantly.
- When your purpose, passion, and sacrifice are flying in unison, there will be no challenge you can't overcome and no ambition you can't make reality.

IN CASE YOU MISSED IT

- "First, they ignore you. Then they laugh at you. Then they fight you. Then you win." —*Mahatma Gandhi*
- If people are trying to bring you down, it only means you are above them.
- There will be naysayers, haters, doubters, nonbelievers, and then there will be you, proving them wrong.
- You can't expect the world to come to you on a silver platter. You must continue to pursue and create your own breaks and opportunities.
- Hope is about taking your next breath, it's about conquering your mountain. Hope is everything.
- "The scariest moment is always just before you start." —*Stephen King*

EMOTIONAL RESILIENCE...MENTAL TOUGHNESS

- "It is really wonderful how much resilience there is in human nature. Let any obstructing cause, no matter what, be removed in any way, even by death, and we fly back to first principles of hope and enjoyment." —*Bram Stoker,* Dracula
- "Success is not final, failure is not fatal, it's the courage to continue that counts." —*Vince Lombardi*
- Mental toughness is being able to find fuel in an empty tank.
- You didn't come this far to only get this far!
- Ambition without mental toughness is like trying to drive a race car with an empty gas tank.
- Mental toughness will ultimately define who you become.
- You're never too old, or too young, to summon your mental toughness. It's there if you have the courage to call on it.
- If you are not passionate about your WHY, how can you ever be resilient?
- It's not how good you are, it's how good you want to be.

KNOWING WHY

- Don't focus on what you want, focus on how it will make you feel. Focus on the benefits you'll achieve rather than just the goal itself. That's WHY you want it.
- Write out your reasons why in detail and spend time with them every day. Your WHY should be your cause, your belief, and your purpose.
- Celebrate your success, large and small. That will ensure that your internal flame never dims.
- You have to know WHY! Take the time to clearly define why you have put your life on this course. When the WHY of your life is in focus, the HOW often takes care of itself.
- When you know WHY, your reservoir of mental toughness is always full.
- You will forever need to move your goal posts and recalibrate your WHY. What's important to you today will not have the same sense of urgency three years from now.
- Your goal might be material, but your WHY is always emotional.

- Don't let yourself get stuck in the world you've already outgrown.
- Define it. That's the vision. Describe it. That's the feeling. Demonstrate it. That's the action.
- An impassioned, emotional vision of WHY is the best motivation to take care of your health, which is your greatest asset to achieving anything.

NEVER LET YOUR FEARS CONTROL YOU

- When a door opens, and your Grey Zone is sensing opportunity, you have to confront whatever fear might be stopping you from stepping through that door. Everything you ever wanted could be one step away.
- How many fears do you have that could be cured by a little education?
- I believe that the world doesn't owe us anything. It has provided unlimited opportunity, and the rest is up to us. Do you have the courage?
- What is provoking that sense of fear in your imagination now? Have you ever conquered such a fear before? If you could do it then, you can do it now! Listen to your Grey Zone!
- "Fear is being scared to death and saddling up anyway." —*John Wayne*
- "Fear is a reaction. Courage is a decision." —*Winston Churchill*
- Having fear is normal, surrendering to fear is fatal!
- I grew up afraid that I might die with my music still in me, with my voice having never been heard, and my potential forever left untapped.

THE GREY ZONE

- Remember, your Grey Zone is your reservoir of wisdom. Keep gathering the fresh kindling that feeds the fire in the furnace of your Grey Zone. At the same time, vehemently protect your Grey Zone. It absorbs everything so do all you can to keep the input positive. Garbage in, garbage out still applies.
- Don't be afraid to let your Grey Zone dictate to your conscious mind. It knows you better than you do.
- How many things do you do instinctively without thinking? The instinct is your Grey Zone.

- You rely on your Grey Zone. Embrace it, listen to it, feed it, nurture it, respect it! Give it what it needs and enjoy the journey.
- That small silent voice inside you will often be the difference between success and failure. Don't ignore it.
- You may live 100 percent in your conscious mind, but you are at the mercy of your IMAX-oriented, Technicolor, 3-D, Panavision, Sensurround, multidimensional, guided-missile targeted, organic supercomputing Grey Zone. Listen to it!

INNER VISION

- Have the courage to know who you are today, so you can be who you want to be tomorrow.
- Your inner vision knows the coordinates of the harbor where your WHY resides. Follow it and you'll never be off course. After all, it is your internal GPS system.
- Sight without inner vision is like driving blindfolded!
- We all know that hindsight is 20/20. Think of inner vision as your hindsight of the future. Instead of a perfect picture of where you've been, it's the perfect picture of how far you can go.
- "The only thing worse than being blind is having sight without vision." —*Helen Keller*

DON'T COMPETE WITH OTHERS: MAKE THEM COMPETE WITH YOU

- Climb your own wall. You can learn from others and compete with them as a means of improving your skills and abilities, but as you climb the ladder of success, make sure that you are always recalibrating your trajectory so that when you get to the top, it is where you want to be.
- Maintain and improve. Establish the standard that reflects how you will live your life, even on your worst day, then work to get a little better every day.
- To me, hope is kindling. The more you have, the brighter the flame that burns inside you, but remember, you can't live on hope. Action throws the logs on the fire.

- Competition is your measurement against WHY you are competing in the first place.
- Success is a journey, not an event.
- When your feet hit the floor in the morning, make sure you know what you're competing for, and WHY.
- Above all, commit to maintaining your bare minimum standard of good in your pursuit of all the activities on your way to your WHY.
- Action alone is not enough, but without action nothing else matters.

FIGHT PROCRASTINATION: DON'T PLAN TO BE SPONTANEOUS TOMORROW

- A little delayed gratification can eliminate a mountain of stress in your life and improve the results expected of you, where you are, right now. Do what you have to do, when you have to do it, with a plan to stay ahead, and you'll probably have more time for the fun and satisfaction that made you procrastinate in the past.
- If you have a dream, a higher ambition, a vision that you want to live, make sure you clearly understand why you want to make that real and never lose sight of that focus. It will lead you as far as you want to go. Remember, when your WHY is murky, your mind will always remain cloudy.
- If you feel like life is passing you by, that you have a calling greater than what you are living today, take the time to get inside your own head and discover the why and what about yourself that will open your eyes to the life you want to lead. Then follow the second piece of kindling.
- Don't let your procrastination impede your inspiration for accumulation.
- Almost every opportunity you will ever encounter will be the result of someone else's procrastination. How many opportunities have you handed your competition through your own procrastination?
- If you let procrastination become a habit, will it eventually grow into a disease?
- Time only stands still in the mind of a procrastinator.
- Procrastination is the ability to withstand the urge to do anything productive.

- Stop procrastinating today! I promise there will be plenty of time for that later.

THERE IS NEVER A TRAFFIC JAM ON THE EXTRA MILE

- What does your extra mile look like? You are never going to drive on my extra mile. It is a beautiful, magnificent, fascinating place, but it's not in your mind. It will never exist anywhere even remotely close to your most extraordinary orbit. You need to know what your extra mile looks like so that your Grey Zone can navigate the route to that ultimate lane change. You'll only get there when you own it. Get the vision in your mind's eye now and hang on until it's real.

- Take an inventory of your mental transmission. Do you have all the gears you need? Do you need to replace any? Do you need to tighten one or two? Are there some you've invested too much in that you really don't need? A well-maintained transmission gives you tremendous advantages.

- Balance is critical. What is the best use of your time right now? It might be to attend your daughter's recital or your son's Little League game. It might be to have dinner with your spouse. It might be to stop at the gym on your way to the office. It might be to ask forgiveness in advance from those who depend on you and go see that important client or work late and make sales calls. Remember, it all matters. You're not just building a brilliant career—you're building a great life!

- Think of your body as a brand-new car with your brain as the engine. Your engine will be powered by the fuel you put in your tank. What would happen if, every morning before you left for work, you scooped up a big handful of dirt and put that in your gas tank too? How long would that brand-new car fail to deliver top performance? The sand is the equivalent of negative information and energy being allowed into your brain. The question is, What diet have you got your mental engine on?

- Speed bumps are inevitable on the road to the extra mile. Don't let them become mountains of doubt.

- The least appreciated ingredient in the acquisition of wisdom is consistency, which is the cornerstone of any sustainable success.

- The letter *P* in your mental transmission stands for procrastination and it propels you nowhere. Get in gear or get left behind.

YOUR PERCEPTION IS YOUR REALITY

- Remember the words of Aristotle, "Knowing yourself is the beginning of all wisdom."
- Always be developing and improving your skills, knowledge, and abilities. If you pay continuous attention to your own growth and improvement, you'll be prepared for every new opportunity that comes your way while you maximize where you are right now.
- Don't confuse your gifts with your capabilities. You must maximize your gifts, completely exploit them to your ultimate advantage, but remember that you are capable of much more. Even the most gifted among us have had to develop the compensatory skills and learn the supporting knowledge to truly capitalize on our gifts.
- Understanding how others perceive you gives you the ultimate competitive advantage.
- The clutch in your mental transmission shifts you into overdrive when perception is perceived.
- Don't let someone else's perception interfere with your reality.

THE PRINCIPLE BEHIND PERFORMANCE

- Imagine that your entire world is a stage, and everyone is watching, judging, and scrutinizing the performance of your life. From the most trivial to the most monumental, your behavior is the most demonstrative element of how the world judges your character, reputation, and integrity. Make sure you're Oscar worthy.
- The performance of your life must be genuine. Any attempt at acting out your life instead of genuinely living it will always ring false and tarnish your character, reputation, and integrity rather than enhance it.
- Performance is the culmination of your time, effort, and energy focused on the right things in the right way and harnessed to fly in unison to positively impact everyone and everything you ever encounter.
- The ability to perform is not an art, it is a hunger and a passion that you cultivate into an irresistible force.

- At the core of every great life performance is the refusal to compromise your standards for convenience.
- You are not going to live your life in a vacuum. That means that unless you choose to live as a hermit in a cave on the side of some remote mountain in the Philippines, you are going to spend your life interacting with other people. More than any other factor, your character, reputation, and integrity are going to be defined by how you treat those people, and everybody can, and will, observe and comment on that treatment.
- You will earn more in this lifetime, in every respect, by helping others achieve their goals than you ever will by being focused on yours. The reputation for how you treat others will proliferate far beyond your local sphere and will be returned to you in exponential abundance, either positively or negatively. How you cultivate that reputation is determined by the performance of your life.
- The reward of performing with integrity is a good night's sleep.

COMMUNICATION IS EVERYTHING

- Being effectively understood is the first key to being an effective manager, account executive, businessperson, friend, spouse, or child. Remember that a confused mind always says no, does nothing, or does it wrong.
- Effective communication leads to conversation. Effective conversations lead to positive relationships. Positive relationships are the foundation of stable and growing businesses.
- You now have knowledge that I'm sure 80 percent or more of the population never learns. This means that you now have a responsibility. You can never again say, "He didn't get it," or "She didn't understand me." It's not their fault, it's your delivery! By extension, you can never again claim that you failed to connect with someone. If you have taken the time to understand your own style, you can extract the information you need, or lead someone into giving it to you, using the same techniques you would use to connect with them.
- Communication is how I talk to you; conversation is how we talk to each other.

- When I first meet someone, it never crosses my mind what that person looks like. I don't care about what color hair or skin they have, what clothes they're wearing, how tall or short they are, if they're thin or overweight. What I care about is what they say and how they say it because that is what I need to connect with. That's what reveals their inner beauty and gives me clues to who they really are, on the inside. I've always thought, if sighted people could temporarily put a blindfold, or mental blinders, on, perhaps we would not be so judgmental of others when we first meet. We would truly connect with the real person inside.
- I hear you; I feel you; I understand you. Your inner beauty touches me. That's the potential of communication.
- Putting on your mental blinders will allow you to connect with everyone's Inner Beauty, which leads to almost total inclusion regardless of race, religion, creed or financial status.

BUILDING MEANINGFUL RELATIONSHIPS

- "You can make more friends and acquire more clients in two months by becoming interested in other people than you can in two years by trying to get people interested in you." —*Dale Carnegie*
- People do business with people because they choose to, not because they have to. We can always find others doing the same thing or selling the same product. It's the personal connection that makes the difference.
- The cornerstone of a great business is relationships. The cornerstone of a great life is friendships.
- Leaders manifest relationships by demonstrating what they expect without expectation.
- Effective communication establishes respect, which is the foundation of all relationships, but it will be your actions that establish trust. You must be a master of what you say, but it is infinitely more important that you walk your talk.
- A satisfying life has, at its core, a handful of highly rewarding personal relationships that inspire you emotionally and give you your reason for living.

- When relationships grow for all the right reasons, they can last for a lifetime and everybody wins.
- When building a new business, your ability to earn and sustain the trust of new clients is critical. The ability to earn referrals is priceless.

LEADERSHIP

- Leadership is just a title. You determine what it represents.
- You might have a position of leadership, but the real question is, Are people willing to follow you?
- Leadership is the demonstrative embodiment of a lifetime of knowledge, experience, and compassion, focused on the success of everyone who depends on you!
- The ultimate compliment is when everything you do and everything you accomplish makes the people around you better.
- Great leaders empower you to achieve your personal goals for your mutual benefit.
- Leaders have a vision beyond your vision and the ability to elevate your sights to find yourself a higher place in the bigger plan.
- Esteemed leaders earned their position by being the smartest person in the room. They earn their success by surrounding themselves with the next generation of the smartest people in the room.
- If you're the smartest person in the room, and you're not the boss, find another room.
- Respected leaders are perceived to be at the top, but they never look down on anyone, except to admire their shoes.
- Leaders don't set the standards; they personify their own standards and then hire people who can exceed them.
- Leaders should not just give the example, they should be the example.
- Leaders don't have to demand greatness, they inspire it.
- The most effective leaders are able to check their ego at the door.

NO EXCUSES: DON'T ASK FOR DIRECTIONS IF YOU'RE NOT GOING TO START THE CAR!

- An excuse is nothing more than the pathetic rationalization to justify the decision to fail before you even try.

- Nothing stifles growth more than an excuse. Excuses are like weeds, left unchecked they will overwhelm you. Excuses will always be there for you, opportunity won't!
- Excuses are the self-talk of failure. So many people spend more time thinking up reasons why they can't do something than they spend trying to do it, and those who lead with an excuse are justifying their failure without giving success a chance.
- Those of you who are inclined to make excuses are simply rationalizing, justifying, and giving fuel to your habit of procrastination.
- If you're going to make excuses, stop being creative. If you're not going to do anything, any excuse will do.
- Making an excuse today is like writing a prescription for failure tomorrow.
- Excuses are your personal kryptonite. As soon as you utter one, your power to achieve is gone.

ACTION SAYS IT ALL

- Just because you might be on the right track doesn't mean you're going to succeed. If you're not in action, you're going to get run over.
- You can't get to the extra mile if you're living your life in neutral.
- Any action is better than no action, but the proper action would be better, all things considered.
- Nothing is accomplished in business until someone makes the first move. Action is power. What are you waiting for?
- If you're not in action, you're in reaction. Action is offense, reaction is defense, but the best defense is a great offense. Take action!
- Most highly successful people are willing to fail more than most people are willing to try. Oxford defines *try* as "make an attempt or effort to do something." Making an effort requires action
- You can't consistently deliver a high level of performance unless you have a laser-like focus, a mountain of sacrifice, and a heart full of passion.

HAPPINESS

- Remember, someone else is happier right now with less than you have. Never fail to appreciate all the good things in your life because there are always people less fortunate than you.

- A chair with three legs cannot stand. Happiness has four pillars. Do the math.
- The best feeling of happiness is when you're happy because you made someone else happy. Be a candle of happiness. After all, a candle loses nothing by lighting another.
- Happiness is the oil in your engine that keeps all the other aspects of your life running smoothly.
- You can't achieve someone else's happiness. Make sure you're striving for what makes you happy. It's your life.
- Make a conscious effort to start each day in a positive state of mind. Regardless of how you feel when you wake up, you have the power to take control and choose to be in a good mood, if not outright happy. When you learn to do this, your self-lit flame will carry your good mood throughout the day.

AMBITION LIVES IN THE MOMENT

- Action is the differentiator that separates successful people from everyone else.
- Life is not a juggling act. Make a difference in people's lives, don't just entertain them.
- Make life's moments your priority because you don't want to miss the special ones while you're making other plans.
- Remember, the power of now is all about character and reputation. It is about doing what you said you're going to do, when you said you are going to do it, as you should do it, and—this is the important part—with the people you committed yourself to and to the exclusion of outside distractions and influences.
- Athletics taught me a valuable lesson: how crucial it really is to perform in the moment.
- Ambition is the spark that fires the pistons in your internal engine. Without it you can't propel yourself forward toward your dreams.

SADDLE UP!

- Live life to the fullest because you only get to live it once. This is not a dress rehearsal.

- "Change is the law of life. And those who look only to the past or present are certain to miss the future." —*John F. Kennedy*
- Life is too short to wake up in the morning with regrets. So, love the people who treat you right, forgive the ones who don't, and believe that everything happens for a reason. If you get a chance, take it. If it changes your life, let it. Nobody said it would be easy, they just promised it would be worth it.
- "People grow through experience if they meet life honestly and courageously. This is how character is built." —*Eleanor Roosevelt*
- Your life will be a cinematic, big-screen release for every critic watching to critique, and these days, with social media being what it is, most of them will. The creation of this portrayal is beyond your control, automatically and continuously produced by your thoughts and actions. Be grateful that those are under your control because that is your only opportunity to direct the performance.
- Ultimately, your legacy will not be noteworthy for the material wealth you left behind, but for how you used your success and wisdom to enhance others not so fortunate as you.
- Never allow waiting to become a habit. Live your dreams and take risks. Life is happening now.
- Your legacy will carry on through the actions of other people if you take the time to plant the rights seeds in those people while you're still here.
- Be grateful for all the unsung heroes that have touched and impacted your life in a positive way. You may have created your own breaks and opportunities, but you didn't achieve your success without the support of others.
- "You cannot push anyone up a ladder unless he is willing to climb a little." —*Andrew Carnegie*
- The hardest thing to overcome in the pursuit of a successful life is inertia.

CONNECT WITH CRAIG MACFARLANE

Craig MacFarlane is constantly being approached by corporations, organizations, associations (large and small), television networks, local TV stations, radio stations, podcasts, universities, colleges and high schools, executives, and sports teams who wish to hear more of and benefit further from the insight and experience of this remarkable man.

If you would like to get in touch with Craig MacFarlane or book him as your next keynote inspirational speaker, trainer, or coach, Craig has made it easy for you:

You can call him at 727-442-4400.

You can e-mail him at craig@findyourflame.com.

You can keep up-to-date on Craig at www.findyourflame.com.

A
F.R.E.S.H.
Start

— THE —

5 SECRETS
FOR CREATING THE "TOTAL YOU"

**PILLARS FOR SUCCESS, HAPPINESS
AND A BALANCED LIFE**

COLLETTE CHAMBERS OGRIZOVIC

ALSO AVAILABLE!

A
F.R.E.S.H.
Start

WORKBOOK

Get your copy today!

WHAT LEADERS ARE SAYING ABOUT
COLLETTE CHAMBERS OGRIZOVIC

"The five pillars in F.R.E.S.H. is a foundation for success, happiness, and a balanced life that Collette has applied through her personal journey of tragic loss to faith and triumph. Collette's practical advice and tips for each of these pillars is easy to apply and follow. Many of us are not taught ALL five of these important principles. F.R.E.S.H. should be taught as early as possible to live a healthier, happy, and successful balanced life."

—Jennifer Niu, MA, Certified Health Coach, Owner of Faith in God, LLC

"This book was divinely meant for me and the recent life events I have experienced. It gave me hope that there are better days ahead and a road map on how to get there. Thanks for taking the time to put your thoughts and experiences in an easily understood and relatable structure. I thoroughly enjoyed reading the contents."

—Venessa, Founder and President of
Business Strategies and Solutions

"*Total You F.R.E.S.H.* is just what you need to change your life and start moving in a positive direction. Let Collette coach you to greatness by following her solid, road-tested advice!"

—Peter Colwell, Motivational Speaker and Author of
Spell SUCCESS in Your Life

"Collette Ogrizovic has created a model for living a full and fabulous life, and she expertly shares these ideas in her new book, *Total You F.R.E.S.H.* I love her authentic stories of how she has claimed and reclaimed these pillars in her life, and how she provides insights for creating your own inspired life. Highly recommended!"

—Cathy Fyock, Author, *The Speaker Author:
Sell More Books and Book More Speeches*

Published in the United States by Ignite Press.
www.ignitepress.us/

ISBN: 978-1-950710-34-8 (Amazon Print)
ISBN: 978-1-950710-35-5 (IngramSpark) PAPERBACK
ISBN: 978-1-950710-36-2 (IngramSpark) HARDCOVER
ISBN: 978-1-950710-37-9 (Smashwords)

For bulk purchase and for booking, contact:

Collette Chambers Ogrizovic
TotalYouFresh@gmail.com

I dedicate this book to our son, Decosta Daniel Hemord Ogrizovic, who left us too soon, yet inspires me to live on. You taught Mommy the greatest parts of herself; a strength like I've never known. To my dad, Hemord Chambers. A man of strong integrity whose passion for his community transcended beyond his family. He showed me a father's love that allowed me to understand my heavenly Father's love. Even now, I know you are still with me. To my mom, Hazel Chambers, the pioneer, the trailblazer. So strong, so fearless, so full of wisdom and determination to succeed. To my loving husband, Darius, and our beautiful children, Solomon, Ethan, and Elizabeth, thank you for taking this journey with me. My love for you and our children is insurmountable. And to my dear family and friends, I thank you for your support, motivation, encouragement and love. I am truly blessed.

Table of Contents

Introduction

Why I Wrote This Book

Do you sometimes feel that you are doing everything possible to reach a desired goal, but you are falling short in other areas of your life that you feel are important to achieve? Does this overwhelm you? Do you wonder why you are working so hard in one area, for example, career goals or your business, with no time to exercise and eat healthy; yet at the same time, you want to spend time with family, along with making sure that you're managing or building your financial position effectively? You may even feel like you are applying work/life balance well, but you still feel like you are juggling 10 balls and most, if not all of them, are about to fall.

You may even be telling yourself, "Give up...I can't have it all!" I'm here to tell you, don't give up; you **can** have it all! For some of us, we may not have those questions, it may simply be that there was a turn of events in our lives that left us empty or distorted. For me, I felt like I had it and all I needed to do was to hold a steady pace and continue to build on what I considered to be a firm foundation. Life was going well. Work was great. My relationships were strong and enduring. I had a great supporting cast. I didn't have a care in the world. Then, tragedy struck.

It was a beautiful fall Saturday evening. I was planning on going shopping to buy fall clothing for my 21-month-old son. Two of my friends were at the house. They offered to stay with my Daniel while I went to the mall. I was having a wonderful time hanging out with my friends. Hence, I opted not to go. We made brunch and enjoyed playing with my son. We were having such a great time fellowshipping that time got away from us. It was now evening and all of us were just tired. I proceeded upstairs to feed Daniel as my friends went to the other bedroom to take a nap.

I fed my son his milk as he relaxed in my arms. I watched him gently close his eyes in the middle of his feeding. I said, "Oh well, My Love, you must be very tired." I gingerly got up with him in my arms and laid him down to sleep in his bed. I then went to my bed to take a nap, or so I thought. I fell into a deep sleep. I'm not sure what jolted me out of my sleep, but I jumped up into a sitting position on the bed when I noticed it was dark outside. With a tired and anxious mind I thought, "Oh my goodness. I overslept! Daniel must be starving, and he didn't eat much before going off to sleep. What time is it?" I looked at my watch, only to realize that I had been sleeping for almost four hours.

I jumped up and rushed to my son's room. When I got to the entrance of his room, the environment felt strange. I peeped into his crib and he was lying in the exact position I had left him almost four hours ago. "Hmmm," I uttered…"My Love, you've been sleeping just as long as Mommy…time to wake up." As I leaned over and touched him, I realized he was stiff as a board and cold as ice. *Is he? No, is he? Nooo, is he dead?* I SCREAMED: "Daniel! Daniel! Noooo! He's not breathing!" I screamed. Both of my friends rushed upstairs. One of them grabbed Daniel. I watched with hope as she cradled him in her arms, rocked him back and forth, and uttered with a forceful voice, "Daniel, wake up! Wake UP, Daniel!" But my son's eyes remained closed. If anyone could raise someone from the dead with the voice of authority in prayers, it would be her. She is a true warrior in prayer. But Daniel remained motionless.

By now, the ambulance had arrived, and Daniel was rushed to the hospital. The hospital is a 15-minute drive from my house, but that day, it felt like a 10-hour drive. My hope was still active as I thought to myself, "When they get to the hospital, more can be done.

It's a place of help." At the hospital, they quickly carried my son out of the ambulance. Doctors and nurses rushed to our aid.

I watched the doctors and nurses work to revive Daniel. My heart leapt with hope as I saw his little body move, but it was only to the shock of the defibrillator. They tried and tried, but my leap of hope faded as they continued. Then came the words that I never thought in my life that I would hear, "Ms. Chambers, your son is deceased."

It was one thing to think that my son might be dead, but it was another to hear the final word. The "may be dead" thought I had when I initially found Daniel in his crib was giving me some hope, but the formal proclamation was a gut-wrenching, nauseating feeling I would never want even my worst enemy to experience. My son was dead.

At this point in my life, primarily up until I gave birth to my son, I had already incorporated specific strategies I developed over several years. They were creating excellent results for me. Nevertheless, when I met with such affliction, the loss of my son, no one could save me. I had to find a way back to the formula I created for my life to counter the deep pain I was feeling. I wanted *my life* back and I was going to find a way to put the pieces of my life back together again. For some of us, tragedy may not have been the factor that caused our life to veer from its purpose. Perhaps there were other circumstances which got in your way.

My life experiences have motivated me to bring this book to life. An even more motivating force has been coaching many people to apply the principles in this system, and watching their lives be significantly changed. It is a system that never leaves you once you "work it." You may veer off the road at times, but something will always trigger you to come back to F.R.E.S.H.

I went from almost losing my mind and almost everything I had worked so hard to achieve, to being restored to a balanced life with success and happiness. The system is called **"Total You F.R.E.S.H."** The slogan is: **The Blueprint for a Balanced Life, Success and Happiness.** F.R.E.S.H. is an acronym. **F** = Finance, **R** = Relationship,

E = Education, **S** = Spirituality, and **H**= Health. For you to be Total (Total You), goals need to be written and worked on as you apply key principles in all five areas. The F.R.E.S.H. System will be elaborated on further in the next chapter.

Making This Book Work for You

Now that you have an understanding of why I wrote this book, as you read on, my desire is that you will find what most resonates with you. It may be that there are gems from all 5 pillars of F.R.E.S.H. that you'd like to focus on and work through. Or, it may be a specific pillar you find you want to target. If that is the case, be encouraged to focus on that area. Though, I'm sure, you'll quickly see that how you function in one pillar has a direct correlation with some of the other pillars. For example, Finance and Relationship are very much associated with each other, so is Relationship and Health. The point here is to take your time. Moses, one of the greatest known people in the Bible was 80 years old before he came into the fullness of who he was created to be. I am not suggesting that it will take you this long, but you see where I am going. This is meant to be a journey, a marathon of sorts, not the 100m dash. Take your time with yourself through this book. Keep a positive mindset and meditate on all the wonderful possibilities. You are stepping into an opportunity to learn the tools you need to become your Total You.

> "You can't go back and change the beginning, but
> you can start where you are and change the ending."
>
> —C.S. Lewis

F.R.E.S.H. OVERVIEW

Work/Life Balance and the F.R.E.S.H. System

After achieving my MBA and working in the hectic pace of Corporate America, I learned that work/life balance transcends beyond making time for myself and my family. It's more than me just pulling away from the hustle and bustle of the business world to have a social life. Instead, it's about ensuring that the essentials in my life are flowing in unison, thereby creating a physical and mental balance, which in turn fosters happiness and success. I had never given this a lot of thought until I attended a personal transformation program. This is a TD Jakes program called God's Leading Ladies. I started thinking about the different aspects of my life and why things seemed to be going so well overall and which areas I could improve.

> *"Work/life balance transcends beyond making time for myself and my family."*

I thought about how I had overcome obstacles and how I was able to navigate through challenges to achieve my life goals. How do I have such happiness and success as I pursue goals? I began writing down the things in my life that brought me the most happiness and things that I would like to ensure that I continue to work on. After writing down a long list of things in both areas, I then grouped them in the categories of Finance, Relationships, Education, Spirituality, and Health.

I also realized I had been working on all five areas in unison which created a balance as I set goals and pursued them. I soon realized that one area supports the other. For example, life can be more enjoyable when you have good health with which to enjoy the outcome of effective financial management. Hence, I came to realize the importance of taking care of my health by exercising and nourishing my mind, body, soul, and spirit with wholesome foods.

> *"Life can be more enjoyable when you have good health with which to enjoy the outcome of effective financial management."*

Just imagine layering effective management of your Finances, Health, Relationships, and Spirituality as you continue to stay relevant through Educating yourself in your passion or career. This allows for a constant momentum of staying **F.R.E.S.H.** (**F**inance, **R**elationship, **E**ducation, **S**pirituality and **H**ealth). This became my checklist for self-evaluation to build my life, hence the slogan: The Blueprint for a Balanced Life, Success, and Happiness.

Are All 5 Tires Ready for the Road?

One day, while I was driving my car on the highway, I saw an object on the road. I didn't have enough time or distance to avoid it safely. Moreover, it appeared to be a harmless object, so I rolled over it and kept going. A few minutes later, the car began to feel unstable. Immediately, I had a flashback of the object that I had run over a few miles back. "Oh shoot!" I said, "It feels like I have a flat tire." Soon after, it was completely flat, and the car felt out of balance. I had to slow down even more. All the other cars with their four fully inflated tires sped by as I slowed down significantly to take the closest exit.

I was hoping to exit as quickly as possible so I wouldn't damage other parts of my vehicle. I knew from my brother, who is a great mechanic, that it's very important to avoid driving on a flat tire because it damages other parts of the vehicle. You run the risk of destroying the rims. The car can overheat, which can cause damage to the engine. All these problems are because you aren't optimizing the full performance of the car. Repairs can be very costly. The manual for your car will let you know that in order to get the optimum performance, all four wheels must be inflated. In addition, it's not just okay for all four tires to be inflated; the spare, the fifth tire, needs to be ready for use in case you have a blowout.

Our life is like the fundamentals of optimizing the operation of a vehicle. I've learned that life essentials need to be flowing in unison, thereby creating a physical and mental balance for peak performance, which in turn fosters happiness and success. I refer to these essentials as pillars, like those used when building a structure. These five pillars are our **F**inances, **R**elationships, **E**ducation, **S**pirituality, and **H**ealth (**F.R.E.S.H.**).

> *"Life essentials need to be flowing in unison, thereby creating a physical and mental balance."*

All five pillars provide mutual support. What is wealth without health? What is health without finance to support what you need? What is a relationship without spiritual governance? What is health and finance without a wonderful relationship with your spouse and/or children? And if you are single, what good is a prosperous financial situation without wonderful friends with whom to enjoy life? When we have a flat tire on our vehicle, we don't just say, "I have three good ones. Let me keep going at full speed to my destination." That could be miles away, right? If you don't do that with your car, why do so with your life?

This book provides principles for getting and staying F.R.E.S.H.. As you think through all areas of your life, you can agree that you want to be prosperous, happy, balanced, and successful. Finance, Relationship, Education, Spirituality, and Health (F.R.E.S.H.) are areas you can point to so that you can achieve your desires. "Beloved, I desire that in all things thou should prosper and be in good health, even as your soul prospers" (3 John 1:2). Hence, it is possible to prosper in all things. Just like the tires on your vehicle, if you drive with one flat tire, you won't go as far, and you will soon destroy the car. While expensive, you will likely get a new car if needed. You, however, only have one life; you can't buy a new one. Live it well.

"Beloved, I desire that in all things thou should prosper and be in good health, even as your soul prospers"
(3 John 1:2).

Exploring the 5 Pillars

The challenge is we are not taught to think about life in these five pillars and as a result many of us could be missing out on major gains in life. For example, if you don't understand the importance of relationships, you are less likely to forgive someone when something happens. This can lead to living with bitterness of the heart, thinking you are getting back at that person but it's only destroying you and your health. "My people perish because of lack of knowledge" (Hosea 4:6). Education is the way to learn and take care of ourselves to live the best of what life has for us.

Finance: As I mentioned earlier, when I developed the F.R.E.S.H. concept I felt balanced. I was happy and successful. My Finances were on point. I was saving, investing in the stock market, had a financial advisor, and was investing in real estate.

Relationship: I wasn't married at the time; however, I was okay with being single. I had attempted relationships that I dismissed because they were toxic, or they dismissed me because they felt like I was not the right person for them. I was very hurt, but I chose to move on.

Education: I graduated from undergraduate school at a young age because I was able to complete my first year of college while finishing my last year in high school. I earned my MBA at George Washington University in my early 20s. When I went back into the workforce full time, I was continuing my life learning with my employer, where I was able to take classes in Belgium and several other places every year in any city of my choosing. Training in Europe granted me the pleasure of interacting with students from across the world. I worked in Japan for 1 ½ years in a management capacity. While living in Japan, I was flying back to the US in business or first class an average of every four weeks.

Spirituality: I was a part of a major church. As a Christian, it's called hearing and living the Word. I went to Bible Study regularly. I later started a prayer group named Women United in Prayer. We meet every Wednesday morning at 5:30 am to pray. We are still going strong today, since we started in 2003.

Health: I considered myself physically and mentally fit. I had toned muscles and ripped abs. I was eating right and looking healthy and strong. Mentally, I stayed away from drama and nourished my mind with positivity.

When Life Took a Turn

I was living the F.R.E.S.H. life. Then one day, my life seemed like it just flipped upside down when my son was pronounced dead at the hospital. It ripped through my F.R.E.S.H. living. The physical impact affected me significantly, which affected the way I thought and believed. Then there was the rippling effect on Finance; I was sinking deeper and deeper into debt. As I said, my life was flipped upside down. However, I never lost my foundation and was determined to get my life back using F.R.E.S.H.

Even though I questioned my spiritual journey, I never let go. While everything was falling apart, I surrounded myself with some awesome people who allowed me to get to know a greater power than me. That greater power that said, "Beloved, I desire that in all things thou should prosper and be in good health, even as your soul prospers" (3 John 1:2).

My desire is that this book will bring healing and balance to everyone who reads it.

Chapter 1

F – FINANCE:
It's Not About How Much You Make; It's About How Much You Keep

This chapter is for the wealthy, the middle class, and the person who is struggling to find their next dime for food, rent, mortgage, and more. I've learned it doesn't matter how much money you have; you have to know there are principles to live by to stay in balance financially. I've found that it doesn't take much to knock things out of place with your finances if you don't apply basic wisdom which I will share with you in this chapter.

Sometimes it's easy to get so caught up in the moment of a financial challenge or hope for financial prosperity that you forget there are guidelines which must be adhered to no matter what. Unfortunately, sometimes hope is used as the sole plan to become financially secure. You must apply action immediately to that hope. Time is limited and it waits for no one. How long have you been hoping? Has your hope provided you financial increase? I've learned that financial peace is not so much about how much you make; it's about spending wisely, with a goal and actions to save and build assets instead of liabilities. While you can delay investing as you save, it's not okay to delay savings unless you are paying off debt, especially if you have high-interest debt.

> *"Financial peace is not so much about how much you make; it's about spending wisely, with a goal and actions to save and build assets instead of liabilities."*

The Humble Beginnings of Saving

First things first. You must learn how to save. When I was a kid, my bank account was a washed-out, empty condensed milk can with a slot at the top my dad cut with a knife. The can sat on top of a shelf. Whenever I received money, I asked my dad for the can and dropped the money in. He would then place it back on the shelf above my head, far from my reach.

Looking back, I realized how important that small arrangement was with me and my dad. I was learning to save, and I felt a sense of accomplishment when I did. I felt proud I was doing a good job. I didn't know it then, but this experience was shaping me for the responsibility of saving and being responsible when it came to my finances. My dad putting my savings out of my reach was also symbolic in that if my money was too close and easily accessed, I would justify an "in the moment" use of it. I believe a significant amount of money set aside to build your financial wealth should not be easily accessible.

> *"Money set aside to build your financial wealth should not be easily accessible."*

Each Drip Eventually Fills the Bucket

While your story of saving may not include a condensed milk can, the takeaway is to **save**. It should come with a detailed *financial success plan* which will help you to spend responsibly. Just imagine if you were to pick up and save every coin you saw lying around, how much you could accumulate over time. It may not be $1,000 – it could be $20 – but all the same, it's yours to save or make purchases as needed. The thought of picking up a coin off the ground may sound impoverished but it's money, right? It has a value.

As children, we are very happy when we see a dime on the floor. That's a lot of money because we know if we keep finding dimes or pennies here and there, we will eventually have enough money to buy that candy bar. For me, my reward was a pack of peanut-butter-filled cookies from the corner store.

Unfortunately, for most of us, that mindset as an adult is hard to sustain. An exception is my mom, who would often say in her Jamaican accent and dialect, "Mi still pick up di penny if me see it on de floor because it will eventually add up … if I go to de store and mi bill is over by 25 cent de cashier is not permitted to give mi di food mi pick up … mi hafi lef some-ting behind … so every penni add up … so pick up e off di floor and put it in a yu paket every time yu see one." Try to save, no matter how small it may be.

It's not so much about the amount of money but rather creating a habit of financial building. Have you ever seen a pipe dripping or leaking? You put a bucket down to catch the water because you know eventually the area becomes saturated, right? It's the same concept with your money. You may forget that a small drip from a pipe into a bucket eventually fills the bucket. This applies to spending or saving your money *and* spending it arbitrarily. Saving fills up the bucket; spending looks more like a dripping pipe with no bucket.

"It's not so much about the amount of money but rather creating a habit of financial building."

Put Saving into Practice

Simply put, we must learn how to save. This requires focusing on our needs and not our wants. A great example: you need a car, and you want a Mercedes Benz. Maybe you can afford the Mercedes Benz. Are you living paycheck to paycheck with a big enough amount to afford it? If the answer is yes, then you are not saving. A high car payment does not include the insurance coverage, gas, and repairs needed to maintain this luxury item. Not to mention the risk of your ability to pay changing with a different job or a home repair emergency. It doesn't mean that you won't ever be in a position where you can afford such extravagances, but you must learn how to save to get there, especially if you are thinking about starting your own business, having a family, taking a vacation, or purchasing a home. You need to learn how to plan, spend wisely, and save to become financially independent.

Say, for example, that your monthly income is $3,000 per month and your average monthly expenses are $1,500 per month. By savings alone, your total savings for the year could be $18,000. Just imagine, in five years, you could save $90,000! In some cities, that's the price for a house. You may say, "How can I possibly save half of my paycheck?" You must think about your biggest expenses. Does it make sense to room with someone in your humble beginnings so you can afford the things you want later? You must consider these things to build financial peace. The practice of saving early (or even now that you are gaining the wisdom) can allow you to have financial peace.

Some may ask, "How can I save when I'm struggling financially?" Even saving $1 per week may seem unattainable at some times in our lives. There is always something to cut back. If you're a cigarette smoker, how much money do you spend on cigarettes each week? You may not be ready to quit smoking yet, but at least start by cutting back; hence spending less on buying cigarettes. This applies to any addiction, not just cigarettes. It could be shopping. Start to save by shopping less.

If you buy Starbucks coffee every day, consider going to Dunkin' Donuts or brewing coffee at home. The point is simply to weigh the options that will save you money. Think about it: Can you cut your cable bill in half or eat out less? I've advised clients about making small changes and they have been amazed to see how it all adds up in their bank account at the end of the year. I told one client who was rarely at home to cut her cable bill for a year and put that money in a separate account. Her savings totaled $150 per month. At the end of the year she had $1,300 to show for her efforts. What would you do with $1,300 at the end of a year? Could you use some savings to make an investment? Build the future you want. Savings plus investment is a win-win! I will discuss moving from savings to investing later in the chapter.

Forego Short-Term Benefits for Long-Term Gain

Meet Kent. Kent graduated from an elite university a few years ago and got a job with a Fortune 500 company. He works to maintain his livelihood through well-roundedness in all five areas of F.R.E.S.H. Kent often speaks with me when any of these areas become a challenge. His parents, who are fairly financially secure, took out a loan for his college education. However, it was Kent's responsibility to pay it off once he finished college.

Like my mom, his parents were teaching him to manage his responsibilities. I'm sure they could have easily paid off his loan. But what financial benefit would he gain or what would he have learned? After college, Kent decided to stay at home. As life progressed, he saw all his friends moving out on their own, getting married and starting their families or working and taking these adventurous vacations. He began to feel a little stifled, "not grown up," in comparison to his friends.

He came to me and said, "Collette I want to leave my parents' home, but I know if I stay with them another two years, I could aggressively pay off my college loan."

What do you think I said to him?

If you think I told him to stay with his parents, you're right. I told him, "Kent, keep your butt at home and pay off that loan." And he did! Three years later, Kent's loan is paid off and he is also engaged to a wonderful young lady. He and his wife-to-be have begun saving to purchase a home.

I've seen where school loans have plagued so many people. It can turn into a never-ending life-time debt. Unfortunately, things in life happen that cause financial challenges and school loan payments get delinquent impacting credit scores. Kent's decisions, along with the proper coaching, made the difference. Congratulations, Kent!

The point I want to emphasize is: Seize the moment to save. The situation might be uncomfortable, but you will make it. It will pay dividends later. If you can get a roommate or live with a family member for a short period of time with the goal of improving your financial situation, do it! There is nothing like financial freedom. Recognize that the uncomfortable situation you are in is only temporary.

Don't Give Up When Financial Challenges Hit

Often financial challenges hit and in haste to find an immediate solution, there is a missed opportunity to get proper advice and direction. Most often, people file bankruptcy unnecessarily without giving thought to the financial implications. Because of their financial struggles, some people may even turn to substance abuse and give in to increasing stress which causes health issues. I'm here to tell you, don't give up and resort to negative solutions. Set a goal on where you want to be. Seek sound advice and work your plan.

"Seek sound advice and work your plan."

Meet John. John is a single dad with four children, all above the age of 20. Three of them are living at home as they pursue their education. John has been working for a well-established company for 25 years. He was driving a company car and therefore had zero automobile expenses. What John did have was primary and secondary mortgages on his home. In addition, he was inundated with credit card bills and various other expenses.

One day I got a call from John saying, "You won't believe what happened to me. I'm here waiting for a taxi to go home because I was fired from my job. They asked me to remove my belongings from the company car. They took the keys and sent me home." John was devastated. He was mentally hit below the belt. His self-confidence was shattered. John expressed that he felt lost without a job and no means to pay his bills.

I told him to come see me immediately. I didn't go into what happened on the job but focused my attention on discussing the five pillars for him to have a healthy life balance. The two most challenging areas for John were his finances and relationships. Right there on the spot, I had him work with me on a spreadsheet of all his expenses, debt, income, and savings. I needed to begin outlining how he would pay off the two mortgages and credit card debt. He had no savings; just a retirement account at his now former company.

John was in debt prior to the termination. No job and no savings looked like it would finally drag him under. I set out to negotiate his second mortgage for him. The total of his secondary mortgage was $108K. After weeks of going back and forth, with my counsel he was able to reduce it to $33K, which he paid using his retirement savings. Fast forward ... within two months he got a new job, purchased a car, and began to rebuild his life. It has been about two years and John has not fallen behind in his mortgage. He has a savings account now and has been able to take care of several other financial matters. He quickly learned the concept of keeping versus spending. John is now living a better, happier, and healthier life.

John and I also discussed his relationships and their impact on his finances. As I coached John, I encouraged him to get rid of an awful relationship he was in. I generally see a link between finances and relationships. I often see that when people are going through major financial issues, there is often a bad relationship in the mix or vice versa. John eventually ended the bad relationship. He embarked upon another one later but had learned enough not to subject himself to relationships in which he was mistreated or underappreciated.

From Savings to Investing

After you have saved some money, it doesn't matter how much, start to look at how to make this money multiply. You might connect with a financial advisor or do some research on your own. You might take that money and apply it toward the down payment on an investment property. I encourage everyone to own a piece of real estate and establish that momentum to make money while you sleep.

Author David Ramsey describes that "saving is the 'baby steps' of developing financial peace." It's the early stages of appreciating your money. What you don't appreciate, you will never learn to manage. Hence, let's not despise the humble beginning of financial peace. However, there comes a time when you must move beyond savings and move into investing. Saving is like a squirrel finding a single nut and burying it in a single hole during the summer with the hope that it will be there when he comes back to eat it in the winter. The squirrel in this case has one nut hidden in one hole. When we put a single dollar into the bank, our hope is to come back and find that dollar in the future intact and ready for use.

However, when a farmer plants a seed, they are expecting multiplication, duplication, and exponential growth. From one seed comes much fruit. This, in a nutshell, is investing. You may invest in real estate or the stock market. If you don't find a way to make money work for you while you're sleeping, you will have to work for money until the day you die.

She Made It Happen

Meet My Mother. My mother, born in Jamaica, moved to the United States to give her family a better life. She never made over $35K per year. Would you believe that even with that amount she was able to purchase two homes in a now high-demand area?

How did she do it?

She cut her spending to focus on her financial goals. When she purchased the first home, all her children were living with her. The youngest of us was 15. My mom took this opportunity to show us responsibility by asking all of us (five sons and two daughters) to contribute to a utility bill or the mortgage. We all thought it was a bit harsh. We were young and we wanted to have the freedom to do as we pleased with our money. But looking back, that was brilliant! I'm so glad she did. I learned responsibility and accountability.

Eventually, we all left home. By then, there was a subway line about three blocks from the house. My mom didn't stress about how she was going to continue to pay the mortgage. She decided to rent out rooms. It wasn't easy, but she made it work. Sharing your space with renters, in this case strangers, is risky, but mom was determined because she had a plan for her money.

One day to my surprise, she called me to inform me that she would like to buy a second home down the street. I was in shock and wondering where she would get the money to make such a purchase. She gleefully told me she had been saving the money from the rent she collected from tenants over the years and had enough for a down payment. I asked her, "Mom, how are you going to financially maintain a second home?" She said she would rent the entire first home and rent some of the rooms in the second home. Mom purchased the second house and did exactly what she said she would do. I can happily say that her nonstop efforts to plan and save led to her now being retired and living a financially secure life.

Put on Your Oxygen Mask First Then Invest

Meet Sharon. 45 years old and a 20-year business owner of a small IT consulting company. Sharon will tell you in no uncertain terms that she has no problem making money. Her problem? Keeping it.

Sharon shared with me that she used to make up to $800,000 per year in profit, which is equivalent to about $1M now. Unfortunately, she couldn't show where her money went. She spends and spends and spends without paying herself. No money in her bank account nor investments to show for her hard work. She generously took care of her brother, nieces, nephews, and friends but neglected to make any substantial deposits into her own account.

Many people make this mistake. They don't build up themselves first before attempting to build up others. Sharon didn't put on a life vest or get the oxygen she needed first before trying to help the person next to her. Sharon's business requires her to rent commercial space in a commercial business. Each year the rent continues to increase significantly. I wonder how the course of Sharon's life would have changed if she had purchased a building and rented out the spaces to other business owners. It's never too late to correct your course of action. Sharon and I discussed the F.R.E.S.H. system, she is now positioning herself to rebuild her finances and focus on building assets instead of liabilities. She is now looking at the potential of buying a building.

Meet David. Like Sharon, David is a business owner. David, on the other hand, did understand the importance of saving and was always looking at ways to increase financially. For example, he and his wife in their 20s owned their own home. They rented out the basement of their home for several years. They could have easily not done so because their privacy as a young couple with small children was disrupted. However, they had their vision set for long-term gains and not short-lived pleasures. They turned their home into an asset versus a stressful liability.

Being able to save, David (with my encouragement) took a portion of his family savings and opened an investment account. I shared with David the difference between saving and investing; the pros and cons. When he was ready, we went to the investment institution together and opened an account. David took a few thousand dollars and invested some in a mutual fund and some in stocks. Years later, his account grew significantly. Within that period, it so happened that the building where David was renting space to conduct his business was up for sale. The owner came to David. He and his wife were ready for this opportunity. He sold his stock and mutual fund and became the owner of a prime piece of real estate. Since then, the property is now valued about 10 times higher than what he paid. David went from savings, to stocks and mutual funds, to owning a piece of commercial real estate. He also rents the space to other business owners. He, his wife, and children have since moved from their original home into a newly built beautiful home. David moved from saving to investing and from renting to owning.

Kick Fear – Embrace Your Passion and Increase Your Income

I believe that when you have a passion, you are innately skilled to do it well. And with the right guidance, you can be financially rewarded. Some people let fear stop them. The fear of not being successful. The fear of not winning others' approval. All these factors can kill our drive or ability to take a leap of faith – to take that first step. I refer to this as needing to Just Start!

This can be as simple as updating your resume and sending it out. Seeing what comes back to you. Approaching that potential first client to start a business venture. Or developing a website to showcase a product that you are selling.

You may say, "I don't know my passion." I implore you to think about the one job you would do if no one paid you. Is there something that you would do for free even if you had to work 10 hours a day five days a week? Whatever the answer is, that's your passion. I'm not advocating for you to not get paid for your gift. You should ensure that you do. Often, we simply need a big push from someone to take the leap of faith.

Meet Jane. I met Jane while she was working as a receptionist. She was working to recover from a challenging period in her life which impacted her in every aspect of F.R.E.S.H. Jane had become very comfortable in her position as a receptionist. She didn't have to work a full day. She was not challenged mentally. Jane relished in the flexibility of working half days so that she could do whatever she wanted to after work. Jane had a passion to always want to help. She always liked the idea of being a Personal Assistant, thereby helping someone else to be successful.

It so happened that she became friends with a lady who owned several properties but needed some help in communicating with the tenants. I began coaching Jane on the pursuit of her dream, suggesting she work as a property assistant to someone for a nominal fee. The thought of her venturing out into big corporate America sent fear rushing through her. She had been very comfortable working odds and ends jobs. I saw tremendous potential in Jane. She had weathered some very difficult property management responsibilities, so I knew this could be a career path for her if she so chose to pursue it.

Jane was in court almost every Friday for an entire year assisting the property owner with various cases. She collected outstanding debts from tenants who didn't pay their rent on time. Jane contacted tenants relentlessly but with excellent professionalism. One day, Jane and the property owner ran into a tenant behind on their rent. The property owner amicably went over and introduced herself and

Jane. The tenant looked amazed and said, "That's Jane!" He was amazed to see that this person who looked so laid back was the same person who pursued him with such passion to collect on the debt he owed. This wasn't Jane's dream job, yet it was her passion for her work that gave her the tenacity to get results.

Jane quickly became knowledgeable about property management. She was then able to construct a resume showcasing her experience. While Jane was undergoing this life training, her financial needs increased. She needed her own place and a car to get to work. She had basic needs, which were impossible to fill with her part-time salary as a receptionist and the nominal fee she was getting from the property management company. I advised her to send out her resume and not long after she was contacted by a temp agency who wanted to interview her for a Fortune 500 property management company.

Jane was scared and very nervous at the thought of embarking upon an opportunity to work for a major corporation. This would be her first corporate job. I coached her on the interview process and Jane got the job! Not only that, they liked her so much, they moved her from a temporary employee to full-time permanent status making more than twice what she was making as a receptionist. She moved into her own place, rebuilt her credit, purchased a car and was able to maintain it all with her new job. She has since gotten her real estate license and various certifications in commercial property management.

Financial Management Helps You Live In Your Passions

Jane loves music. With all that she had accomplished , she later realized she was stifling her gift for writing music because of the financial burden she was carrying before landing the corporate position. Now that she had income to fulfill one of her dreams, she began to write and sing again. Her passion for singing could have been destroyed by her previous environment. I was determined to help Jane realize her dreams could become reality. I encouraged Jane to connect with people who had answers to the questions she had on meeting her life goals. Additionally, I emphasized the importance of getting mentorship in any area of interest she might have.

I recall when Jane told me about her desire to work with entertainers in her preferred genre of music. Her thought was, "If I could even carry their bags, I would be so happy to be in their environment and learn as much as I can." Jane eventually connected with a well-known recording artist and began to assist her for free without a hidden agenda. Jane just yearned to be amidst her passion. Eventually, Jane began to get paid and coached by the artist and her husband in the music business. She was even asked to write a song for them with the potential to be on one of their albums in the future. Today, Jane is taking vocal lessons, working with other recording artists and investing more time into her dream. Jane minimized her spending, invested time into her dream, and it is now paying dividends.

Create a Financial Plan

I encourage you to have a financial plan. Not having a financial plan is a plan to be financially challenged. Who wants to live a life of being financially stressed? No one, right? Start your financial planning by simply writing down your financial goals. It doesn't matter how big or how small. Then get an understanding of where you are currently by writing down all your monthly expenses. Next, subtract your monthly expenses from your income. You would be amazed to know that most people have been operating in a deficit from month to month, which leads to rapidly increasing high-interest credit card debt.

The final major step in this process is to start executing financial wellness by getting out of high-interest debt and begin looking at ways to increase financially. I like Dave Ramsey's 7 Baby Steps. It shows you how to build an emergency fund, pay off all debt, and build wealth. It may sound impossible, but it can happen. It takes discipline and I believe you can make it happen. Live in financial freedom!

> "*Not having a financial plan is a plan to be financially challenged.*"

Financial Words of Wisdom

Financial Wellness Good overall financial wellness starts with an awareness that the more logical you are in the process of planning and the fewer emotions you allow to be involved, the better your success will be.

Be Charitable Put the purpose in your heart to be charitable. It feels great to give. I try to practice never giving an empty greeting card. It doesn't have to be a large sum. It could be "here is something to purchase your favorite sandwich." Now I know why the Bible states "…It is more blessed to give than to receive" (Acts 20:35 NKJV).

Handle Your Business For a business to be successful, its expenses must not exceed its income and the business should always be looking for and executing opportunities for growth. Manage your money; you are the business.

Don't Lend Emotionally Think with a clear head. For example, if you know that Johnny has a poor track record of not paying his debts, don't give him a loan with the expectation that it will be returned to you. Decide to make it a charitable contribution or don't give at all. Protect your hard-working money without any apologies. Don't ruin your friendship with loans.

Avoid Emotional Spending Google definition: "Emotional spending occurs when you buy something you don't need and, in some cases, don't even really want, as a result of feeling stressed out, bored, underappreciated, incompetent, unhappy, or any number of other emotions." Emotional spending will break your wallet. Again, the more you spend, the less you get to keep.

Keep Your Eyes on Your Credit Score A low credit score can cost you. The lower your credit score, the higher your interest rate will be when you borrow. I'm not a strong advocate of always borrowing. I minimize my borrowing. However, check on your credit scores. Keep an eye on your financial power! Act to achieve it. The goal is to work on being the lender and not the borrower. Empower yourself!

Develop a Plan for Your Money Do you have a plan for your money? Not having a plan is actually a plan; a plan to be broke. Your money should always have an assignment to fulfill. Whether it's to purchase something important, be saved for something later, to invest, to donate, or to loan, there must be a plan. When you have a plan or assignment for your money, it becomes a lot easier to do things with purpose and not for momentary satisfaction. It will be a lot easier to say no if that faithful borrower comes knocking. It will be a lot easier to not make a purchase and to deposit the money into your future. Don't go another day without giving your money a plan and an assignment!

Chapter 2

R – RELATIONSHIP:
You Are Worthy

Who Gets the Chipped Cup?

I travel extensively to various cities and countries to conduct business. After my work is done, I often purchase a coffee cup for my husband and me. It became a bit of a collection to mark all the places I had traveled. My husband and I had a favorite cup set that I purchased in Canada. It's elegantly painted in red and white, the colors of the Canadian flag. At home, my husband and I take turns making tea for each other. Over time our lovely Canadian cups aged and one of them began to chip. Initially, I was the tea maker in our home. I consciously always never gave my husband the chipped cup. There were two similar Canadian cups, but the one that I would give him was intact while I used the chipped cup.

Later, my husband became the primary tea maker in our home. I just knew that would be the end of my favorite mugs from Canada. My husband doesn't like to use things that look old. He will purchase new items to ensure we have the best quality of anything that we use. When he didn't bring the cup to my attention, I surmised my husband just hadn't seen the chip in the cup. I figured I could at least keep it around until he noticed and asked me to throw it out.

Month after month, I continued to drink from a flawless cup. "Hmm, he must have purchased a new cup, maybe online, because he sure didn't go to Canada," I thought to myself. "What an awesome guy, he secretly purchased a new cup without my knowledge because we both enjoy drinking from those mugs so much." One day, I decided to sneak a peek at the cup he was drinking from. To my surprise, he was using the chipped cup. I asked, "Honey, why do you keep putting your tea in the chipped cup? I know you don't like to keep old things around." He said, "I don't want to give my honey the chipped cup and I know how much we both enjoy drinking from these cups." My heart melted. Even more, he also felt the sentimental value of keeping the original cups we purchased. What is my point? My husband and I were thinking that giving each other the best demonstrates the *value* that we place on each other in *our* relationship.

It took some work to get to this stage in our marriage. It's an individual effort to be the best you can be to yourselves and it requires teamwork to be the best for your partner. We both held onto the chipped cup. Although neither one of us knew it at the time, it was a demonstration of our humility and respect for each other. This goes a long way in any relationship.

Don't Let Anyone Steal Your Values

Should someone try to steal your purse or your wallet you would rush to do everything in your power to hold on to that possession. Why? Because *you know* you have things of value in that purse or wallet. You have confidential information you don't want exposed to someone who is going to abuse it and could literally clean out your bank account. Because you know the value of *what's in* your purse or wallet, and even the value of the purse or wallet itself, you will do everything to protect it from being stolen. Why should your life be any different? You are valuable; you are a prized possession.

I have a dear friend. She loves purses. If you want to see her get upset, put her purse on the floor and see what happens. You would have thought you stole it and threw it in a pile of garbage. She literally feels disrespected. Some people will endanger their lives to protect and keep their purses. It's because of the value they have placed on the purse *AND* because what's inside, both mean something to them.

Meet Janet. One afternoon Janet went to visit her dear friend Elaine at her place of business. The building is located on a very busy street. When Janet got there, she immediately pulled into a parking spot directly in front of the building entrance. "Awesome! I don't have to walk too far," Janet thought. She knew this was a quick stop to say hi and bye. Janet ran up the steps, opened the entrance door to the building, closed the door behind her, and began greeting Elaine. During the greeting hug, she heard a big thumping sound as if someone was trying to break a window.

She immediately thought, "That's my car!" Then she said, "Oh shoot, I left my purse on the car seat!" She ran to the window only to see someone taking a second hit at her car window. She yelled, "Stop! That's my car!" The car window smashed. The thief snatched her purse from the car seat and took off running. To his surprise, he was not the only one running. Janet took off running after him. A few steps before catching up with the thief, Janet fell. By now, the violator had gained some distance on her. Janet ran back inside the building and grabbed her car keys.

There was an onlooker outside and Janet asked them which direction the thief ran. The onlooker pointed in the direction of a one-way street. Without hesitation, Janet drove up the one-way street the wrong way chasing after this guy. She was determined to claim what belonged to her. She thought of all the valuables in her purse. Janet aggressively went after this person. She ran red lights and drove the wrong way up one-way streets and alleys. By no means was she going to let this person rob her of her valuables!

At this point in the adventure, Elaine stood in amazement. She had no idea what to do but to jump into her car with the intention of following behind Janet to ensure that she was okay. Janet was nowhere in sight. When Elaine caught up to Janet 20 minutes later, Janet had her purse in her hand. Turns out, Janet pursued the thief with such aggression, he got scared and dropped the purse. She was determined to get back *what belonged to her*. Janet went into a zone. All she saw was someone taking something of value from her and she was going to get it back. This was serious because she endangered her life and the lives of others. It wasn't until much later I found myself laughing so hard at her story because all had turned out well. I was impressed with her boldness and aggressiveness to prevent her valuables from being stolen.

Don't get me wrong. I'm by no means telling you to risk your life as Janet did if you should see someone stealing your valuables. The point I'm making here is this, she KNEW she had valuable items. She had an iPad, a cell phone, credit cards, bank cards, cash, and several other personal items in her purse and someone had the audacity to try to steal them from her.

Moreover, for this to happen in broad daylight on a very busy street was downright wrong. "Such disrespect. I felt so violated, even when I saw him and told him to stop, he was still bold enough to take my purse. Dealing with identity theft was not an option for me," Janet said. One might say, most of these things are replaceable. Why risk her life like that? I agree. However, these were HER valuables and she refused to let someone steal them.

Know That You Are Valuable

If you have a low sense of value or none, you can never become the great person you are destined to be. We are created in the image of God (Genesis 1:27). You may have been through intense abuse, battered mentally and physically, or feel like you are worth nothing. I'm here to tell you that's a lie. The abuser knew how valuable you were, that's why they came after you. You are fearfully and wonderfully made (Psalms 139:14). You are made to soar like an eagle (Isaiah 40:31).

No matter what happens to you in life, you need to **know that you are valuable**. You may have been mistreated and left to feel worthless. Don't believe it! No matter what it feels like during a dark time, your feelings and the truth often differ. You are not garbage. The truth is, you are a human being that God put on this earth to live an impactful life. You were born with gifts and talents you may not be living up to because life happened along the way and you got derailed. You can get back on track. You are neither too old nor too young. Where there is life, there is hope. A hope for better things and greater things… and you can do this! You are created in the image of the Creator. He creates nothing but EXCELLENCE and so you are! Don't give into the lies of your abuser. You've likely heard that saying, hurt people hurt people. It is a true statement indeed – one you can use to assess what really may be happening in relationships.

Even when you are at your weakest, loneliest, and most fearful, know that you are valuable. You were born with worth. A baby's way of communicating is through crying. They will let you know loud and clear when they are hungry, wet, or tired. Or they just want love and to be held. *Those are the things a baby values; don't go silent now as an adult.* Those values are still in you. Tap into them, get to know them, and don't be quiet when they are being violated. I'm not saying you must yell or cry (know both are okay for the purging of those emotions), but learn to not let *your* values be violated and diminish *your* self-worth.

> "*Even when you are at your weakest, loneliest, and most fearful, know that you are valuable.*"

Establish and Write Down Your Values

I strongly encourage folks to write down their values, especially if you find your values in a reshaping process. Start small with three to five values. This is highly recommended whether you are working to establish a relationship with someone or looking for a new job or career. Your goal is to live a balanced, successful, and happy life. Additionally, it's important for you to identify your values which will foster those goals. When you locate what you believe you are looking for, review your values list to ensure that things line up. If you don't put this check system in place, your emotions may lead you down the wrong path. Why do you believe a company has a mission statement or a motto? It's so that their employees and clients can know what the company stands for, so its values can be met. A client or a customer of a company can challenge the company on its values if the customer is not pleased with a service. This helps the company to stay in line and provide stellar services.

Unwritten values can be forgotten values. Writing them down helps you to take the time needed to focus on the journey. It also helps you to establish a mindset to stay the course. You must spend the time to get to know what's in you. It is key in protecting and recovering a strong self-worth.

Meet Kevin. Kevin was broken from a previous marriage; there had been infidelity. Kevin was so broken, he was losing weight, his skin was breaking out, and he wasn't getting enough sleep. He had lost so much weight that when he was required to take off his belt through airport security –you guessed it – his pants fell to his ankles.

Kevin and I would often meet at our favorite tea spot to talk. On a couple of occasions, Kevin found it difficult to hold back his tears. I encouraged Kevin to know that while this was a challenging time for him, we all go through hard times and we all can make it out the other side. One day, I noticed him crying on at least two occasions. Each time, I offered to let him have a private moment in my office while I stepped away. I encouraged Kevin to know that while this was a challenging time for him, there would be a point in his life where he would be in a better place.

Sometime after Kevin's divorce was final, he began to talk about going out on dates. He said he wasn't good at attracting the right girl. I told him, "Just go out as often as you can. Don't put a label on anything; just have fun." Kevin struggled for a while, but he did begin dating. Kevin was also a part of a community of people in his age group who would often hang out together for dinners, brunches, or just simply to meet up to have fun. There were a few sweet, single ladies in this group.

There was one woman in the group that he liked, so I began asking him a few important questions. Does she show appreciation for your values? Does she show appreciation for you? How comfortable does she make you feel when you are hanging out with her? Her friends? Her family? Do you feel respected? This began the process we shared as he began to get to know his dates and his own expectations. After answering the questions for each person he dated, I was able to help him focus on what a person holding values most important to him might be like. The woman he was at first most drawn to didn't meet those values.

One day while Kevin was out with the group, an issue came up and several people in the group pointed blame at Kevin, except one young lady who came to Kevin's defense with very strong convictions. Kevin looked at her in amazement and appreciation. When Kevin told me this story I immediately said, "That's the one to watch as a potential girlfriend." Kevin quickly responded by explaining he was not attracted to her; although he did think she liked him. I said, "Kevin, keep your eyes on her, she is the one that I like based on what you've shared with me."

A few months later, Kevin told me he thought about what I said and began looking differently at the woman who stood up for him. He said that he couldn't forget what she had done, plus, she appreciated his weird sense of humor. A year and half later, I received a wedding invitation to attend their wedding. Five years later, they now have three children and are living their "happily ever after."

My point to Kevin was that he is valuable. The woman that came to his defense despite what most of the group may have thought knew something about Kevin and was ready to fight for him. She understood and appreciated his values. When I told him to pay attention to her, I was really asking Kevin to tap into her values and see if there was a match and mutual appreciation. And there was. Value brings about respect; respect can blossom into love and honor.

Surround Yourself with Like-Minded People and Those Smarter Than You

Research has shown that our environment has a major impact on us, considerably more than we think. I read an article entitled "You're the Average of the Five People You Spend the Most Time With," a celebrated quote by motivational speaker Jim Rohn. The article goes on to state that we are greatly influenced by those we spend the most time with. This environment affects our way of **thinking**, our **self-esteem**, and our **decisions**.

Regardless of who you are around, you exchange thoughts, recommendations, ideas, and your stories. These things program us. It's okay to want to hear the positive things, that's ideal, right? However, you don't just want to have "yes" people in your circle. Your best relationships should have a balance that includes real, constructive thoughts. Why is this important? It's one key path to growth. If you don't know what to improve, how do you know what to fix? That's why you see so many corporations, even churches, asking folks to fill out surveys. An article in the Harvard Business Review states that research has shown "novices have a preference for positive feedback, experts want negative (constructive) feedback," this is so they can make improvements, and thereby make progress.

You may be thinking, "Collette, why are you talking about novices and experts? I'm just starting out." I'm glad you asked. I've brought this to your attention in order to evaluate where you are in your journey and your desire to set your mind to become an expert. Checking oneself to know whether you are open to constructive feedback is extremely important; keeping in mind that such feedback is not alway rosey. No one wants a Debbie Downer or a Dream Terminator. I think we all know what types of folks those are. That's not what constructive feedback is, at all. I'm talking about someone who is experienced and is willing to provide areas for improvement and recommendations. Find someone that you hold in high esteem and seek to get constructive feedback from them. When that does happen, write down the feedback and put a plan in place to improve or work on the recommendation. Don't take it personally, just DO it!

> "*Checking oneself to know whether you are open to constructive feedback is extremely important.*"

My Story. Not too long ago, I had a major speaking event – an event designed to take me to another level in my goals. Prior to the event, I asked two people I highly respected to attend the event with me. One of the individuals plays a major role in selecting keynote speakers in her place of employment. The other is an accomplished author who also has expertise in event planning and facilitating speaking engagements. I asked them to take copious notes and be prepared to give me some feedback.

While speaking, I totally forgot I asked them to observe me for the purpose of providing input afterward. They, however, did not forget what I had asked. After a reminder, a few days later we scheduled a conference call. You know the saying, tell me the good, the bad and the ugly. Neither one of them minced any words as they provided their feedback. Trust me on this, it wasn't easy allowing myself to be in this position after working late nights and long days for perfection, but I knew I had to allow them to provide their constructive feedback. What they shared ranged from, "Collette you knocked the ball out of the park!" to "Collette you did fantastic!" to "Here are a couple areas that you need to work on." I had to brace myself for the not-so-great parts of their feedback, but I knew it would only benefit me and I wanted to get better. I listened to the recording from the event, and I mean *really* listened to myself. And they were right! I had areas that needed improving. I have had many speaking events since then, and I made sure I made those corrections. My point is, never be afraid to get constructive feedback from the people you value and who value you in whatever you are doing. That requires being around like-minded and smarter people of value. Remember, "You're the Average of the Five People You Spend the Most Time With." It is also a form of being coachable without having a formal coach. This often requires us to be fairly humble. Again, it's not easy hearing the not so rosy guidance, feedback and instructions; but we all can learn so much from each other to make us better.

Keep Your Surroundings Toxin-Free

It is almost impossible not to encounter toxic relationships. "Bad company corrupts good character" (I Cor 15:33). Therefore, it is imperative we learn how to manage them. Earlier, I mentioned that the management of your relationship should align with your value system. When you have a set of values established, it can make life easier in managing toxic relationships. If someone understands you won't stand for something, they will remove themselves and never attempt to befriend you. You know the saying: Birds of a feather flock together? This applies to both good and bad relationships. Good people will leave and the not so good, if they think you are like them, will stay.

Sometimes it's easy to sit, justify, ponder, and make excuses for a person's bad behavior to the point where it becomes accepted. If something disrespectful is taking place, you should respectfully speak up and/or take action without apologies. You won't spend time sitting around dwelling on a matter because you have already addressed it and moved on. This approach prepares the path toward establishing good and rewarding relationships. A Harvard 75 year study surveyed people about their lives (including the quality of their marriages, job satisfaction, and social activities) every two years and monitored their physical health (including chest X-rays, blood tests, urine tests, and echocardiograms) every five years. They came away with one major finding: **Good relationships keep us happier and healthier.**

When is a Relationship Toxic?

Toxic relationships bring about behaviors that go against your values and have some of the following elements:

1. Gossiping or speaking ill of others
2. Wasting time or being unproductive
3. Being condescending
4. Conversations that encourage the dream crushers and the non-supportive

Build Trust, Stay Healthy: Gossip – The Root of All Evil

There is one thing I strongly emphasize. Stay away from gossiping. If you want someone not to trust you, gossip with them about others. Think about it. Why would someone trust anyone who is always telling them about others? It won't be too long before you become a victim. Furthermore, listening and harboring negativity towards people is allowing someone to dump garbage on you. Don't allow yourself to be a "dumpster." This is very toxic and not good for your state of mind or your health. These things lead to stress, anxiety, and fear, which lead to other illnesses.

"There is one thing I strongly emphasize. Stay away from gossiping. If you want someone not to trust you, gossip with them about others."

Stay true to yourself and others. Live your life in such a way that others can trust you. People are looking for someone they can trust. Is that you? Often, people go through challenges alone because they feel others will judge them or think less of them.

Stay Respectful

We live in such a diverse society. It's very difficult to get to know all the dos and don'ts of a culture, race, religion, and so on. Hence, there will be times when we may innocently hurt another person's feelings or disrespect someone. It has happened to me. To rebuild that relationship is very difficult because the person may think you intentionally behaved that way. I know in my case I didn't. The best you can do in those situations is apologize, work on not repeating such behavior, and stay kind.

Sometimes, you have to take a step back until you get a better understanding before you even put a pinky toe back into the waters of the relationship. However, while taking a time-out, it's important that you do not speak ill of the person or gossip. It will not help you or them. Spend some time to get to know *yourself* even more. Take what happens as a learning tool to get to know your traits and habits. These experiences help to shape your values.

Regardless of what happens, the goal is to maintain a respectful relationship no matter what happens. Even if you don't like the way a person does something, you don't have to be disrespectful. You can choose to agree or disagree. This applies to family, friends, as well as coworkers in your work environment. You never know how you both will learn and grow.

Value Yourself. Don't Wait for Others

When the quiet times come, and it's just your thoughts that govern you and no one is around, that's when it's most important that you play the good tapes of what you think about yourself in your mind. It's disappointing to say, but people can be fickle. Not a judgment, but more of an acknowledgment that we are all human. You could be talking to a coworker who has just gotten off a frustrating call or a friend may have said something that you don't like. It's important in those times that you remember your values. No one, not even a parent or spouse, should dictate how you value yourself. That has to come from within.

Meet Taylor. Taylor was born in an environment where her daddy gave her everything she wanted. Her mother loved her dearly, but Taylor and Daddy had a special relationship. She was "daddy's little girl." As a little girl, she went to a private school. She learned how to play the piano. She took ballet. She learned how to play golf. She went on international trips with her daddy, including Paris. She was involved in various sports. She had every little girl's dream. Taylor even had a Strawberry Shortcake decorated room with a big dollhouse loaded with toy furniture. Her parents did everything they could to value and cherish her.

As she developed into her teenage years, she eventually lost the closeness she had with her dad. He divorced and married again and it would be ten years before she spoke with him. The pain and disappointment she felt eventually helped lead her down a dark path of sex, drugs, and alcohol. It was easy for her to have access to all these things because she connected herself to people and an environment where she felt the most valued. It would be this same environment that found Taylor raped by a close cousin at the age of 18. This affected her in such a way that she didn't tell anyone for years and her drug abuse got worse.

All Taylor ever did was give love. She thought if she could show her graciousness by being a loving and kind person, she would receive it back. She wanted to be valued. She eventually met someone who she thought did love and value her, so she married him. Her pain was too deep and, she later learned, so was his. The enabling of alcohol abuse between the two was toxic. Taylor did eventually wake up and realized that she didn't want to be this kind of person anymore. She eventually filed for divorce.

Through much coaching and praying, Taylor began her path to recovery. I often let her know how valuable she was, but it was hard for her to see or accept this because she was living in an environment in which she was undervalued for so long. She felt like she was the savior to all when she herself needed saving. Everyone looked up to her, and that gave her a sense of value in a very toxic environment.

Taylor always wanted to do better, even in her darkest of times. Her fight led her to continue to come to me even though she wanted to duck, run, and hide. She kept coming and I kept listening and speaking into her life. She still works hard at staying out of those dark places; the major difference now is she has tools which she didn't have before. Taylor works out and prays regularly. Her relationships, spirituality and health were the main pillars she focused on in her F.R.E.S.H. journey. It was working on those areas that made her successful in finding happiness. Now, she does not isolate herself. She has cut out toxic relationships and is surrounding herself with great people. I am so proud of her progress.

Don't Feed Yourself Poison

The power to forgive is the power to live. The only person that unforgiveness hurts is the person who needs to forgive. This could be the offended or the offender. The act of forgiving is like cleaning out a wound so it won't get infected. Hence, if the offended is hurting, they must clean out their wound. How? First, acknowledge the fact that you are hurting. Second, set in your heart that you need to clean out this wound so it won't get infected. Third, develop a plan as to how you are going to forgive this person. It could be face to face or a phone call to simply say, "I have forgiven you." Make sure you really mean it. How to check to ensure you meant it? Ask yourself, "Can I, with a willing heart, help this person if they have a need?" The answer may be, "I'm not ready as yet." It's ok. At least the word "yet" is there. It's a process and you are on your way.

"The power to forgive is the power to live."

On the other hand, your answer may be, "No." That too is okay. However, recognize that you have some work to do. Remember, you are cleaning up a wound that *you* have so it won't get infected. There is a famous statement: time heals all wounds. I would like to tweak such a statement by saying: time heals all *clean* wounds. Otherwise, you run the risk of an important part of your body being amputated.

Unforgiveness fosters resentment, bitterness, and hatred – all of which are ingredients for living a very unhappy and stressful life. This needs very careful consideration when this relates to a very important person in your life. You see, if you live, there will always be offense. You need to arm yourselves with knowledge about how to deal with it when it does happen. The goal is to not allow oneself to be held hostage by a person who offends us. Don't allow your wound to fester. Clean it out and go on and live your life. Unforgiveness is like drinking your own poison and expecting someone else to die.

Lead and They Will Follow

When you step up your game, those who want to be in your life will follow. First, we must love ourselves. The Bible says, "Love your neighbor as you love yourself" (Matthew 22:39). If you don't know how to love yourself, how can you love others? And not just other people; I'm talking about family also – our husband, wife, sister, and brother. Discover you, embrace you, and if there is something you need to work on within you, it's okay. Take action and work it out.

Sometimes, we beat up on ourselves or live in fear because we make a mistake. If you don't make a mistake, you are not making anything. This happens in business and in relationships. Life is a process and through that process, you will hit some bumps in the road. You can't walk in fear because of the bump you may or may not hit. No need to fear to love again because the previous relationship was a failure. No need to fear trying that business endeavor again because the one before didn't work out. No need to fear taking that class again because you failed it before.

As a matter of fact, you didn't fail. You were in training. You learned what not to do next time. Embrace that lesson and go for the win. Along the way, love yourself. Don't focus on the naysayers. Know that you are worthy and valuable. When we do this for ourselves, it is just a matter of time before we attract others in our lives who will respond to us with that level of respect. Don't worry if the ones who knew you prior to you taking action to live your best life don't understand who you are now. *It's not for them to understand.* It's for you to understand where you are going. You take the lead to love yourself and others will follow. Be FEARLESS!

Relationship Words of Wisdom

1. **Be Free! It's for You!** Forgiveness is not for the other person; it's for you. Don't put chains on yourself. Forgive and be free.

2. **Don't drink the poison.** Unforgiveness is like drinking your own poison and expecting someone else to die.

3. **Impact in seconds.** It takes seven seconds to form an impression about a person and six months to change it. If the first impression is the lasting impression, as the saying goes, then make the first seven seconds count.

4. **Tips on dealing with difficult relationships:**

   - Don't gossip; it makes matters worse and causes unnecessary stress.

   - Step away and take time to quiet down.

   - Remain kind.

   - Focus on the present issue and let the past be the past.

   - Agree to disagree.

   - Apologize.

   - Forgive.

5. **But How?** How do I begin to forgive? Every time you think of that person, say, "may God bless them." I know, we want to curse that person out instead because the pain is so deep; hence saying such a statement is very difficult. Don't hold onto the pain. Practice releasing the pain and say, "God bless you <name>." Remember, practice becomes perfect.

6. People you must forgive who may have hurt you:[1]

- Our parents; otherwise, you always remain a child.

- Relationships that didn't work out; no forgiveness can threaten our self-esteem and self-worth.

- Ourselves; we should stop carrying past mistakes around with us. It stunts our growth.

---

[1]   Tracy, Brian (2005). Change Your Thinking, *Change Your Life: How to Unlock Your Full Potential for Success and Achievement* (1st ed.). Hoboken, NJ, United States: Wiley.

Chapter 3

E – EDUCATION:
Get Relevant & Stay Relevant

My Mother and Education. I believe my mother is a wonderful example of a life-long learner. She grew up very poor. Her childhood education stopped at third grade. Unfortunately, her mother didn't understand the value of education. Grandma thought being domestic defined her daughter best as a woman. Therefore, my mom would only go to school after all the housework was complete. Her duties included cleaning, cooking (parching the coffee), feeding the animals, washing the clothes, and the list goes on. All before my mother left home for school. The rule was that all her chores needed to be completed first; school was secondary. Can you imagine how taxing that would be on a child physically and mentally and then trying to learn afterward? Unfortunately, most of the time school didn't happen because the chores took too long. Due to poor attendance, my mother eventually had to drop out in third grade.

My mom never gave up! She left home as a teenager to venture into the world to educate herself through self-taught reading and writing. Her business savvy began to kick in, buying produce from the locals and taking it to the main market squares for sale. First, she depended on drivers to take her to the market and after a short while later realized that it was best for her to get her own vehicle. With a third-grade education and some self-taught learning, she passed her driver's test. She purchased her own vehicle, a blue truck with an open back. My mom was one of a hand-full of female drivers in Jamaica at that time; moreover, driving what's considered an industrial vehicle.

Eventually, my mother migrated to the United States. She began working as a housemaid. Going from an entrepreneur to becoming a housemaid was not her calling. She had a plan for better things. She later decided she would attend school to become a beautician. My mom is a risk taker. She left her housemaid job to attend school during the day and worked at a seafood restaurant making salads at night.

After completing her schooling, my mom passed the state board exam and became a licensed beautician. She didn't stop there. She continued to work her evening job. Her zest for learning pushed her even further to become a nursing assistant. Because of her dedication for learning, it ultimately afforded her the benefit of improving her income.

As a little girl, I watched my mom fight for her education. She didn't blame anyone for her limited childhood education; she made up her mind to pursue learning to better herself. Today, my mother is the owner of two homes in a now highly valued neighborhood with next to no debt and now leading other ventures. Even until this day, my mom continues to learn, asking thought-provoking questions to experts about real estate and building projects. Her zeal for learning inspires me on my educational journeys.

Nothing to Lose by Continuing Your Education

Education is the process of increasing understanding and wisdom through receiving or giving systematic instructions. The benefit of continuing to learn is that it keeps you relevant because new trends and technologies are introduced to us almost every day. Why do you need to remain relevant? Relevant means "closely linked or significant to what is being done or considered." Therefore, if you're not receiving a fixed (systematic) set of instructions you can't remain plugged in (connected). No one wants disconnection, it relates to something being broken. You want to be encouraged to have an enriched life, career, and development. A broken life is not one we want for ourselves, our children, dear friends, and loved ones. You and I know when there is disconnection, something is broken. That's a broken life, career, and development.

> *"The benefit of continuing to learn is that it keeps you relevant because new trends and technologies are introduced to us almost every day."*

Education has a strong correlation to our happiness and, therefore, our success. Being enlightened is true continuing education. Continuing from when you were a child, the behavior you exhibit as a child is your natural state. Watch children. They have a zest for knowledge. They are very curious; they want to touch everything. Children tend to have no boundaries. Parents often connect their children to a physical niche that correlates well with their mental zest for knowledge. The curiosity and the exploration are endless. It is in our nature to crave learning. It's innate. However, things happen throughout our life that get us off track. I want us to regain that natural state, that innate ability, and continue learning. Moreover, for us to succeed, we need to grow. Growth comes through learning and application.

Society has pinned a negative view on the concept of education for some of us: it's called an exam. Most people tend to avoid pain and stress at almost cost all. From grade school onward, exams are used to grade how well an individual retain information. For some of us that is too much stress for comfort. To change that behavior, you must equip and empower yourself through education. Remove the stress and reclaim your mind to be excited about the benefits of learning new paths, new ways, and new things.

In order to succeed, you need to grow. For you to grow, you need to educate yourself. Often, failure happens because we are not willing to educate ourselves. I am by no means saying you should go back to school and get a four-year degree. What I *am* saying is to tap into an environment where you can learn. Whether it be reading, volunteering, or attending seminars – grow your skills in the learning channel(s) of your choice. Study your craft and study your passion. Studies in neuropsychology have shown how our brain craves learning for us to grow. Let's not deprive ourselves of such a powerful natural opportunity.

Don't Lose Your Zest for Learning

School is often revered as the foundation of our learning. Yes, this is true. However, that association leads to the false assumption that you stop learning because you are no longer in school. After graduation, some think, is a time to enjoy life. Unfortunately, the studying stops for many of us right there. You land a job and work and work and work, becoming too busy to delight in the joy of learning. How many professional development courses are you taking on the job? Or do you find those courses to be a pain in the butt rather than a great opportunity to advance your skill sets? Never mind the fact that phone calls and meetings interrupt the day and you just don't have the time. That's because we are disrupted and that learning time for many of us no longer holds as much value. We must ask ourselves if we are doing a disservice to a "free" opportunity to develop our livelihood.

Meet Joyce. She was unhappy in her current profession. She felt there was more to life but didn't know how to tap in and no matter what she tried to do, it was overwhelming and unfulfilling. She expressed her concerns to me and came to see me for a F.R.E.S.H. coaching session. Our discussion included goals and aspirations in all five areas of F.R.E.S.H. and actions required to achieve them. However, I don't just stop at goals and aspirations; I encourage my clients to dream. What was that special dream you had as a child that you have not been able to attain yet? There are so many people with hidden and untapped dreams. So many times, they are reluctant to say what they are because they often feel that it is too late, they are too old, or it's just plain impossible. They are often amazed after they begin to have an exploratory conversation and take action based on our discussions. They begin to see how that childhood dream is achievable.

Joyce was doing well in her current profession, but her passion had always been to dance and help people. Her desire is to become a dance therapist. As Joyce continued her coaching sessions with F.R.E.S.H., she decided to sign up for professional dance lessons to improve her craft. Later that year I got a call from Joyce.

"Hi Collette ... you won't believe this!"

I said, "Please share."

"Collette, I'm currently en route to New York."

"For what?"

"I'm going to an audition for a dance therapist."

I was so very excited for her. The glee in her voice was as if she were a kid again and living her dream. Joyce waited patiently for weeks as she continued dance training.

A month later, Joyce called, "Collette, I got the position!!!"

Joyce is now on her way to living her childhood dream as a dancer. Joyce is not a 20-something year old; she is 40-something years young. You see, age is just a number; it's the desire of the heart and taking action that brings about results.

Initially, Joyce was concerned about changing directions. What would people think or say to her for making this move at this point in her life? I told Joyce to focus on herself! This is about *your* happiness, pursuing *your* passion. Sharpen *your* gift. Build *your* talent and use it. Joyce is continuing her dance education. She recently shared with me that she would be doing a ballet certification program in New York. Go, Joyce!

Be That Curious Child Again

Do you remember as a child always being curious? It's probably the main reason why our parents had to tell us "Don't touch that" or "This is how this works, my love." A child is always curious, always researching everything around them. Their little hands and feet constantly busy and wanting to explore. Let's reclaim the thirst for knowledge again as though we are children. You still have it. It is innate. For my children, I do my best to allow them to familiarize themselves with guidance. Instead of saying "No," "Stop," and "That's dangerous." If it's an activity that's not going to endanger their lives or health, I give them "Yes," "Go," and "Give that a try." Those supporting words will lead them to success. I'm teaching them to not be afraid with my guidance.

Lifelong Learning

Become a lifelong learner. This requires disciplining the mind by making the commitment to learn again. We often stop learning because we are no longer required by the government to attend learning as we do up to high school. Some of us move on to higher learning after high school. However, after graduation from those places of higher learning, some say, time to enjoy life. For many, that mindset seeped immediately after high school; others immediately after college.

It happens often that work-related mandatory classes are looked at as a pain in the butt, because work is consuming. I believe we should make every effort to respect learning in our work environments so we can continue to develop our professional skill set. I encourage you to take another step beyond the mandatory learning. How about the companies that pay for college education? I've never seen a case where it harms our professional development. I have seen nothing but successes from people who take this extra step.

Meet Simon. He is a very hard worker. Each year he gets the highest professional ratings. His company had a program allowing him to complete an MBA for free. He began working for the company immediately after undergraduate school and always wanted to pursue his MBA. After ten years with the company, Simon decided this was the time and submitted his application. He applied for the program knowing the selection process was intense. To his surprise, the company selected Simon. Now, he had to commit to both the program and his long work hours. The discipline of the two, both work and school, required Simon to delegate so he could manage. Well, Simon did just that. Two years later, Simon achieved his MBA. Simon went on to increase his salary by more than double. Not only was Simon living out his Education goals in F.R.E.S.H.; he was also balancing his relationship. His lifestyle of living on the road away from his family was now a distant memory. He now has a job that allows him to go home every night to be with his wife and young children. He improved his financials and relationships. Go, Simon!

Apply What You Study: Methods of Learning

It is vitally important to apply the knowledge that you gain through your learning channel as quickly as possible. I often see people go to seminars or motivational talks and don't apply at least one thing they were taught or inspired to do. Take all that substance and apply it. If you spent the time on it, it's yours to use. Don't leave anything on the table. Keep the studies going.

> *"Apply the knowledge that you gain through your learning channel as quickly as possible."*

There are many paths to continuing your professional development beyond taking classes or getting a degree. While I strongly support these methods, there are other effective educational means. The focus here is to improve your personal and professional skills based on your area of interest and profession. It is very important to lay out a plan.

1. **Professional Organizations** – the best way to access professional organizations is through the organization in which you work. Whether self-employed or not, it's important to seek organizations that will keep you up-to-date on what's going on in your industry. Often, you'll find those organizations want to support your human equity, i.e. professional growth and development. When you grow with the company, opportunities open up aiding in your advancement. If your company does not offer an organization for you to join, there are websites that host lists of organizations by industry. Locate the industry in which you work or one you'd like to grow into in the future.

2. **Mentorship** – has a couple of different angles. Have you ever seen a professional or celebrity that you would like to be your mentor? In your current professional environment, it's okay to reach out to someone within your organization that you'd like to learn more about. You may have questions like, how did you get to this level? What would it take for me to advance within the company? The main point here is to ask. Also, if you have a celebrity that you'd like to understand how they got to where they are, do some research. If you search, many are willing to offer information free or have books for purchase with a plethora of information to help you build your own outline.

3. **Seminars** – like professional organizations, seminars can often be accessed within your professional organization. Some may be financially supported by the organization and others may have a fee. If your employer sees professional

relevance between the knowledge you want to attain and the benefit to a client team and the company, it could be supported even if it's associated with cost. There are also online resources that list seminars cross-country. Explore what is available, and locate seminars (some are free) within your area.

4. **Internet** – sometimes all it takes is a Google search. It's important to find trusted websites to source information you want to pursue. Scholarly websites are important. You may even have to Google what you Google, but it's worth it to make sure you're accessing resources that are of value.

5. **Reading books** – bookstores and libraries still exist. I know, it's old school, but they do. Both bookstores and libraries have staff that can aid in narrowing down the myriad of resources at your disposal. Resources are also available for purchase online, once you know what you're looking for. Whatever your choice, decide what topics garner your interest and read up on them.

6. **Listening to Podcasts** – podcasts are easily accessible with the Internet. You can search podcasts by name (if you know it), industry, topic of interest, and more. With any type of learning platform, you want to find the style that works for you. Some podcasts may be formal or informal. Whatever your desire, find the type that works and listen on your computer, smartphone, or tablet. Once you have access to what you're looking for, listen in at work, if your environment supports that, on the ride home or at home.

7. **Develop a Mastermind Group** – a mastermind group may sound grandiose; however, it is quite easy to do. Bring together a small group of three or four like-minded people that want to tackle life's challenges and find a way to work

through the solutions together. This isn't meant to be just a informal meeting. You want it to aid in achieving results. Set the rules – meet weekly or monthly, leave the group with homework that must be completed before the next meeting. This is a high-level of accountability that you can enjoy with people who also want to advance.

8. **Mandatory Classes for Work** – professional organizations now require professionals to participate in mandatory courses. It is imperative to take advantage of these opportunities. Webinars and workshops are just a couple of opportunities offered. If the company is offering, they have tapped into an area they want their employees to utilize. If they aren't mandatory, still try to participate. It offers a networking connection to colleagues and more opportunities to learn and grow. Remember, these classes are free so make them work for you.

9. **Hiring a Coach** – coaches are an excellent resource. If it's an expense that you can afford, I highly recommend it. Make sure you find a reputable coach. Do the research. Remember, they are working for you to teach positive life tips to aid in your development. Ensure that the person is living the lifestyle they are teaching you to live. Ask questions and observe vigorously. Make sure your coach is the right fit.

Learning is NOT a two-step forward, one step back proposition. Learning how to do something is not the end; it is the end of the beginning. In most cases, also learning how NOT to do something will speed the process of success! Beginning with the end in mind confirms that you must be willing to change, understand the how-tos of improving, and finally put into practice what you learned.

Whoever said, "Knowledge is power," didn't finish the statement! Knowledge is merely information if no action is taken. A car without an engine is no more valuable than an engine without a car!

You can't change your location in life in an instant; however, you can change your direction with simply a thought.

Education Words of Wisdom

1. **Make the time to gain.** Taking the time to learn can provide access to knowledge that can unlock so many doors to your success.

2. **No age limit.** Who says that learning stops in your youth? There is always an opportunity to learn. Continuing education courses are always available. A quick search on the Internet can also provide you with free resources on any subject matter of your choice.

3. **It's not overwhelming.** Why make it hard? Relax and enjoy the building process. Learning can build the life that you want to live. If it's an area of growth you want to explore, go for it! Your weakness is an area of strength you have not yet explored. Identify it, embrace it.

4. **Think positively as you learn, pave the path to growth.** You can't change your location in life in an instant; however, you can change your direction with simply a thought.

Chapter 4

S – SPIRITUALITY:
Making The Decision To Overcome

Even to this day, I sometimes wonder how I made it through the death of my son. As I look back, I recognize it is my relationship with God. I asked God to give me strength because it was far more than I could handle. I had family members and friends who supported me. My dear brother, with the support of his lovely wife, was very instrumental in getting me through this difficult time. He came to my aid when I didn't even know what I needed and took great care in making sure things were being handled. I had a dear friend who stood strong with me every step of the way. He would often find me in tears of pain. My friend knew when to step back so that I wouldn't use him as a crutch, so I could grow in strength. To get that inner strength, I had only to tap into a power greater than me. I've reflected on that time in comparison to where I am now and it's as if I'm resurrected from the dead.

"How could this be?" I asked myself. "I went from happily laying my son to rest in his bed after a full meal to now laying him to rest in a field of dead people." Facing this reality was one of the most disquieting feelings. Initially, I couldn't take part in making the funeral arrangements. I asked others to make the arrangements as I lay in bed dying of a heartache, which wasn't apparent to me until my next-door neighbor's visit. She pleaded, "Collette, please get up. You need to get up. Don't do this to yourself. Just last week, someone I know died of being heart-broken from losing his son. It started out by him lying in bed for days fretting over the loss of his son. Just like you are right now and four weeks later he died."

I could easily see how that could happen. For a few days I didn't care to eat. Eventually, a couple of my friends and family aided me out of my bed and sat me at the dinner table. I could barely make it out of bed. I was so weak, both physically and mentally. I didn't have the will or strength to lift a fork to my mouth. I sat there staring at the food as I sobbed. Eventually, I saw a fork rising to my mouth. I looked up and one of my friends had begun to feed me. I managed to take a few bites.

After having a few morsels of food, I went back to my bed. Later that evening, it dawned on my friends that I hadn't taken a bath for days. They came to my room and asked me to take a bath. The thought of doing such a simple task was tiring. I had no desire or energy and it was very apparent. My friend left for a few minutes then returned to let me know that my bath was prepared, and they were escorting me to take a warm bath. They gingerly removed the blanket from my upper body and aided me to sit up in the bed. I reluctantly turned and placed my feet on the floor. They pulled me up from the bed and walked me to the bathroom. The walk felt like a 10-minute run, but the bathroom was only five seconds away. Eventually, I was in the bathtub. I remember sobbing as they gingerly washed my back and spoke encouraging words to me. They were also my prayer warriors.

The Decision: Six Feet Above, Not Under

It was close to bedtime, so it was fitting for me to go back to bed after my bath. The next day (day four), as I was lying in bed, I heard a soothing inner voice; "Mommy, Mommy, get up Mommy...only you know where to lay me to rest Mommy." I thought about it for a few seconds and said, "Ok Daniel, I think I can do this." As soon as I said, "Do this," I felt a jolt of energy. I immediately called my friend who was assisting me. "I'm ready to go and visit some of the places that you found," I said. He said, "Are you sure?" "Of course…I need to do this…I have to be involved." I got up and went to a couple of potential cemeteries. None of them felt suitable. I began to search for a few on the internet and went on a couple of site visits. Eventually, I found a location I felt at peace with. Even though it was about an hour drive from my home.

Before I knew it, I was busy and fully absorbed in making my son's funeral arrangements. It wasn't easy, but I had to. That morning when I heard that inner voice it was a jolt in my spirit saying, "Rise and take care of business; do not grieve yourself to death…you have a lot to live for." When I responded, I made the DECISION to live and not die, to stand six feet above instead of under.

After the Rest

After laying my son to rest, there were other areas in my life that I had to face which had been on hold for 21 months. From birth, my son was in and out of the hospital for challenges that he faced. My life was dedicated to him being better. It was extremely stressful, but I couldn't give up. I had to hold down a full-time job in a leadership position at a large consulting company, as well as make every attempt to keep some real estate ventures alive.

Again, I had to DECIDE. "I cannot give up," I said. "This has to get better!"

Faith – Water the Seed

You must be personally accountable. What I mean by this is: I had friends and family there for me, yet I had to have the ability (even fully knowing it was not in my own strength) to want to be in a better place. It wasn't easy. Giving up seemed a lot easier. So I had to dig deep and lean into faith; hence, the belief that there is better even though you can't physically see it or feel it. I soon realized that working through a problem is like planting a seed that you expect to grow.

"You must be personally accountable."

When you plant a seed in your garden, it requires proper care for it to grow. While caring for it, such as watering, the seed is getting stronger beneath the surface. You cannot see the roots getting deeper and stronger, but due to your knowledge of what's required each day for a seed to sprout, you nourish it, knowing that someday it will start to sprout. Your faith is like a seed. You can't see it sprouting initially; however, it will grow if you nourish it daily. Your faith allows you to envision, speak, and eventually live that which once seemed impossible.

"Your faith allows you to envision, speak, and eventually live that which once seemed impossible."

Making the Seed Grow

Just like a seed, the same care is required to work through problems. As I walked through those dark periods in my life, I did my best to live by these principles:

A gentle answer deflects anger, but harsh words make tempers flare (Proverbs 15:1 NIV). When the initial challenging period with my son arose, I was away from my family and friends living in a different state. During that period, I was treated very poorly by a young lady I thought would have been there for me. However, I believe the stress that I was going through was more than she could handle. Her response was to no longer welcome me into her home after I was in the hospital with my son.

I could have gotten very indignant with the young lady, but it would have just compounded the stress and heartache. At the time, I was thinking how to survive the nightmare. I was at a breaking point. My brother was my rock, my voice of reason. He encouraged me to stay calm in the most unbearable circumstances.

Often, we are too quick to give someone a piece of our mind. It is worthwhile to take a moment to think if it's worth spending the energy or if it is best to focus on a strategy to move forward. If it's not going to change the direction of the challenge to a more positive situation, let it go. Sometimes it's a test to see if you're going to go low when someone else goes low. I call those distractions. They are there to take your focus off the most important matter at hand.

Accept help. People generally want to help without you even asking. I believe they are angels that are assigned to you. Often, people let pride get in the way. Don't push your angels away. You see, you have been assigned to accomplish a greater purpose and their job is to ensure that you are on the path to success. Especially when life throws you a curveball. One of the best pieces of advice is you must allow people to bless you. It's their gift from God to you. Don't deny them the ability to be used in a great way.

Write down the outcome you desire, not the pain. I could have easily written how painful each day was, but I kept hearing, "Focus on what you want to see, Collette." So, my diary was filled with words of hope and vision. That was extremely difficult because I had more that was going on deep down within. One day, I passed by the mirror and just happened to look over and I was horrified because I didn't recognize myself. I felt like if I smiled my face would crack because I hadn't smiled in such a long time. I wanted to see if I could smile just to camouflage the pain, but my facial muscles couldn't even move. I kept going, barely glancing at myself. Despite the pain, I still had to write thoughts of hope every day. I strongly feel that writing the pain would have sunk me deeper. It would have been a self-fulfilling prophecy of a road filled with more pain.

Connecting with a team of hope. One night I had to rush my son to the hospital. It was about three in the morning. I went alone. I was at the hospital until 7 am. At the time, my mom was at home. When my son was discharged from the hospital, I called my mom and let her know that I was going directly to church. At that time, I didn't care what I looked like. All I knew was that I was taking my son to church. I needed to hear some words of hope because I wasn't feeling hopeful. I arrived for the 8 am service on time. And no, I wasn't wearing my Sunday best. I wore exactly what I threw on to rush to the hospital that morning. When I got to the church, I carried my son inside in his car seat. I discreetly sat in the very back of the church. I didn't want to be seen, I just wanted to hear a good message.

I also connected with a smaller church group. I would be encouraged by pastors to push my way to church no matter how difficult it may be and not to let anything get in the way. At this church I met some wonderful people who are still a part of my life today. We spent time praying and believing and praying and believing some more. Even though my son still had some challenges, I began to get my joy back. I was able to smile again. I was able to laugh again. I felt hopeful. My faith was growing stronger and stronger.

Take care of your temple. The worst thing you can do when you're going through challenges is to neglect your body which is a temple. It should be treated as holy ground in what you use to fuel it. When I was initially going through my loss and I couldn't eat, it was my support system that kept me going with encouraging words, scripture, prayer, and just being present. They, in a sense, became nourishment because they were speaking positivity into what was a broken body. I may not have been able to recognize it as such then, but I believe it had an impact.

Once I was able to eat again, I got back into prioritizing my health. Mental stress alone is enough to wipe you out if you don't counterbalance it. I returned to eating fresh fruits and vegetables and going to the gym. I learned early on that what I did physically helped me mentally. I needed it to rebuild me again.

"Mental stress alone is enough to wipe you out if you don't counterbalance it."

Your P.A.L. (Prayer and Meditation, Action, Love)

It has been my experience that **P**raying and meditating, taking **A**ction, and operating in **L**ove gives us an optimal outcome. Whether you are going through a challenging period or not, collectively each of these activities work together. At the beginning of my coaching and workshop sessions, I share the importance of finding quiet time to stay connected with your P.A.L.

Pray and Meditate

It is vitally important to apply prayer and meditation in your life. Some of us already know how to pray but often dismiss meditation. The distinct difference is while prayer opens the door for that one-on-one communication with God, meditation clears your mind and positions you to receive what God is saying to you. I've learned that prayers are most effective when we combine both. For example, you may pray, "Dear God, I want to start my own business. Please help me to do so." However, it's meditation that opens the mind and heart to receive the directions He will give you on how to start and who you need to connect with for your business.

In the quiet time of prayer, there's an instinctive nature or gut feeling that you get when you hear what God is saying. If He says, "Write down what you desire for your business," a gut feeling allows you to hear the instructions on what to do. When you meditate on the instructions given to you, you're freeing your mind of the clutter that would prohibit you from believing what you're hearing is real and therefore it can easily be taken for granted.

Let's look at the example of writing down your wishes and goals. First, you must know you were given an instruction for a reason. Now, when you receive it, and begin writing, you create an opportunity for God to show you what He wants you to see. You may be thinking, "It's just an idea...I don't have much to write," but you will be amazed by what happens when you begin to write, hence following the instruction.

One best practice of most successful CEOs is traveling with a notebook to write down ideas and future plans for their companies. Speaking from experience, insights and ideas begin to flow when you transmit what's in your head to paper. Those initial thoughts are no longer occupying space in your mind. So when you move them from mind to paper, you can make room in your head for more innovative thoughts.

Pray and Meditation Reduces Fear

Another reason why prayer and meditation is important is so we don't allow fear to consume the vessel of our innovative thoughts, which is the mind. Fear of the unknown or just fear in general can be very crippling. Though when the mind is clear, there is a certain boldness and "got to do it" attitude that dominates our thinking. It's as if you downloaded a road map for your future and are able to trust the lights illuminating your path.

You may say, "Collette, I don't know how to mediate." Yes you do. Do you often wonder how a bill is going to get paid? Or how an issue is going to get resolved? You feel overwhelmed about all that's going on, so much so it becomes all you think about. You see, that is meditation, but it's meditation on the problem. I'm asking you to meditate on the positive things; meditate on the solution. When you pray, fill your mind with all the great things that can happen. You are now taking a step towards a mind shift to success.

One of my favorite quotes from the Bible says, ".....my friends, fill your minds with those things that are good and that deserve praise: things that are true, noble, right, pure, lovely, and honorable" (Philippians 4 v8 Good News Translation – GNT). Take time to think of all the wonderful things in your life. I practice this by getting into a mode of gratitude. By counting my apparent blessings – I can speak, I can hear, I have a roof over my head – I am focusing on the things I do have rather than focusing on things that are not available to me. We have to do our best not to take what we have for granted even during our darkest moments.

If meditation is challenging, start by writing down each day two things you are thankful for and review them all at the end of each week. Within one week, you will have 14; in two weeks you will have 28; in three weeks you will have 32; and in one month, you do the math...that's right, 56 things for which to be thankful. Over a month's time you will have a list that will reflect how many blessings you have when you are able to shift your mind from focusing on the negative to counting the positive. Rather than trying to find an affirmation, you will begin to think, "What am I thankful for today?"

Action

Receive is analogous to accept, which leads to taking action. For example, if you are hungry and someone presents to you a meal to eat, you cannot satisfy that hunger by looking at the food. You have to accept (receive) the food then take action by placing the food in your mouth, right? It's the same thing when it comes to praying about starting that new business. God will give you instructions; it's when you take action, next steps become clearer. It's a process. Just remember, every invention starts with an idea. The car you're driving today was an idea. During the time of horse and buggies, someone took action to figure out the next best thing.

Many times we fill our thoughts and notepad with ideas, but how often do we spring it into tangible items? It may be a matter of knowing where to start. The thing we have to think about is if we don't start, it doesn't happen. Even the smallest step leads you closer to the goal. You begin to add up those small steps and before you know it, you have one major step in the right direction.

Even though you have the strongest of faith, without action nothing will happen. You can have the most beautiful vision of your future and a well-documented plan, but without action it will stay a vision and the plan will stay a plan. Years and years can go by; nothing changes. Let's be productive. Take those beautiful dreams and ideas and have them come to life by taking action. Someone is in need of your dream coming to fruition. They are waiting on your services, your invention, your creativity. Better yet, someone is waiting to help your dream come through and into the world. Don't keep them waiting! You can do this!

Love

I heard a story about a set of twins raised in a home where their father was an alcoholic and was very abusive. When the boys got older, one was asked, "Why do you drink?" He answered "Because my father was an alcoholic." The other one was asked why he didn't drink. He responded, "Because my father was an alcoholic." Same experience, but chose a different path in life. I want to encourage you not to let challenging life experiences make you bitter; instead, let them make you better. The Bible says, "…. all things work together for good, for those who are called according to his purpose" (Romans 8 v 28 ESV). All of us are born with a purpose to fulfill. As we live our lives, some very painful things will happen to us; as I shared some with you in previous chapters. It is love that conquers the pain no matter how difficult the situation. That's why we must find it in our hearts to live peacefully with everyone. Yes, you will find those who don't want to live in peace with you. Remember, you are only responsible for your response. Keep the peace and operate in love.

Love will always win. It's about keeping yourself in perfect peace so you can execute your purpose. What is love? In 1 Corinthians 13:4-8 it describes it this way, "Love is patient, love is kind. It does not envy, it does not boast, it is not proud. It does not dishonor others, it is not self-seeking, it is not easily angered, it keeps no record of wrongs. Love does not delight in evil but rejoices with the truth. It always protects, always trusts, always hopes, always perseveres. Love never fails." You must know that love isn't about perfection, but a willingness of the heart. It'll get you through the most difficult of situations. And, I truly believe that love frees the mind and heart to operate more fluidly. A real love for others will chase worries away.

Oftentimes, it's the thought of being punished which makes us afraid. This shows we have not really learned to love. 1 John 4:18 Contemporary English Version says, "There is no fear in love; but perfect love casts out fear, because fear involves torment." The New King James Version says, "But he who fears has not been made perfect in love." You are not entrapped in fear. Your ability to love can help you face any challenge.

Peace in Love

Find it in your heart to live peacefully with everyone. Now you know a challenge will be difficult people, we all run into them. Armed with this knowledge, you can respond not with a harsh reaction, but with a calm, love-filled counteraction. Keep the peace and operate in love.

I've found that even in church, in *the* place of love, I've had to find my peace and forgive rude actions or words. In any environment, you will run into some challenges. Why should church be any different?

One day I was at a church service. I was having a wonderful time clapping and singing to the songs with the choir. There was a lady directly in front of me who was jumping and clapping, enjoying the songs right along with me. I felt like I was in great company as we girls sang, jumped and danced to the songs. There was no shame in this time of fun. I thought to myself, "This young lady seems to have such love and joy in her heart I would like to connect with her outside of church." I travel a lot for my job, so surprisingly to me, I realized that I had been attending this church for over 10 years and I barely connected with anyone.

When service ended that day, I went over and tapped the lady on her shoulder. She turned around and I introduced myself. I told her I traveled extensively for work and hardly knew anyone at the church. She responded, "You need to join a ministry at the church that's how you connect with people and until you do such, I won't give you my number...I too travel for work and I'm a part of a ministry."

I thought, "This can't be the person that was jumping, dancing, and praising in front of me thirty minutes ago." Maybe she didn't understand me clearly. I continued to share, "My schedule is very very hectic, I fly out every Monday morning, waking up around 4am, return on a Thursday or Friday with only a day or two to spend with my family before I have to pack again to get on the road." I tried to have small talk with her to better understand why she wasn't welcoming. I couldn't believe what I was experiencing and was shocked by her unfriendly behavior.

Looking for a sense of understanding, I asked about her and learned she often treats people poorly. I was concerned her behavior could bring about unforgettable pain towards others. I attempted to reach out to her so that I could speak to her in love. The purpose wasn't to be mad at her, it was to understand so we could find mutual ground and both attain a peace about the encounter. When you're introspective, the focus is keeping yourself in perfect peace so you can execute your purpose.

Our overcoming is a process. Each day we take a step, it is toward a better and better version of ourselves. When we pray and meditate, if we take action and be sure to operate in love, we will be getting closer to who we want to be.

Spirituality Words of Wisdom

1. **No fear.** For God has not given us a spirit of fear, but of power and of love and of a sound mind (II Timothy 1:7 NKJV).

2. **Love.** ....There is no room in love for fear. Well-formed love banishes fear... (1 John 1:18 MSG).

3. **Overcoming through Faith.** You are equipped with the tools that will carry you through if you exercise faith. Believe that you can overcome! Read about overcomers! Listen to overcomers! See that you can overcome! Speak as an overcomer! And you will overcome!

4. **Peace.** Quiet down. Find your tranquility and bask in it.

Chapter 5

H – HEALTH:
Health Is Wealth

Make a Decision to Be Healthy

Meet My Father. As a little girl, I was often awoken in the morning by my dad's footsteps as he'd open the door closest to my bedroom to head into the kitchen. As I lay half-asleep, the aroma of fresh mint tea steaming in the kitchen drew me out of bed. Some mornings, it was the smell of spices: nutmeg, vanilla, and cinnamon in Jamaican porridge. If I stayed in bed too long, there would be a gentle wake-up call by my dad. "Collette," in a quiet, deep tone. "Collette, it's time to wake up dear." Oh, I can still hear that inviting tone of my father's voice, even today as I think of my childhood. I believe sometimes I used to pretend that I was asleep just to hear him call me.

One morning, there were no aromas, no gentle calls. I thought, "Something must be wrong. Where is Papa?" I got up and rushed to my dad's room. I said, "Papa, are you ok?" He said, "I'm not feeling well, my daughter." This was the beginning of a journey that I will never forget. My dad not getting up before me was simply abnormal. It disrupted every excited feeling I knew about my mornings as a little girl. I had no understanding of what was going on, but I knew whatever it was it would change my life forever.

Soon after, I had to migrate to the United States to be with my mother. I remember asking my dad with tears in my eyes, "Why are you allowing me to go to the US?" He said, "So you can have a better life." "But how?" I asked with tears in my eyes. My "But how?" pertained to the fact that I knew he was not 100% well and he needed me there with him. The thought of going to the United States to live was very intriguing. The flip side was leaving my security blanket, my dad. You see, my dad was the one who I would tell all my secrets to, all my stories, especially when I got teased at school. He would tell me, "Never mind," and give me a confidence boost, letting me know it didn't matter what anyone said about me; I am bold, beautiful, and strong. Most of all, he believed in me. I learned sometime later, after my move, that my dad was struggling with diabetes.

No one wants diabetes, but for my dad, this was now his new life; he was living with the disease. My dad was strong and never a complainer. Sometimes I wish he was, maybe he would have received the right help early on. As an adult, I recall another morning when my grandmother went to his room and noticed he was not feeling well. He was weak and could barely speak. They rushed him to a nearby hospital. Once again, I didn't know the extent of his illness. A couple of days later I learned my dear papa had died.

When Did the Change Begin?

Losing my papa changed me forever. Growing up I was chubby and taller than most of the young ladies my age. Yep, people placed me in the "big girl" category. It didn't feel good, it felt downright awkward at times. I recall the unpleasant nicknames. I was always at the back of the line with the boys as they lined us up from the shortest to the tallest. This happened throughout elementary school, middle school, and high school. I would often watch my friends who were thinner and shorter get favorable attention from others, especially the boys.

I often felt there was a cute-girls club and I was never going to be a part of it. My self-confidence was low, and I became more of an introvert. Which in a way, I was happy and confident with not having to say much. I was too fat and too tall. I was taller than all the boys. By middle school I was 5' 9" and hating every bit of the extra three inches. By today's standards, 5' 9" is close to average. Back then, that was not the case. I would literally pray to God to be shorter, but nothing happened when I woke up in the mornings. I was still at the same height I measured myself on the wall the night before. Sounds silly, but it's true. We all have something that we tried to pray away as a kid; but thank God He knows best.

By high school, I eventually gave up praying to be shorter and began to look at what was in my control to change. I quickly found out that I could change my width and stop focusing so much on my height. I began to read more about what to eat to make the change and soon realized there were many foods that I was eating that were negatively contributing to my weight. At the lovely ages of between 12 and 16, I wasn't thinking too much about health; I was thinking more about appearance. I knew that I had to do something with my diet to change the way I looked.

The first thing I did was cut back on the amount of sugar I put in my daily breakfast of cornflakes and whole milk. My goodness, it was the most insipid taste! But the more I practiced eating this awful tasting food, the more it became normal. It was an acquired taste. This was at the tender age of 14. That wasn't enough. I had to make other changes as I struggled with my weight issues up to 11th grade. The summer before my senior year, I began to read more and more about health and fitness, which then led me to cut out meats and added exercise to my quest gradually.

I would go for long walk/runs in the evening from my house to the track at my old middle school. There, I would also run bleacher steps. If I missed my running, at nights I would run up and down the stairs at my house. Then, I'd do leg raises to further build my core, something I learned from one of my brothers. Soon I began to see results. By the time my senior school year began my peers noticed me as the tall, thin girl with no glasses and flawless hairstyles. As mentioned earlier, my focus was about appearance and I made a decision that summer that I would not begin the school year as a shy and insecure teenager.

The journey wasn't easy. In high school, I was ridiculed when I didn't eat the oversized cookies for dessert like the rest of my peers. I had stopped eating meat. It was not easy because in the Jamaican community, we know how to cook and eat all types of tasty meats such as oxtail, curry goat, jerk chicken, and roast pork. My mother cooked all of them very well. In fact, chicken was the last meat that I stopped eating and that took a while.

I had to make a change. As I got older and went out to eat, the ridicule intensified, especially when I would go out to a restaurant with a group and asked the server to "bring the salad dressing on the side; no cheese, no croutons, no bacon bits please, and extra lettuce. Thank you!" Oh, and I would ask, "Can you please cook my salmon with less butter? If there is a sauce, bring it on the side." It all seemed high maintenance to others, but I knew my family health history, my body, and my end goal. In my mind, I was paying for my food, I needed to be served the way I asked. And you know what? I haven't gone to one restaurant that did not serve me based on my requests. I'm always polite and respectful in my interactions with the waiters. You would be amazed how accommodating restaurants are, especially lately with all the diet awareness in the media.

Another Wake-up Call

One day I got a call from my mom. "Hi, Mom!"

"Hi, babe," as my mom would amicably call me. "I don't know what's going on. Today I was driving, and I felt dizzy." She said, "I must be getting older."

"Of course, you are getting older, Mom, you're alive."

She chuckled and said, "I'm going to stop driving because I don't know what's wrong." At the time, my mom was 55 years young. She went to the doctor and a few days later she went back in to get her blood work report. I received the phone call, "The doctor said I have diabetes."

By now, at the age of 20-something, I read about diet and nutrition, basing my lifestyle on healthful habits. Immediately, I said to Mom, "I'll teach you how to eat well." Up until then, my mom used to think that I was nuts when I wouldn't eat those starchy, high-carb Jamaican meals. I grew up on those meals; I just now approach everything with awareness and moderation. My mother now listens to my food recommendations for a low-sugar, high-protein, and vegetable-eating lifestyle; 25 plus years later, my mom never had to take insulin injections. She still takes the pills, but she manages the diabetes primarily through her diet.

Lifestyle change when it comes to eating is not easy. Even though I was no longer overweight, I was battling sugar cravings. There were certain types of candy that I had to have. For some, it may be salty treats. Whatever it is, know that you can find ways to manage those cravings in a healthy way. It's not that you give up everything you enjoy, just find the healthier alternative.

I went on a sugar fast with a close friend. We held each other accountable. The 40 days led to 60 days then another month and another. Before we knew it, we finished a one-year fast from sugar where we cut out candy and sugary desserts. We even removed some of everyone's favorite carbs such as chips, white rice, and pasta. Instead, we ate more of the good carbs from green vegetables, berries, fruits, nuts, beans, lentils, quinoa, brown rice, and other high fiber carbs to improve our overall health and stabilize our blood sugar.

The original garden story in the Bible says, "Behold, I have given you every plant yielding seed that is on the face of all the earth, and every tree with seed in its fruit. You shall have them for food" (Genesis 1:29, ESV). We are whole food deficient because convenient processed foods are found in so many countries now and we are getting away from the Original Garden when the plants were fresh and vine-ripened. Benjamin Franklin said, "An ounce of prevention is worth a pound of cure. A little precaution before a crisis occurs is preferable to a lot of fixing up afterward." Look up his quote online. My goals were to avoid the inherent possibility of diabetes in my life since I had seen it affect my parents.

Mental Health

I thought burying my dad was the darkest time in my life. That is until the period I gave birth to my nearly dead son only to unexpectedly bury him at 21 months. A mother should never have to bury her child. Unfortunately, I did. The pain was real. I wanted to die with him. "How could he leave without me? Who is going to take care of him there?" These were the questions roaming in my head. I lay in bed for days not wanting to eat or bathe. I remember getting assistance to take a bath. I remember someone putting a fork to my mouth to eat. The mental anguish was beyond anything anyone could imagine. "My one and only son is no longer with me." "What happened?" "How could I allow this to happen?" "He depended on me and I failed him." "Dear God, help me to make it through this!"

At this point of my life, there was no F.R.E.S.H.-ness within me. My Finances were challenged; I was getting in more and more debt with the properties I owned and barely collecting any rent. Relationships were challenged because I found myself wanting to run away from everyone I knew, having a strong desire to move to another country. Education – "What's that? What is there to educate myself about, life is not worth living." Spirituality: I did cry out to God, but I couldn't feel the strong connection, I knew it was a must, so I kept trying.

There was one thing that allowed me to start building the F.R.E.S.H. pillars back up – Health. This discovery came about somewhat by accident. I pushed myself to go to the gym one day and after working out I felt a slight change in my mood and my thoughts. "Hmm, there might be something to this," I thought. I was going to church, I had friends praying for me, I had family members checking on me, but I had to dig for more.

One night around 11 o'clock, the pain hit hard. My heart just ached as if someone was using a knife to cut into me. That's how it felt to me mentally. That night I managed to find a 24-hour gym. I worked out for 45 minutes, took a shower, and headed home. I felt a boost inside of me. Before I knew it, the gym became my medicine. I could easily get into the scientific explanation of how I was pushing the negative hormones out by increasing the positive hormones as I worked out, but that could be another complete book.

I knew this: without the physical nourishment of working out, I would not have been able to optimize on the Spiritual. Mentally, I had to get to a place where I was ready to receive all the good that would come from the challenges that I was facing. My health was no longer about my physical appearance. It was about my mental appearance. No one knew what was going on inside me but me. To this day, I have not stopped taking my dose of workout medicine.

Your story may not be about burying your child, it could be a parent, a friend, or even a pet. It could be a broken relationship. Whatever it is, something threw you for a loop mentally and you are still trying to regain who you are and whose you are. My recommendation is, get into a workout regimen. Compliment a good workout with eating live foods from juicing to eating a rainbow of fresh fruits, vegetables, salads, avocados, and raw nuts. These provide the brain food that your mind and body need to operate at its optimum.

"Get into a workout regimen."

Meet Jennifer. Her very best friend, her dad, had not been in contact with her for years after he pursued a relationship with a woman who would become his wife. Jennifer was hurting deeply. As she attempted to build her F.R.E.S.H. pillars, life threw her for another loop. There was one financial setback and then another. Her relationship with her husband was totally dismantled. Her zest to increase her knowledge (Education) was dwindling. Feeding herself spiritually was an uphill battle.

She recently had surgery that would challenge the health of her 30-years-young body. Life continued to throw her one curveball after another. One day she contacted me amid it all. "Please go get a workout in," I advised. Her response was how unmotivated she was and she didn't feel like it. I checked back in with her later that week. I asked, "Did you go to the gym?" No, she hadn't gone. I literally begged her again to go. Eventually, she started back up again. Now, she is at the gym at least four times per week. Her mental outlook has made a 180-degree turn. Additionally, she is going to therapy weekly, understanding that the importance of her mental health and her physical health go hand in hand.

Powerful Meds: Laughter (Free, No Side Effects)

Another dose of medicine that I apply is laughter. The Bible says, "A cheerful heart is good medicine but a crushed spirit dries up the bones" (Proverbs 17:22). Along with all the other nourishing things that I push to do during challenging times, I do my best to get into an environment that motivates me to laugh. I said "motivate" because, when tough times hit, no one feels like laughing. Our inner person gets sad as we begin to feel a sense of hopelessness, pain, guilt, and disappointment. Push to get out of that slump. Remember, such a mood does not improve your situation.

Laughter vitalizes the body's organs with oxygen. When you laugh it increases the intake of oxygen to heart, lungs, and muscles. Moreover, it activates the brain to release more endorphins, according to the Mayo Clinic. Endorphins are chemicals produced by the body that relieve stress, anxiety, and depression. We have all these wonderful things in us to fight off negativity. Let's use it! When we create environments that provoke laughter – funny movies, nostalgic moments with our friends and family – we are counterbalancing negativity with a smile.

My Eating Lifestyle

I don't diet. I mostly go organic and eat foods in their most natural state. I lean on eating this way. No one wants to be hungry. It's not that I deprive myself; I just learned to love the best stuff for myself. I often make super-size salads with spring mix, spinach, shredded carrots, and avocado. I roast sweet potatoes, zucchini, and cauliflower in coconut or avocado oil (olive oil heated isn't as good and can become carcinogenic, so maybe use some coconut oil or avocado oil which has a higher heat tolerance).

Olive oil is best used in cold dressings not heated, so mix it in when you can. My salad dressing is often apple cider vinegar with olive oil and a little mustard. My breakfast is often two glasses of a smoothie which contains a lot of organic greens, berries, chia seeds, vegan protein powder, and almond or any plant milk with about two ounces of 100% pomegranate juice. Sometimes I do oatmeal or millet porridge. I avoid cakes and cookies. Most of the time if I do indulge, I make my own at home with mostly organic and wholesome ingredients.

Even though I aim to eat as much whole food, plant based and clean ingredients as I can, I know our food source is depleted of nutrients due to pollution, depletion of nutrients in the soil, and our produce not being vine ripened. So I take a clinically proven powdered product with research published in reputable medical journals to bridge the nutritional gap. This is very helpful because many of us are not harvesting from our own gardens anymore.

When you eat plant foods in their most natural state, not only do you get the full benefit of all the vitamins and minerals, but also the phytonutrients, antioxidants, and enzymes found in fruits, vegetables, berries, beans, and whole grains. Plant foods process through your system a lot quicker. It doesn't allow the ability for it to sit around and store fat resulting in weight gain. Again, it is not easy at times, but the more you practice, the more it becomes a part of your daily routine.

"Eat plant foods in their most natural state."

Exercise - Divorce Feelings, Engage Future Self

I've yet to find a person who just loves to exercise. The people I know who have made it a lifestyle don't usually do it because they enjoy it. They do it because they enjoy the benefits of it. I am one of those people. For example, this morning I woke up feeling very tired. Every fiber of my being wanted to stay in bed. The temperature in the room was just right and I was covered with fresh, clean sheets. I had all the ingredients for another two hours of sleep before I had to wake up for work. But I had set my mind the night before that I had to wake up early to get some exercise in to start my day.

You see, learning to appreciate your future self means that you must think ahead to how your future self would feel. If I didn't work out, my future self would be upset that my current self didn't take the opportunity given. Simply put, I never want to look back at my missed opportunity. So, I got up, got two miles in, a five-minute plank, and some stretching. Now I'm charged up writing this chapter. You see, I had a goal and I didn't want to disappoint my future self again.

One of my favorite workout routines is Pilates. The movements in pilates are very subtle but very impactful; especially to your core. It's very important to have a strong core. It trains the lower back, hip, pelvic, and abdomen to work in unison; thereby you are less prone to back and hip injuries. The results I see in my physical appearance in less than six months of taking classes two days per week after pregnancy was just amazing. CORE, BALANCE, NO ACHES or PAIN, weight loss, muscle tone, stamina, and flexibility. I know I wouldn't be feeling this great without Pilates.

Exercise - Don't Defeat the Purpose

It's very important to have a good workout regimen; but while doing so, you must nourish yourself very well. Otherwise, you will defeat the purpose of working out by exposing your body to cumulative effect of exercise induced oxidative stress over time. Oxidative stress occurs when there is an imbalance between free radicals and antioxidants in your body which can lead to many degenerative diseases. Free radicals are unstable molecules and they have an uneven number of electrons so this allows them to easily react (connect) with other molecules and they scavenge the body to seek out other electrons so they can become a pair. This causes damage to cells, proteins, and DNA.

The best recommendation for antioxidants and exercise is having a balanced diet rich in natural antioxidants and phytonutrients (plant nutrients). Regular eating of vine ripened and, rainbow variety of fresh fruits and vegetables, whole grains, legumes and beans, sprouts and seeds, is a great way to get many antioxidants in physically active people and athletes. Don't stop exercising; just be sure to compliment your workout with rich nutrients.

https://www.ncbi.nlm.nih.gov/pmc/articles/PMC4393546/

Dodging the Happy Weight

I often hear people talk about the "happy weight" after marriage or being in a happy relationship. If you have experienced neither, that stage in happiness is real. When I got married nine years ago, my husband was accustomed to eating a certain way. Men metabolically burn fat at a different rate than women, so I really had to be mindful. Of course, I enjoyed the moments; I just had to find my balance. One day I figured it out. Add about 75 to 80% wholesome natural foods in all that "love eating" and I would be okay. He eventually began to eat with me in the same manner.

Traveling and Health

I travel extensively for work. I have been doing so for over 15 years. There are major health risks associated with extensive traveling. Harvard Business Review states, "frequent business travel, especially long-haul travel, accelerates aging and increases the likelihood of suffering a stroke, heart attack, and deep-vein thrombosis." It also exposes travelers to pathological levels of germs and radiation. The Harvard Business review states, "If you fly over 85,000 miles per year, you are absorbing radiation levels above the regulatory limit of most countries." I fly out on Mondays and return on Thursdays or Fridays. I had a work assignment in Japan for about 1½ years. I would fly home every three weeks. While in Japan, I had to attend some very important business meetings in the United States. I flew in for the day and flew back immediately after the meetings. On one of my business trips, I remember taking seven flights that week that included my round trips.

With such a rigorous flying schedule, it was very easy to be a victim of those statistics. Airport foods are not the best. I could have easily gone for broke at the hotel breakfast buffets and gone out with the team for lunch and dinner daily. After late dinners with my team, I would get back to the hotel with just enough time to sleep and wake up at 6 am. It is so typical when I start an assignment to hear, "Collette, before I started traveling to this assignment, I was 10 to 20 pounds less." Or, "Since I started traveling, I've been diagnosed with diabetes or high cholesterol." These stories are very frightening.

I had to force myself to make time to work out. Studies have shown that the best time to work out is in the mornings. It stimulates healthy hormones for clear thinking and energy to start a productive day. I totally agree. However, while traveling, I make it a rule to get in three to four half-hour workout sessions into my schedule. Sometimes, my sessions are in the mornings. Some evenings I will skip the dinner gatherings and go to the hotel fitness facility to ensure that I get in all my sessions. You will be amazed how quickly thirty minutes go by. Five minutes to warm up. Fifteen to twenty minutes on the elliptical or treadmill or bike, then stretch and off to be refueled with a healthy dinner or breakfast, depending on what time of day I work out.

For a long time, I traveled with a jump rope in my bag; 10 minutes of jumping rope is equivalent to 30 minutes of running. Not only is it one of the best exercises that gives you an overall body workout, it is inexpensive, and you can do it anywhere. In addition, if you were to do 10 minutes, three times per day, you would burn about 2,000 calories for the week, says this website: https://www.healthsomeness.com/benefits-of-skipping/.

After a while, I learned to apply the same eating habits that I used to avoid that happy weight gain. I decided not to fall back into bad habits. If I know I'm going to be on a long-term (three months or more) assignment, there are a few things I ensure that I do:

1. I invested in a juicer and/or a portable blender that I lock away in the client's office or keep at the hotel. One might say that's a lot, but, trust me, your body will love you for it later when you take the time to take care of it.

2. I make time to find a local grocery store that sells organic produce and purchase a few things for breakfast, lunch, and dinner that week.

3. I take the most well-researched powdered produce in concentrated, dehydrated form on travels; it is convenient and affordable with clinically proven published studies that show the nutrients are bioavailable (easily absorbed) into the body since the majority of people do not eat enough fresh vine-ripened produce.

My travel schedule makes it more feasible to purchase a small amount of groceries to have on hand. I keep my meals simple so that grocery shopping isn't overwhelming. It's a great way to stay in control of what I put in my body. Breakfast consists of either vegetable juice or a smoothie of three or four ingredients. Juice is typically carrots, kale, and celery. Smoothies are typically a vegan protein powder, almond milk, organic berries, and kale. Lunch: a salad of spring mix, avocado, tomatoes, red and yellow peppers, with a protein (tuna fish or non-GMO tofu). Dressing is usually mustard and olive oil with apple cider vinegar. Dinner is typically like lunch. You may say that's no fun. My body is having fun eating all these nutrients to fight off illnesses. I keep in mind that if what I eat is not nourishing my temple, it is destroying it.

There are times I grab breakfast at the hotel. I have plain oatmeal without all the toppings, unless they are raw nuts. I skip the granola toppings. It's loaded with so much sugar. What about the fruit toppings, you might ask? I avoid berries (strawberry, blueberries, raspberries) unless they are organic (these are loaded with pesticides if not organic). I'll do a medium size not over-ripe banana. The riper the banana, the higher the sugar content, which I work to minimize, keeping in mind the history of diabetes in my family, hence sticking to low glycemic foods.

All This Talk About Health

By no means do I have all the health answers. I will tell you this, the benefits of a healthy lifestyle will trickle into all other facets of your life. It motivates. It encourages. It gives perspective. My story and journey in healthy eating and exercise is not one I'm asking you to mirror. What I do know is that an investment in your health will pay off in the way you think. A healthy mind and body help build a strong foundation for further success in our lives.

According to the Centers for Disease Control and Prevention (CDC), heart disease, cancer, unintentional injuries, lower respiratory diseases, and stroke make up the top 5 leading causes of death. In some cases, how you treat your body can help to avoid these diseases. Without good health, productivity decreases significantly in our lives. Ask the person who is self-employed and out with the flu for a week or two. Or the person pushing so hard, only to be stressed, leading to high-blood pressure, which leads to other illnesses and not being able to take care of other responsibilities in their lives. This is just a reminder that we get out of our bodies what we put into it. Making health a priority will serve our bodies and the other areas of our life best.

Family, Career, Health - What Will You Choose?

Many times, I see where a person is put in a position where they have to choose between family, career (money), or their health. These choices can be very difficult in situations where you have to choose one thing over the other. For example, if a woman is pregnant it's very important for her to minimize her activities to preserve the health of both mother and baby. However, she shouldn't have to feel compelled to push and stress herself prior to giving birth or after giving birth, thrusting herself back in the hustle and bustle of the workforce because she feels that she may lose out on career opportunities.

Let's be real, careers matter. Isn't that what we use as a gauge of financial security? Introspectively, a career can be the driver to financially support family. By that same admission, we are saying, we need to make a certain amount of money. Men also must look at this very same situation. Paternity leave is fairly new and perhaps not as easily accepted, yet cannot be overlooked.

More corporations are and should work with their employees giving consideration to both women and men who are working to create balance between work and taking care of their fundamental life needs of family, finance, and health. Unfortunately, a lot of times work responsibility or dare I say "work guilt" leads us to believe that we are going to miss out on opportunities that will improve our financial position.

Meet Doreen: For over 20 years, she has been traveling extensively for the major corporation in which she works. Additionally, she works long nights almost every night. Her clients are often demanding, therefore so is her schedule.

Doreen didn't have much time for a social life. Of course, she wanted to meet someone, get married and start a family, but didn't know how that could be possible. It so happened that Gayle, who works with Doreen, met a wonderful guy. They had a wonderful relationship and got married. One day Doreen asked Gayle in amazement, "Gayle, where did you find the time to meet someone. How did you manage to make the time to spend such quality time that leads to marriage?" She later learned that Gayle and her husband started a family. That too was a surprise to Doreen. She asked again, "How did you make all this happen given the intense schedule that we have?"

Doreen learned that Gayle made a mindset shift. Although work was important, so was creating a life with someone to share it with that would eventually lead to having children. She prioritized her goals on starting a family. She researched her company's support on family issues, and took a bold step to manage both her career and her family.

Gayle later returned to work without skipping a beat. She even had a more rewarding position when she returned. The point is, there is a shift that's taking place in the workplace. Unfortunately, it's not yet the norm. However, we are the voice of corporations. I know, it may not seem like it; but if more and more people take advantage of these opportunities and speak out regarding their needs to establish a secure family; I believe corporations will move along with us. We should be able to balance life, career, and family without it negatively impacting our financial security. The key is, it starts with us.

Our Health and the Workplace

Those of us who desire to be successful will often think, I wish I had more time in the day to get it all done. We are being pushed to do more in our work environments and it can easily take a toll on our health. We have a lot of technology that makes us readily available for people to reach us, but there's nothing like the human factor of assistance. I have learned that as technology increases and human interactions decline, more people are sharing their stories of becoming chronically ill or even dying due to stress in the workplace.

I can't emphasize enough that taking time to focus on your health is important. You will not be able to go to work if you're ill, so you can't allow yourself to let the pressures of work take you down. Such was the case of Nigel whose wife found him collapsed after having a stroke early one morning after he returned home from work sometime after midnight. Nigel had to retire from his work after this incident due to some disabilities. Let's not wait for an illness to force us to pause. Do it now! Work will wait!

Some ideas on how to pause/lower anxiety/lower stress:

1. **Spend Some Time Away:** There are several ways you can stay away from work. Plan vacations; sometimes, all we need is a staycation. You decide what's best for you to get a mental break. Another approach is to take a half day off from work to decompress, especially after a tough day. When you are away, stay away; that means do not check emails, social media, or even call anyone that provokes stress. All will still be there when you get back. Just shut it down and take time for self-care.

2. **Walk your meetings:** Sometimes you can invite a person that you need to have a discussion with for a walk as you discuss some challenging topics. It's far more difficult to get uptight and tense when you are walking.

3. **Block Out Time on Your Work Calendar for You:** We live by our work calendar. Block-off your work calendar for your workout, family time, and whatever self-care activities you do to decompress. Don't miss your own appointment! If you miss, reschedule! Stay with the plan!

    While working out - Break A Sweat: There are many forms of exercise, don't forget to incorporate aerobic exercises. It improves the health of heart and lungs. Doing aerobic exercise can lead to a longer life span. There was a recent study of 1.4 million people who found that "high amounts of aerobic exercise were linked with a reduced risk of 13 types of cancer. And a large study of more than 660,000 people found that the people who did 150 minutes of moderate aerobic activity per week were 31% less likely to die over a 14-year period than those who did not engage in any physical activities" (https://www.livescience.com/55320-aerobic-exercise.html)

4. **Breathe:** Deep breathing helps you to relax. Scientific studies have shown that it has a positive effect on the heart, digestion, brain and even your immune system. This can be done anywhere – at your desk, while heading to the next meeting, and even while in a meeting.

5. **Delegate:** Don't hesitate to share the workload. Ask for help and don't back down from your stance.

We need to take back our lives and learn how to be effective in the corporate world (or any industry for that matter) without hurting ourselves. When you are truly balanced, you are productive. When you are more productive, you are happier. When you are happier, you create the environment for success. Nourishing yourself creates a flow and this flow begins with you. You have to take charge and *Just Start!* I'm not saying it's easy, but you can make it happen!

Health Words of Wisdom

1. **You.** There is only one you. You only have one temple. Take care of it. Nourish it! Love it! Exercise it!

2. **Make the appointment.** You make an appointment or note on your calendar to attend very important events. You are important. Make that appointment to exercise!

3. **Fall in love with the real deal.** We all love to eat. Often, the love is for sugary and processed food which is reeking havoc on our health. I encourage you to fall in love with real food; that's wholefoods...your fruits and vegetables.

4. **Laughter - the free meds.** Good laughter makes the heart merry; moreover, it is free and has no side-effects.

Conclusion

F.R.E.S.H.:
You Can Do This

You've Already Begun to Get F.R.E.S.H.

I conclude this book with tears of joy looking back on where I was in comparison to where I am today. It was a long and arduous road at times. However, I'm grateful to have overcome and just as excited for those I've seen firsthand experience transformation through my coaching to live a F.R.E.S.H. lifestyle. Be encouraged that as it did for us, it can happen in your life as well. By the mere fact that you have gotten this far in the book, you have already begun your F.R.E.S.H. journey.

Self-examination is extremely important; especially if you are feeling overwhelmed with life's expectations. The five pillars of F.R.E.S.H. are an internal reflection on how to attain a balanced life, success, and happiness. All of which is achievable when we prioritize our focus area, examine our goals and act. If you are at this point in this book, you now know it's not simply a choice of maintaining our financial, physical, and mental well-being. Like anything worth having, it requires work and there are times when that work is challenging. It's especially in those moments that it's important to remind ourselves, the effort that is put into each area of focus, is what we will get out of it.

> "*The five pillars of F.R.E.S.H. are an internal reflection on how to attain a balanced life, success, and happiness.*"

Financial prosperity is learning how to manage what you earn in order to keep it. Relationship success is about creating value. It is not just the value you see in other people it is also about the value you see within yourself. Education allows us (and presents us) the opportunity to stay relevant in an ever-changing world. Spirituality is the basis of managing those changes, especially when life throws us a curveball. Health supports each of the preceding pillars because, as we know, without our health we lose the opportunity to put them into full practice.

Here's a quick recap on how to zero in on the five pillars of F.R.E.S.H.:

> **Finance** – stability, saving, investing
>
> **Relationship** – value, respect, self-worth
>
> **Education** – focus on an area of F.R.E.S.H. that needs work, prioritize, set goals
>
> **Spirituality** – assess the spirit within you, surround yourself with hope, establish your PAL (Pray and Meditation, Action, Love)
>
> **Health** – mental, physical, fuel the mind

This is a simplified breakdown, yet powerful in the sense that if you can look at any of these areas and one or two words pop out at you like, "yes, that's something I want and need," then you have done a key part. Identify where you want to focus your attention. Be reminded not to get overwhelmed by working them all at once, find the one or two that starts your foundation and build on it. You can do it!

As I reflect back on this book, I would be remiss if I didn't share a story. It is very dear and special to me as I give thought to the impact of the coaching I was able to share with this phenomenal young lady. Below is something Olivia wrote about her experience with me and gave me permission to share:

> My life was never the same. I didn't know exactly what I was looking for or asking for but I knew I needed change. I needed to feel better. I needed to see things clearer. I wanted to dream again. I wanted to live again. I missed....me.
>
> Initially I didn't know anything about the Total You is F.R.E.S.H. concept. It would be months, almost close to a year, before a formal introduction to this lifestyle dawned on me. Everything I learned and understood I received from watching the real life of Collette. When I first met her I thought she was such a refreshing person to be around. I instantly fell in love with her son and our relationship pretty much grew from there. After he died I really thought it was all over. ONE week after he died and one day after his burial, I watched her walk into church with a bag instead of a car seat and she had the biggest smile on her face. I didn't understand this emotional stage she was in for several reasons.
>
> Reason number one is that we kept in touch via email most of the time. When I was leaving for a trip she informed me she was going to spend some time with friends in Florida and go on a cruise. A cruise???
>
> Reason number two is that when I returned from that trip she encouraged me to join her at the gym. She knew I was in desperate need to get my health together. She would pick me

up and would have the biggest smile, excited about the gym. We would discuss things I should eat and things I could do at home. Not one moment did she cry or seemed depressed. I didn't understand this at all!

Reason number three came when I began assisting her with her business endeavors. My first assignments were to organize mail and gather any and all remaining medical expenses for Daniel. I would always hear, "I don't want any debts. Anyone I owe will be paid." I didn't understand this at all. She had every reason to fall behind in any and everything, but she didn't.

Now, between her son's death and her assignment in Atlanta ending, she accepted an assignment in Pennsylvania. OK. I get it. She's going to leave the area. That way she won't have to be around anything that reminds her of Daniel. Her job will cover her expenses so, no need to come home. This all made sense until she told me her plans. Four to five days in PA and back home. "I want to sleep in my own bed." Really??? And on top of this she would be in her room (the place she spent most of her time with Daniel) studying to perform better on that project. By this point I was delightfully baffled.

I have said all of that to say this: I was introduced to Total You F.R.E.S.H. by way of someone's successful lifestyle. I had hit the lowest I had ever been in my life. I came from New York a very independent, financially stable, responsible person. After two and half years my life had flipped upside down. I was totally dependent on those I was around (another story within itself), in debt, very sickly, out of shape, isolated, and totally at a loss about my next steps.

Now things weren't all peaches when I arrived. I had some struggles and issues that were with me prior to coming but I was still able to make sensible decisions. Total You F.R.E.S.H. helped me to understand that the only way to get to where I wanted to go, to be and be able to sustain, there had to be balance. Prior to Total You my life was totally consumed by church. I was in church on Sunday, Tuesday, Thursday, Friday, and Saturday. Every so often I had to be there on a Wednesday. Things had gotten worse when I was employed there. Now please don't take this as a negative attack on the church. I'm just painting a picture and giving you my experience. I was totally separated from my family, stopped doing music, forgot about school, unhealthy, broke and had no social life. Suicidal? You know it!! I remember thinking one night, I should just run into oncoming traffic around midnight. They would never see me coming. This all changed when I began hanging around Co (the nickname I gave her; short for Collette).

I saw this balance which I had never seen before. This lady really had her stuff together. She truly and successfully lived Total You F.R.E.S.H. This gave me the drive to go after the things that I wanted in life. I realized the dreamer in me was still alive and wanted to show me some things and how to get to them. So, for one full year I decided to live out this concept. I figured that if it could work for her (with every blow that she was dealt) then surely I could be successful too.

I immediately changed my diet and began exercising. The weight came off. I began going to other places instead of 'LIVING' at church. Hello DC and Silver Spring MD! Nice to meet you Florida and the Bahamas! I had lived in the Silver Spring area all of this time and only knew the city the church was in. I then got a new job and a new place to live. I was no longer living like a pauper. I began to pay off the debt I had accumulated and increased my credit score. Then came the change in church. I joined a church that represented Christ the way it was intended. I felt loved, welcomed, and like myself again... There, scales began to balance out nicely.

I now have a good credit record (finance), am going out more and traveling while becoming more social and spending time with my family (relationship), have a renewed true relationship with God (spiritual) working out and eating healthier (health) but there was something missing. I wanted to do more, be more, get more. I then decided to work hard to get my responsibilities increased as I assisted Co.

Here I stand seven years after learning about this concept; I'm pretty much debt free and have adopted a lifestyle that keeps me away from doctors. I am more energized and healthy, I got out of a relationship that was mentally, emotionally, financially, and physically draining, learned so much in assisting Co that I landed a great job. I'm pursuing my dreams and have created balance in my life. I know what I want and now have the tools to go get it. Whenever I feel like I don't have the energy or drive to do something, I think of F.R.E.S.H. Then, I realize that if one thing is imbalanced then everything is affected. It's not worth it. This concept has changed my life forever.

I have another short success story to share with you. There is a young man that has been a part of the F.R.E.S.H. program since its inception. We would have a Total You F.R.E.S.H. check-in on Saturday mornings while he was away at college. It was a routine for his development so that he could be successful while in school and continue long after he graduated. When I would call to check-in, he would often say, "I'm getting F.R.E.S.H.". I understood that as his way of saying, I am working the principles and incorporating them each day. I am proud to say that he is a college graduate and has moved on to the professional arena. The F.R.E.S.H. pillars have never left his thoughts as he develops his blueprint for his life journey. He is now doing extremely well for himself.

Change Your Mindset and Hit Start

There is nothing more impactful than a changed mind. You may change your address, your zip code, your size, your clothes, your job, your car, your hairstyle. You may even change your spouse, but nothing beats a changed mind.

I remember when I was a kid in Jamaica, between the ages of 8 and 11, there was one boy in the neighborhood by the name of Harry that would tease me to tears by calling me derogatory names. It felt like every month he would find a new nickname for me, as if this was his mission in life. The more I cried, the more he repeated the nickname with laughter. I would just cry and cry helplessly until he left or I would run away from him. At times, it got so bad, that I would see him coming and I would run in the other direction. Basically, I would do whatever I could to keep my distance. Despite my efforts, it didn't stop Harry from yelling out a nickname. Before long, it got worse because the other kids would hear him and began doing the same thing. It was a completely mortifying experience.

Then one day, I got hold of something. I made up my *mind* that the next time I saw Harry, I would be unbothered by his latest nickname for me. I said to myself, "I won't try to avoid him. I won't run away from him. I will stand my ground and look totally unbothered by his name calling and laughter." Did that day come? Yes, it did. Shortly after this self-declaration, I saw Harry in the distance walking towards me as I was out playing. I knew he was coming and I continued to play as though he were not. As soon as Harry approached me he began the name calling. The more I ignored him, the more names he found to call me. When he realized he couldn't get to me, he left. "Yes!" I said gleefully. "I won this round."

Harry was a very determined person and I knew that he would be back for a few more rounds, either that day or the next day or next week. And he did come back over and over again, but my mind was still made up not to let him get to me. I remember how victorious

I felt in the previous rounds. As I won these battles, I eventually won the war. After a period of time, Harry's approach became more welcoming. Why? It proved to me each time that making up my mind to not let myself be defeated was the best choice I could have made for myself.

I encourage you to make up your mind not to accept *less than* in your life. Fix your mind to go for that change. It *is* possible. Don't let predisposed situations keep you in a rut. Make the mind shift to see better, do better, and renew your mindset for greatness. Take the F.R.E.S.H. principles and apply them to your life. Time waits for no one. The time is now. Don't be afraid to leave your comfort zone. I know that you can do this! You can change your mindset for success.

You are now equipped with the pillars to build and reshape the best you. When the F.R.E.S.H. pillars are built, no one can take action in these areas for you. It is for you to look within yourself and start to execute the change you want to see. As implied on the cover of this book, don't hesitate to rip away old habits. Rip whatever needs to be ripped to get to where you want to go. Fight until you begin to get it right, not only hold yourself accountable for the growth, but celebrate it as you go. Treat it as though you were exploring an island on a vacation or seeing a new play in anticipation of a great ending. The point is to enjoy the process.

> *"As implied on the cover of this book, don't hesitate to rip away old habits. Rip whatever needs to be ripped to get to where you want to go."*

Make this fun – you are working to become your Total F.R.E.S.H. You!

Review Inquiry

Hey, it's Collette here.

I hope you've enjoyed the book, finding it both useful and fun. I have a favor to ask you.

Would you consider giving it a rating on Amazon or wherever you bought the book? Online book stores are more likely to promote a book when they feel good about its content, and reader reviews are a great barometer for a book's quality.

So please go to Amazon.com (or wherever you bought the book), search for my name and the book title, and leave a review. If someone gave you a copy of my book, then leave a review on Amazon, and maybe consider adding a picture of you holding the book. That increases the likelihood your review will be accepted!

Many thanks in advance,

Collette Chambers Ogrizovic

Will You Share the Love?

Get this book for a friend, associate, or family member!

If you have found this book valuable and know others who would find it useful, consider buying them a copy as a gift. Special bulk discounts are available if you would like your whole team or organization to benefit from reading this. Just contact Collette at TotalYouFresh@gmail.com or www.TotalYouFresh.com.

Would You Like Collette to Speak at Your Organization?

Book COLLETTE Now!

Collette accepts a limited number of speaking/coaching/training engagements each year. To learn how you can bring her message to your organization, email TotalYouFRESH@gmail.com.

Endnotes

1. Tracy, Brian (2005). *Change Your Thinking, Change Your Life: How to Unlock Your Full Potential for Success and Achievement* (1st ed.). Hoboken, NJ, United States: Wiley.

About the Author

"Let's begin with your thinking. Once we get your thought process operating in a healthy, forward, positive movement, the rest is an enjoyable walk in the park. Knowing that is half the battle."

This concept opened doors for Collette to travel nationally and internationally coaching individuals to corporations. From Washington, DC to Japan and Jamaica, Collette has generously shared her proven keys to success and happiness and now she is ready to share it with you. She has quickly become a sought after speaker for conferences, workshops, seminars, school, and youth trainings. Her interactive, energetic presentations exhibit that you can be successful and happy all at the same time. The key is balancing, which is possible using the F.R.E.S.H. framework.

In addition to her work at IBM, Collette is also an entrepreneur. She started two businesses. The first, CFC Management Inc., a successful real estate investment and property management company. The second, Total You F.R.E.S.H. LLC, an executive coaching, motivational and transformational speaking business. This company is driving and establishing a movement for a balanced life, success and happiness. Collette has many notable testimonies of clients, family members and friends who have been impacted by the program to date. Total You F.R.E.S.H. – F.R.E.S.H. which stands for and focuses on Finance, Relationships, Education, Spirituality and Health – teaches people to develop a plan for their lives so that they may set attainable goals in any and all areas of concern and take action.

Collette has many accomplishments and continues to pursue success and thrive. She was mentioned and quoted in Diane Paddison's book titled *Love, Work, and Pray*, and was published in the Croatian local newspaper conducting a transformational speaking engagement in the country on Total You F.R.E.S.H. Moreover, Collette has a longtime commitment to healthy eating, a balanced diet and exercise. Her discipline in this area led to her becoming a 3rd Degree Black Belt in Tae-Kwon-Do winning multiple national and state medals and a 2nd place win in Korea.

Raised by immigrant, entrepreneur parents who had hearts to see people do well, Collette found herself with the same exact desire. Led by this desire, Collette put a plan together for her life shortly after graduate school. This plan involved working, saving as much as possible, being active, increasing her Christian faith and having positive social interactions. She had no idea that she was creating a blueprint that later would be known as Total You F.R.E.S.H., The Blueprint for a Balanced Life, Success and Happiness.

Collette can be reached at: http://www.totalyoufresh.com/.

Made in the USA
Middletown, DE
23 November 2020